Praise for Knowledge Works

"Knowledge Works is a very practical book that provides proven solutions for important knowledge-related problems in organizations including: how to convince managers that knowledge is important, how to create a knowledge-sharing culture, and how to improve the quality of conversations. A must-read for all managers of knowledge-intensive organizations."
Daan Andriessen, Professor of Intellectual Capital, Inholland University of Applied Sciences, The Netherlands

"To be successful as a manager, you need to make better decisions, be more innovative and to do more with less. In this highly practical handbook, Christine Van Winkelen and Jane McKenzie offer new ideas to challenge your current thinking and achieve this. Their work is soundly based on 10 years collaborative research with the Knowledge Management Forum at the Henley Business School."
David Gurteen, Founder and Director, Gurteen Knowledge Community

"This book shows in a very inspiring and hands-on way how knowledge works. This is an utmost important understanding in the growing intellectual economy for increased operational knowledge effectiveness. The book has in an impressive way systematized many challenging K-works perspectives, from knowledge mapping and flows to social media and knowledge creating conversations. It is demonstrating a number of insightful real life stories and projects during 10 years of the Henley KM Forum, as well as providing valuable reading notes. Happy Knowledge Work . . ."
Leif Edvinsson, Honorary Chairman for the Henley KM Forum, The World's First Professor of Intellectual Capital

"Christine and Jane are attentive tour guides on the never ending journey of learning, improvement and change charted in *Knowledge Works*. Together they have compiled an invaluable collection of grounded research and practical, real-world examples from a wide range of organisations. This is a book which you will find yourself dipping into repeatedly; be sure to have an ample supply of bookmarks before you start – you will use them all!"
Chris Collison, Business Author and Knowledge Management Consultant

"Christine van Winkelen and Jane McKenzie have developed a practical framework that links together a decade of research by the KM Forum. It should be useful to any organization where knowledge is a key asset."
Richard McDermott

KNOWLEDGE WORKS

KNOWLEDGE WORKS

THE HANDBOOK OF PRACTICAL WAYS TO IDENTIFY

AND SOLVE COMMON ORGANIZATIONAL

PROBLEMS FOR BETTER PERFORMANCE

CHRISTINE VAN WINKELEN AND JANE MCKENZIE

A John Wiley & Sons, Ltd., Publication

Registered office
John Wiley & Sons Ltd, The Atrium, Southern Gate, Chichester, West Sussex, PO19 8SQ, United Kingdom

For details of our global editorial offices, for customer services and for information about how to apply for permission to reuse the copyright material in this book please see our website at www.wiley.com

Library of Congress Cataloging-in-Publication Data

Winkelen, Christine van.
   Knowledge works : the handbook of practical ways to identify and solve common organizational problems for better performance / Christine van Winkelen and Jane McKenzie.
       p. cm.
   Includes bibliographical references and index.
   ISBN 978-1-119-99362-9 (pbk.)
   1. Knowledge management. 2. Organizational learning. 3. Problem solving. I. McKenzie, Jane. II. Title.
   HD30.2.W563 2011
   658.4′038—dc22

                                                                                    2011007716

A catalogue record for this book is available from the British Library.

ISBN 978-1-119-99362-9 (hardback), ISBN 978-1-119-97108-5 (ebk),
ISBN 978-1-119-97781-0 (ebk), ISBN 978-1-119-97782-7 (ebk)

Typeset in 10/13pt Trebuchet by Toppan Best-set Premedia Limited, Hong Kong
Printed in Great Britain by Antony Rowe Ltd, Chippenham, Wiltshire

CONTENTS

Section V   Become more agile   175

By creating the conditions that help people adapt their knowledge and understanding to the constant turbulence in the outside world, the organization can become more responsive to new challenges.

Section VI   Make change stick   233

By developing key knowledge-sharing behaviours and using effective communication approaches you show people why a knowledge approach matters and what they need to do themselves to contribute.

INTRODUCTION

"Knowledge Works" came about as a result of reflecting on a decade of highly applied and collaborative research at Henley Business School in the UK. Those associated with the various projects have benefited from the insights, approaches, tools, and methods that came from the work, as their comments throughout the book show. However, until now further distribution has been limited to an academic audience. To mark the 10th anniversary of a Forum that examines knowledge issues in organizations and

> actively challenges current thinking by encouraging new ideas, exploring links with other disciplines, and expanding the boundaries of the subject

it seemed appropriate to share the practical aspects of what we have learnt with a wider audience.

Where does the content of the book come from?

The Knowledge Management Forum (KM Forum) was established in 2000 at Henley Business School. Its members are large organizations, both multi-national private sector firms and major UK public sector bodies. The intention from the outset was to create a community where business professionals could think together with peers facing similar challenges about knowledge related issues. Since then, the KM Forum has established an international reputation for thought leadership in the field.

Each year, we use a consultation process to surface pressing and topical knowledge related challenges facing organizations. From these, projects emerge which inspire working groups of members to congregate around them. The research approach is relatively unusual because it is always highly collaborative from start to finish. In addition to the consultation process and the working groups, each project is co-championed by an academic *and* an experienced KM practitioner. The research has been "with" rather than "on" the organizations involved. All the projects have benefited from remarkable access to senior people facilitated by the representatives of the organizations that belong to the KM Forum. Interviews with senior directors and functional leads have been at the heart of most of the projects. A constant balance of academic and practice input produces findings that are both rigorous and relevant.

Research relevance is a topic of considerable debate in the field of business and management. We set out to embed relevance into both the design and project management principles of our research. On the whole, the research has been exploratory and qualitative, which means we have looked for patterns and indicators rather than proof or categorical "truth". One notable exception is the Knowledge Sharing Behaviours research which was highly quantitative and the researcher was awarded a PhD at the end (see Chapter 15). The more usual exploratory approach for the projects described in the other chapters reflects the diversity of organizations involved in the KM Forum. What happens in a public sector body such as the Ministry of Defence or Department of Health is unlikely to be the same as for a private sector firm such as Vodafone or Syngenta. Nor are they likely to benefit from exactly the same answers. However, the value of participant diversity is that the principles, illustrative examples, models, and insights coming from research across different contexts can be adapted and adopted more easily in other large organizations.

We believe this is the strength of our approach. Our proposition is that by involving many different types of organizations in the research, the outputs will be more broadly relevant and applicable. Although useful approaches to managing knowledge have been generated by many other writers, our view is that sometimes the very important influence of context isn't fully taken into account. What works for an organization which needs to make long-term capital investments (such as in the car or oil industries) may not work for a high-technology firm that sees six months as a long planning timeframe, or for parts of the public sector.

Who is it intended for?

We have written this book for managers who want to do more with less by improving productivity and stimulating innovation. Whenever knowledge and learning are factors that affect organizational performance, our intention is that there will be ideas to stimulate thinking and some practical approaches in the book. Managers responsible for distributed and international teams, increasingly a prevalent feature of organizational life, will find several of the chapters particularly useful for considering how to achieve more productive learning processes.

Those with functional responsibility for knowledge, organizational capability building, or learning (including knowledge and information managers, strategists, human resource managers, and organization development specialists) are also likely to find the content directly relevant to their activities. The topics and the way the research was formulated and carried out came from people with just these functional responsibilities.

What's the best way to use the book?

The book has been created as a handbook that you can dip into according to your needs. Alternatively, you can work through it in a more systematic way to create a plan to improve your organization's performance. The six sections organize the chapters around essential objectives for any business. The sections build cumulatively from strategy to action. Each section starts with a short introduction which offers an overview of the theme and explains the rationale for what is included. We can't claim that every section provides a completely comprehensive view of that theme. The material is simply a reflection of the research projects identified by and prioritized by the business professionals working with us.

The structure of all the chapters is the same and is intended to make it as easy as possible for you to navigate around the material. When your time is limited, you just need to know why the issue matters and what to do about it. We include information about the way the research behind each chapter was carried out too, as well as a few final reflections of a more conceptual nature in case you are interested. The real life examples included in each chapter were collected at the time of the research. They have been selected for inclusion here because the principles they demonstrate remain relevant even though some time may have passed. Where the organization's name is provided, we are grateful that they have given us permission to use the material.

Will a static book be enough?

Knowledge work is a context-specific mix of creative insight and scientific investigation. As academics, we have enjoyed the search for viable solutions to the various challenges posed by managers working in the field. What has been achieved together has come about through those at the sharp end of business practice thinking together. Conversation and interaction have been a critical source of inspiration. In truth, they are a vital way to combine knowledge and intellect and inspire insights that can improve organizational performance. In that sense, the contents of this book can only be a starting point for further knowledge work. We invite you to continue the conversation with ourselves and with other like-minded individuals facing the same challenges. Share your experiences as you grapple with key activities of each section and start to apply some of the thinking. We have set up a website and a blog where together we can continue the process of improving the impact of knowledge work on business performance:

www.knowledgeworkshandbook.com. On the website you will also find further resources that may help you improve the knowledgeability of your organization.

Knowledge work is a never ending journey of learning, improvement and change. We hope that the material in this book provides some inspiration and invigoration along the way!

Christine and Jane

Section I

Establish strategic priorities

Chapter 1 – Identifying valuable knowledge
Chapter 2 – Making a comprehensive assessment of knowledge flows

In a rapidly changing world, current success and future survival depend on constantly learning to do things differently and better. Knowledge is both the raw material that is the foundation for learning and the output from it, offering new opportunities and new sources of revenue. Arguably this means we would be neglecting our strategic responsibilities if we did not review organizational priorities in terms of the knowledge available to the business and focus our management and leadership practices on creating the conditions where knowledge can be used productively.

What do we mean by strategic priorities?

Even when you accept the importance of taking a knowledge perspective on the organization, it is still a challenge to prioritize time, attention, effort, and financial resources to improve the way knowledge delivers results. Often people tend to be more drawn to immediate task requirements and don't sustain the longer term perspective required to join up areas of knowledge activity smoothly and seamlessly. There is an additional challenge too: judging the returns on investments in knowledge-related initiatives can be perceived as highly subjective because the link between action and result can be very diffuse and slow to become visible in any measurable way. Unlike other resources which are consumed with use, knowledge tends to increase the more it is used in different contexts; its impact is amplified through sharing. Both of these attributes create huge potential for value generation. However, the consequences of knowledge initiatives are often difficult to measure directly without considerable effort and focus. Careful thought is needed to make evident the connection between knowledge initiatives, the results they produce, and the ultimate impact that these have on something that matters to key stakeholders in the organization.

As an example, a knowledge initiative could involve investment to establish and maintain more effective networks of people across the organization. One consequence could be speeding up access to the knowledge needed to put together proposals for new business, resulting in higher quality and timelier bids. These can be judged as the immediate outputs of the investment; it is possible to quantify in hard financial terms the increase in bid to win rate, growth in sales, or profit generated as a consequence. However, the final step in any strategic assessment should be checking that this is a strategic priority for the organization. For example, if resources are really limited, have the knowledge-related initiatives addressed what matters most? Is it really the highest priority for the organization to win new business, as opposed to delivering an excellent service to existing customers? If both are important, have resources been distributed between initiatives to improve them appropriately?

Potentially valuable knowledge comes from many sources, not all of which lie within the organization itself. The people who work closely with the organization (through whatever form of contract or relationship) are the main source. However, tapping into knowledge from the outside world in terms of suppliers, customers, partners, competitors, and other players in the sector is essential to supplement this and to provide early signs of the need to evolve and change. Finally, embedded knowledge that helps make the organization productive and unique is also valuable. We should not ignore what is special and distinctive about the way the organization runs, from the use of technology to the design of effective processes, and from the way people are managed to the culture.

By understanding from the outset what knowledge makes a difference to organizational performance, you can focus limited resources on the things that will have the most impact and generate the most value. Initiatives could range from increasing access to knowledge in an area where there is obviously a gap, to improving the distribution of critical knowledge to those who need it when they need it, or even to intervening to protect certain knowledge from reaching competitors because of its unique value. Some knowledge may even need to be shared freely to influence the way thinking and practice evolves in the sector or industry in general; this can grow potential opportunities for everyone. However, it is the piecemeal approach to knowledge initiatives which fails to help organizations make more meaningful and informed strategic choices. Lack of a structured approach also means that it is easy to overlook vital areas in which a knowledge perspective would help achieve the organization's strategic objectives.

How do you establish them?

The starting point is to understand what makes the organization able to survive and thrive in the face of competition and external change. By viewing knowledge as a resource we can make choices about how far it can be characterized as valuable and how much investment should be targeted at developing, maintaining, and protecting it. However, this isn't sufficient because we also need to determine the organizational capability to use that knowledge. How readily can knowledge flow around the organization and to and from the outside world? Do the management and leadership practices create the conditions to enable this to happen?

The two chapters in this section provide complementary approaches to help determine strategic priorities, as shown in Figure I.1. The first offers a way of mapping and evaluating valuable knowledge and the second includes a structure to evaluate the priority of key knowledge flows and whether they are working well or are blocked by certain barriers.

The fact that both "value" and "knowledge" are not absolute ideas that everyone can agree on, means that it is best to involve as many interested parties as possible in these strategic explorations. Those who have a stake in the outcome of the investments need to contribute to the assessment, particularly if they are interested and have influence on what is allowed to happen or how the results are interpreted.

Although these two approaches will get you started, a completely predetermined, structured approach is not necessarily feasible or desirable. Opportunities arise to try things out; success stories emerge that can be used to bring attention to a different way of working; someone with enthusiasm creates a momentum around something that was unforeseen. All of these are the realities of a complex organizational environment and sufficient flexibility is needed to respond. The value in using these models and frameworks to structure thinking about the organization from a knowledge perspective is that it is easier to recognize these serendipitous opportunities and evaluate them relative to others already underway. The challenge is to use the approaches described here to shape rather than constrain thinking about strategic knowledge priorities.

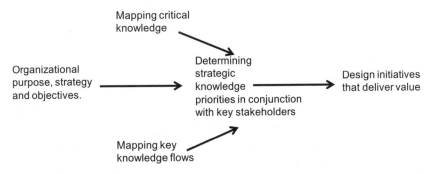

Figure I.1: A strategic approach to designing knowledge initiatives

The knowledge strategy will need to evolve as the organization becomes more collaborative and knowledge-sharing behaviours become embedded. Organizational priorities and external drivers also change continuously. Thinking about strategic priorities is an ongoing activity and using knowledge well in the organization needs to become a dynamic capability which is recognized and valued.

Key questions to ask yourself

As you start to use the ideas in the next two chapters:

- Ask *who* needs to be involved to both ensure that you can make sense of the situation properly and so that there is buy-in to the proposals that are generated.
- Think about *when* you should do this structured thinking about knowledge priorities and how you can keep an up to date view of what matters and what has changed.
- Be clear about *why* you are trying to improve the use of knowledge in the organization. Keep close attention to the generation of value for the organization.

Chapter 1

Snapshot

Valuable knowledge can be found in many places in organizations, from unique business models or solutions, key value-adding processes, core technology competencies, to business support systems that integrate knowledge across the organization. Identifying an organization's most valuable knowledge is the first step in deciding how to prioritize investments in projects designed to retain and develop that knowledge.

A systematic plan of action can be created by mapping key knowledge resources and then evaluating their importance and accessibility. There is a series of questions you can use to help you with this process. The approach works for different levels of detail. You can adapt it depending upon whether you are looking to create an overall strategy or to develop specific initiatives. Three case studies show how different types of organizations applied the approach and what they learnt from it.

Why this matters

Knowledge is widely recognized as a strategic resource. Current thinking goes further than simply acknowledging it as a source of competitive advantage: experts argue that turning knowledge into value is the main reason for firms to exist.[1] While there may be agreement that a knowledge perspective should underpin an effective business strategy in today's fast moving, global knowledge economy, many organizations have no process for identifying their most valuable knowledge and creating a plan to manage it. There is little evidence to suggest that organizations commonly adopt a systematic process to determine whether they are focusing effort and investment on their most valuable knowledge.

Valuable knowledge relates to an organization's competitive position, how it differentiates itself, and even how it manages itself and reinforces its culture and

"One of the reasons it's difficult to identify valuable knowledge is that value is in the eye of the beholder. That's why it's important to involve as many different stakeholders as possible in the process."

Dr Judy Payne, Henley Knowledge Management Forum

sense of purpose. In the public and not-for-profit sector, it relates to the identity of the organization and how it best achieves what it exists to do.

The Institute of Value Management makes the following observations about value:

> The concept of Value relies on the relationship between the satisfaction of many differing needs and the resources used in doing so. The fewer the resources used or the greater the satisfaction of needs, the greater the value. Stakeholders, internal and external customers may all hold differing views of what represents value.

When approaching the task of identifying valuable knowledge, this definition suggests two important dimensions. The first is concerned with the importance of the knowledge (how well it satisfies an organization's needs and therefore its potential benefit to the organization). The second is concerned with the accessibility of the knowledge (the ease and cost of capture, use, maintenance, and replacement).

What this means for your organization

In the field of strategy, various frameworks and tests have been created to assess the value of resources, including knowledge.[2] Despite the publication of such frameworks, anecdotal evidence suggests that they are not widely used.

The reasons for using a systematic process to identify and evaluate the knowledge resources of the organization are:

- To understand what knowledge the organization has;
- To understand what knowledge is needed – a gap analysis;
- To add structure to thinking and action;
- To create a view that is robust against organizational change and over time so that sustained initiatives can be justified.

At a practical level, there are three main activities involved in identifying valuable knowledge: identification and mapping of knowledge resources; relative valuation of knowledge resources; and using the results. The resulting process therefore has three stages:

1. Developing a knowledge map;
2. Valuing the knowledge in the map;
3. Using the output.

All these activities are best achieved by involving key stakeholders who have experience in critical areas of the business, although the exercise could be carried out by a single person.

Creating an action plan

Developing a knowledge map

The objective of this stage of the process is to map the domains of knowledge that are important to the business. Without this mapping exercise, critical knowledge resources for the business may be missed later when conducting the valuation exercise. The knowledge map is not an organizational chart or a process map. It is a representation of the key areas of knowledge that are core to the business over time and will be robust against organizational change.

> "People intuitively see that certain kinds of knowledge – such as the organization's R&D related knowledge – are valuable. But what they are usually much slower to see is that knowledge about how the organization manages its projects or even its facilities can be just as valuable."
>
> *Naina Visani, Head of Knowledge Management, Atomic Weapons Establishment*

To identify valuable knowledge resources, there are some trigger questions that can be asked about the organization:

- What differentiates us in the market place?
- What are our important markets?
- What are our key value-adding processes?
- What are our key competencies?
- What are our important products and services?
- What is important about our brand and identity?
- What are our key business support systems?

It can also be helpful to establish a hierarchy of value, namely:

Strategic – what differentiates us in the market place? Our unique *business models*.
Market – how do we present ourselves to our customers? Our *business themes/ solutions*.
Business processes – how do we operate? Our key *value-adding processes*.
Core competencies – who are we? Our core *technology competencies*.
Basic – what are our business support systems? Our *corporate processes*.

A decision about the level at which you are carrying out the analysis needs to be made. This includes the part of the business/organization involved, whether you intend to stay at a high strategic level, or whether you intend to drill down

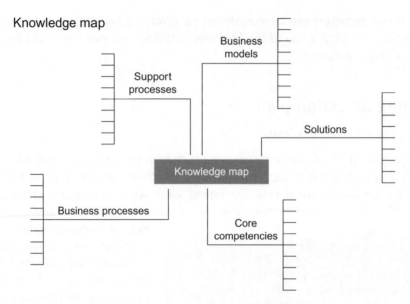

Figure 1.1: Possible structure for a knowledge map

below this to identify important categories of knowledge so that you can design projects in particular areas to retain or develop specific types of knowledge.

An example of the kind of knowledge map that might be created is shown in Figure 1.1.

We have already suggested that the value of knowledge is a function of its importance (its potential benefit to the organization) and its accessibility (the ease with which it can be applied, including the cost of capture, use, maintenance, and replacement). Table 1.1 includes some useful questions to determine importance and accessibility in relation to each type of knowledge identified in the map.

One of the challenges with knowledge mapping is making sense of a large amount of information and making the findings useful for everyone. Visualization of the results helps both to generate insights and communicate key points. Consequently, it is worth trying to organize the knowledge identified into a structured format that allows graphical representation. There are three basic kinds of scale that you can choose to use:

- Nominal scale – classify each body of knowledge as high importance/low importance and easy/difficult to access.
- Ordinal scale – rank the bodies of knowledge to indicate their importance and accessibility relative to each other.
- Rating scale – score the knowledge (e.g. on a scale of one to ten) to indicate its importance and accessibility.

You can then choose to represent the findings in an appropriate way. One approach is to represent them in a two-by-two matrix (using a nominal scale for both impor-

Table 1.1: Determining the importance and accessibility of knowledge

Importance	Accessibility
Is the knowledge critical to the business?	How easily can the knowledge be shared?
Does it impact on reliable and efficient operations?	How easily can the knowledge be applied?
Does it add value to the business?	Can it be used to make other knowledge more accessible?
Is it unique to this organization?	How accurate and reliable does it have to be?
Is it difficult to copy?	How quickly does it change with time?
Is it likely to be relevant for a long time?	What is the cost of maintaining it?
Could it be replaced by some other knowledge?	Can the right people access it?
Is it in demand?	Is the knowledge owned by the business?
Does it represent something we excel at?	
Can it be patented?	
Is the knowledge critical to the business?	

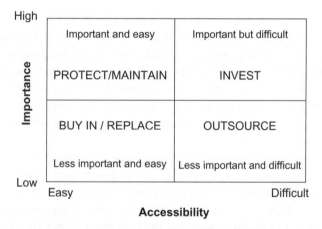

Figure 1.2: Presenting the results as a matrix

tance and accessibility) to create groups of knowledge resources with generic actions for each group (Figure 1.2). The same results can be represented with a cut off below which the value of the knowledge does not provide benefit from management investment (Figure 1.3).

Real life stories

The following three examples have been selected because they show how the knowledge mapping can be taken to different stages and used for different purposes.

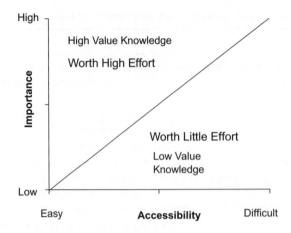

Figure 1.3: Presenting the results using a cut off line

R&D Technology Solutions Provider (TechSol)

TechSol is a UK-based technology solutions provider employing around 9,000 staff on a few main sites plus a substantial number of smaller sites throughout England, Scotland, and Wales. There is also a rapidly expanding business in the USA. The major part of the business is research, development, and evaluation for the defence sector and in this context the organization has in-depth expertise and knowledge over a very wide range of technologies. This extensive knowledge base is exploited to deliver advice and solutions over a very broad range of problem areas.

Identifying valuable knowledge has always been an important part of the development of the technology strategy and the business plans; knowledge is both a raw material and the product. Different types of knowledge were identified (functional, technical, business, market, and tacit) and mapped under seven main headings using the principles developed through this project (see Figure 1.4). The importance and difficulty of building this knowledge under each of the headings was evaluated.

Lessons and observations from carrying out this mapping process and then evaluating the importance and accessibility of the knowledge included the following:

● There were no items of low importance because, by definition, the knowledge map contains important knowledge. However, the discipline of asking the questions caused the manager involved to make some improvements to the knowledge map and he commented that one should not regard the process elements as purely sequential. The ease with which one might access and build knowledge did yield some low scores (easy to build/acquire) and this might suggest that, although the

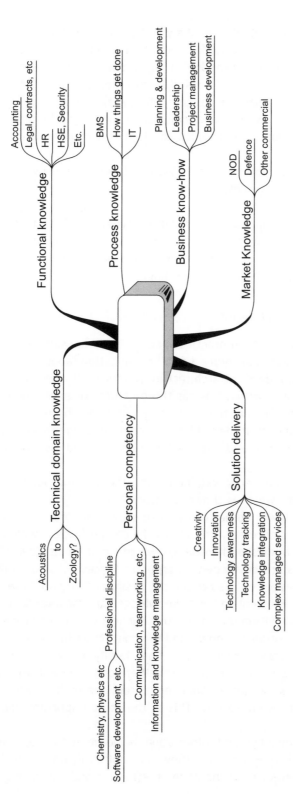

Figure 1.4: The knowledge map of TechSol

knowledge was important, it is unlikely to be the main source of sustained competitive advantage. Such knowledge could be outsourced if necessary.

• The most valuable knowledge in the organization, and the most difficult to create, is the highly tacit knowledge concerning how value is generated; it might be described better as a competency and relates to the capacity to combine collective knowledge and experience with a good understanding of customer needs and supplier capability to create innovative solutions to difficult problems.

• The process has potential as a tool for those developing strategy and plans at many levels in the business.

• The process also has potential in training programmes; in a large, agile, empowered organization such as TechSol everyone needs to understand the way the business functions, and in particular how value is created and the sources of competitive advantage. Going through a process such as this could be a very effective way to develop such personal learning.

Firm of Architects (Architects)

Architects is an architectural practice specializing in housing, with a multidisciplinary capability. Whilst being quite a small organization (about 240 technical staff), it is large by the standards of architecture practices. It operates in the specialist market of housing and within this has three centres of excellence: Regeneration, Private Housing, and Special Needs Housing. Great emphasis is placed on keeping abreast of developments in the field and on continuous improvement, which places a premium on knowledge and information collection and dissemination within the company.

In applying the knowledge valuing model, the starting point was to construct the knowledge map, which is shown in Figure 1.5.

The right hand lower corner of the map shows the "core competencies". This is a very high-level statement, as some of the competencies, such as architecture, include specialist bodies of knowledge which need to be identified in greater detail as strategies are developed. "Corporate Processes" and "Business Process" embody the knowledge required to run the business. They hold the key to mobilizing competences. "External Bodies of Knowledge" and "Market Sectors" encompass the knowledge and information from the outside world which needs to be constantly refreshed in order to understand the context within which the organization has to deploy its competencies. The final family is "Knowledge Integration". This is the knowledge of how to bring together competencies, with the knowledge to deploy them, taking into account input from the outside world, to provide a service that clients want to buy. This is the most important knowledge in the business.

Much of the knowledge and information in the other families can be relatively easily obtained by competitors, but they could not easily understand how to collect it together and present it to clients in an effective and convincing manner.

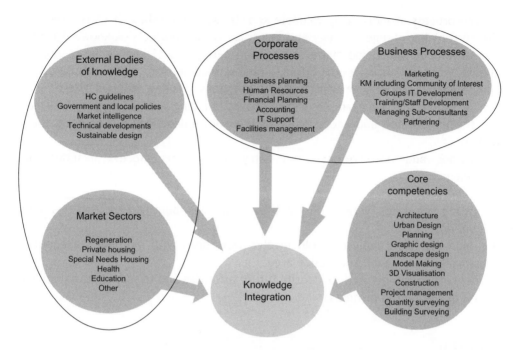

Figure 1.5: Knowledge map of Architects

Lessons and observations from carrying out this mapping process led the organization to recognize that its initial concept of how to manage knowledge was too crude. It was based on visits to other organizations, attending seminars, and reading around the subject. Plotting the knowledge map has provided the basis of a more considered approach. In particular it has:

- confirmed that there are existing Knowledge Management and information sharing tools to meet the organization's most important needs;
- illustrated the gaps in the coverage of the tools and put greater clarity on priorities;
- illustrated the difference between bodies of information and knowledge which should largely just be available, and bodies of knowledge which need to be developed and nurtured.

ICT Solutions and Services (ICT_Services)

ICT_Services is one of the world's leading providers of vendor independent Information and Communication Technology (ICT) solutions and services. It designs, integrates, and manages ICT infrastructures and business solutions for many of the world's largest global and local companies and organizations, helping them maximize the value of their information technology investments.

The process of identifying valuable knowledge was used to check the focus of the current knowledge strategy and prioritize future projects. A knowledge map was developed which identified seven main categories of knowledge resources: clients, global alliances, global offers, global service delivery, global standards and competencies, country operations, and functions. Having mapped these (in a similar way to the two examples shown above), a rating system was used to evaluate the importance and accessibility of the knowledge. Figure 1.6 shows these ratings.

Lessons and observations from carrying out this process included the following:

- Existing initiatives were in line with the priorities identified through this high-level analysis.
- A more detailed analysis would involve workshops with multiple stakeholders associated with each knowledge area.
- The method can be used to identify future priorities and to support the justification of associated projects.

Top tips

The process of identifying valuable knowledge can be carried out by an individual or by a group of stakeholders – people who have experience in critical areas of the business.

Group work has several advantages:

- It builds commitment and understanding.
- Insights are created through discussion.
- It is more likely to produce robust results.
- It is more fun!

If you decide to work through the process with a group, invite people with a variety of skills and backgrounds from different parts of the organization. Consider appointing a facilitator to manage the process and make sure everyone contributes effectively. Consider inviting people from outside the organization – customers and suppliers might be able to bring valuable new perspectives.

The research and the team involved

This research was carried out between 2003 and 2004 by a working group of members of the Henley KM Forum. It involved a review of the literature, focus group exploration of the nature of knowledge value, and an evaluation of the proposed framework by applying it in detail to six case study organizations.

Importance	Clients	Alliances	Global Offers and Centres	Global Delivery	Global Service Centres	Global Standards and Competences	Country Operations	Functions	1	2	3
Is the knowledge critical to the business?	3	2	2	3	3	2	3	1	not critical	important	essential
Is the knowledge relevant to the business?	3	3	3	3	3	3	3	2	low	medium	high
Does it impact on reliable and efficient operations?	3	3	2	3	3	2	3	1	low impact	significant impact	high impact
Does it add value to the business?	3	3	2	3	3	2	3	1	low value	medium value	high value
Is it unique to my organization?	2	2	3	2	2	2	3	1	ubiquitous	differen-tiator	unique
Is it in demand?	3	3	3	3	3	2	3	2	low	medium	high
Importance score	17	16	15	18	17	13	18	8			
Accessibility									1	2	3
How easily can the knowledge be shared?	3	1	1	1	1	2	3	2	easy to access	available	difficult to access
How easily can the knowledge be applied?	3	1	1	1	1	1	3	1	easy to apply	applicable with some effort	difficult to apply
How accurate and reliable does it have to be?	3	3	3	3	3	2	3	2	order of magnitude	important	accuracy essential
How quickly does it change with time?	3	3	2	2	3	2	3	2	yearly	monthly	daily
What is the cost of maintaining it?	2	3	3	3	3	1	3	2	low	medium	high
Can the right people access it?	2	1	1	1	1	1	2	1	generally yes	mostly	generally no
Accessibility score	16	12	11	11	12	9	17	10			
Combined score	33	28	26	29	29	22	35	18			
Priority to focus on	2	4	5	3=	3=	6	1	7			

Figure 1.6: Knowledge map ratings of ICT_Services

The research activities were intended to help managers identify valuable knowledge in their organization to set priorities for management attention and financial investments. It was not intended to provide prescriptive advice for a particular business.

Dr Judy Payne, a member of the KM Forum team and Visiting Fellow at Henley Business School, led the research in conjunction with Brian Holness of InnogyOne, who was the member co-champion. Anna Truch of Henley Business School provided research support. Working group members included representatives from:

Aegis	*DLO*
Getronics	*GlaxoSmithKline*
InnogyOne	*Nissan*
PRP Architects	*QinetiQ*
Unisys	

together with invited associate: John Burrows (formerly Buckman Laboratories).

Final reflections from the research

Case studies have demonstrated the application of this approach across a wide range of organizations in very different business sectors and at varying levels of KM maturity. The working group originally thought that KM maturity might affect the way the guidance should be applied. However, it became clear that organizational culture was more important in determining the way the findings were adopted.

Categorizing knowledge into domains or families helps to identify the different type of knowledge each family represents, hence a different level of impact on the business and potentially a different management strategy. This approach can also identify gaps in the knowledge base that need to be filled to provide the ability to deliver the business plan. Valuing the knowledge in each family allows the creation of a relationship between the level of the knowledge and its potential value to the business. Judgements can then be made on the investment in its management, development, and exploitation.

Notes

1. See for example Grant, R.M. (1996) Toward a knowledge-based theory of the firm, *Strategic Management Journal*, 17: 109-122, or Spender, J.-C. (1996) Making knowledge the basis of a dynamic theory of the firm, *Strategic Management Journal*, 17: 45-62.
2. See for example Collis, D.J. and Montgomery, C.A. (1995) Competing on resources: Strategy in the 1990s, *Harvard Business Review*, 73(4): 118-128 (five tests: inimitability, durability, appropriability, substitutability, competitive superiority) and O'Hara, K. and

Shadbolt, N. (2001) "Issues for an ontology for knowledge valuation", in *Proceedings of the IJCAI-01 Workshop on E-Business and the Intelligent Web* (five characteristics that affect knowledge value: embeddedness of knowledge in a network, knowledge as a means to an end or an end in itself, source of the knowledge, context of the knowledge, amenability of the knowledge).

Chapter 2

Snapshot

Productive knowledge flows increase the potential for value generation. In other words, when knowledge is transferred quickly and easily from where it is generated to where it is needed it has more opportunity to make both a short and a longer term difference to something that matters to the organization. The organization is only one element in an industry/sector-wide system of knowledge-based activity that includes individual employees, customers, suppliers, competitors, and other institutions. Ultimately the knowledge value generated depends on how well connected the organization is within that system and how effectively nine critical knowledge flows work together to influence the firm's performance.

A method has been developed that allows you to build an integrated picture of these nine major knowledge flows and to diagnose what can be done to make them more effective. The approach is based on a two-level framework. The top level outlines the nine flows in some detail (describing the measurable objectives that can be achieved from assessing current and desired status in relation to each flow). This gives you the big picture so that you can make an evaluation of strategic priorities. The second level outlines the common influences affecting how smoothly each of the top-level flows works. It is at this level that you can identify practical initiatives that will have the most impact in reducing waste and inefficiency.

Why this matters

Being well connected affects your organizational capacity to create, access, and use knowledge. Individuals within the organization cannot work effectively in a vacuum. To do their job, they need knowledge to be flowing freely from where it is created to where they need it. Likewise the organization cannot afford to be cut off from the wider world; it is just one player in a sector-wide system of knowledge-based activity, and success comes from actively tapping into, or even shaping, the pattern of knowledge flows.

These connections and interdependencies must be at the heart of a comprehensive assessment of the organizational priorities for knowledge improvement. Yet, it can be difficult to assess how effective knowledge sharing is: the system is so wide, and the discipline so diverse that it can be hard to see how everything fits together. The first level of the framework described here allows you to map knowledge flows both within the organization and between it and the outside world.

Additionally, the nature of knowledge means that context and perception are crucial in determining value and application. Therefore, in addition to understanding the pattern of knowledge flows, the second level of the framework allows you to carry out a more detailed assessment of why each flow matters, what is involved in making it flow well, how it is supported, and the context in which it is happening. This means you can identify where any potential blockages lie and assess where investments need to be made to overcome them. Most importantly of all, it helps you to prioritize individual initiatives whilst still seeing the bigger picture of the organization as a knowledge-based enterprise.

What this means for your organization

This framework provides a tool to bring clarity to issues within the development of a knowledge strategy. Of itself it does not create a strategy, but it does provide a structured approach to an internal investigation of the organization from a knowledge perspective. In particular it places at the centre the proposition that knowledge needs to flow purposefully to improve performance. The method is designed to develop an integrated picture of nine knowledge flows associated with the organization and what enables these to be effective. The original model of the flows proposed by Karl-Erik Sveiby[1] has been adapted and consists of two levels corresponding to two key principles: coherence and alignment. Coherence means how well the nine knowledge flows work together in harmony to support performance at the first level of analysis; alignment is about how well various factors support or obstruct the flow so that at the second level it is possible to design interventions to reduce inefficiency and improve performance.

In the first level of the framework, there are nine different value generating routes along which knowledge can flow within and between three knowledge domains: individual people (I) working for the organization (sometimes called human capital), the systems and processes of the organization (O) (sometimes called structural capital), and the external relationships (E) of the organization (sometimes called relationship capital). This is illustrated in Figure 2.1.

The beneficial purpose of each numbered flow, in other words how it can generate value for the organization, is explained below. Such definitions are useful for creating a common language about the knowledge flows in the organizations.

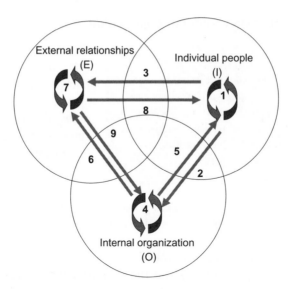

Figure 2.1: First level of the framework – nine value generating knowledge flows associated with an organization

Knowledge flows that start from individuals

> "Unisys has a client account site within its IT systems, to store and share information about each client. No matter who in the organization is talking to the client, or where they are in the world, their learning is fed into that site. So knowledge can flow around the organization easily."
>
> *Alex Goodall, formerly with Unisys, now an independent knowledge management consultant*

Flows between individuals (1): This is essential for individuals to be able to solve problems more quickly and get better answers. They need to be able to build communications across the organization and vertically. This has benefits for employers, as it stimulates learning, enables better use of existing knowledge, and is a potential source of innovation.

Flows from individuals to the organization (2): This ensures individual learning is translated into business knowledge and expands the intellectual capital of the organization. It saves every individual reinventing the wheel when faced with the same problems and builds the capabilities of the organization.

Flows from the individual to external stakeholders (3): This involves individuals sharing knowledge with customers and partners to strengthen those relationships that generate value. It helps the organization protect its competitive position by improving quality, customer responsiveness, and loyalty.

Knowledge flows that start from the organization

> "We have interactive team spaces across disciplines, to allow knowledge to flow between individuals outside of project groups. Users can ask questions, communicate with one another, read resources and use a searchable database of expertise. This is available to both internal employees and external partners such as consultants and contractors."
>
> *Daressa Frodsham, Head of Engineering Knowledge, United Utilities*

Flows around the organization (4): By adopting integrated Knowledge and Information Management systems and processes, the organization can save time and money, and make better informed decisions.

Flows from the organization to the individual (5): By establishing knowledge systems that can be easily accessed, searched, and used, individuals can learn from the intellectual capital of the organization more quickly and relevantly. This improves productivity and the potential for innovation.

Flows from the organization to external stakeholders (6): Using organizational knowledge to shape external conditions for customers, suppliers, and partners enables the organization to influence the environment in favour of the organization and improve its position.

Knowledge flows that start from external stakeholders

> "It is vital to establish knowledge flows with external partners. We have a group of companies we engage with on a mentoring level, including charities and non-profit-making organizations, where we put what we know on the table for them to learn from. It is a two-way process that we gain understanding from too."
>
> *Carolyn Lees, Director of IT, Permira Advisers LLP*

Flows between external stakeholders (7): Communication across the sector or industry drives advances that can benefit everyone in the process. By choosing to influence this, the organization can be a first mover and potentially gain advantage.

Flows from external stakeholders to individuals (8): It is easy to focus on internal dimensions first, and ignore the fact that external knowledge changes all the time. If you don't tap into it, you can become out-of-date very quickly. By improving external connectivity, individuals can gather fuel for innovation and will have early-warning signals for any changes that will affect the business.

Flows from external stakeholders to the organization (9): Establishing and institutionalizing these contacts enables an organization to better exploit its current knowledge or innovate more quickly – most importantly it enhances the organization's capability to learn.

The second level of the model

At the second level of the framework, we rely on research that suggests that there are some basic factors that affect an individual's responses in a situation which need careful attention. When they are in alignment it makes it easier for them to work without confusion, internal conflict, or unproductive stress.[2] People need to be motivated to achieve the purpose of the knowledge sharing that happens along the flow (they understand why it matters), have the skills to complete the task (they know how to do it), be comfortable with and able to take the necessary actions (they know what to do), and feel that the environment is conducive to such action (where it takes place is appropriate). If these four factors are in align-ment, the process of achieving the outcome tends to run smoothly and efficiently because there is nothing blocking it. For individuals, motivation comes from their beliefs and values. We have assumed this applies equally to organizations (through culture which is a set of collective beliefs and values) and external stakeholders (the industry expectations of what is acceptable and achievable). Organizations have core skills and typical behaviours just like individuals and collectively there are industry skill standards and certain behaviours become industry norms. The environment for individuals is the organization, while the industry is the environ-ment for the organization.

These factors are illustrated in Figure 2.2. Like a dam in a river, unmanaged each factor can act as a blockage to the flow of knowledge (illustrated as obstruct-ing the flow along the arrow), or well managed it allows the flow to proceed and generate value (illustrated as raised out of the flow). Value is generated most effectively when all four factors are raised out of the flow. Value is generated most

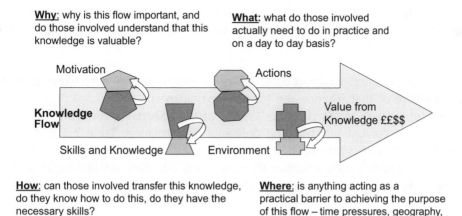

Why: why is this flow important, and do those involved understand that this knowledge is valuable?

What: what do those involved actually need to do in practice and on a day to day basis?

Motivation

Actions

Knowledge Flow

Value from Knowledge ££$$

Skills and Knowledge

Environment

How: can those involved transfer this knowledge, do they know how to do this, do they have the necessary skills?

Where: is anything acting as a practical barrier to achieving the purpose of this flow – time pressures, geography, time zones, culture, incentives, access to technology?

(Henley KM Forum, 2004)

Figure 2.2: Removing the blockages to each knowledge flow (second level of the framework)

effectively when all four factors are managed to support knowledge flows. To understand the nature of these four factors and whether they are blocking or enabling a knowledge flow, we suggest that you ask the relevant questions in Figure 2.2 (why, what, how, and where) in relation to each knowledge flow in turn.

Creating an action plan

The method is intended primarily as a way of gathering and structuring information.

The method can be used to structure interviews with a range of key managers and individuals across the organization. Alternatively it can be helpful to use it as part of a workshop format with groups of people. It depends on who the influential stakeholders are and how easy it would be to get them working together in a workshop. The objective in either case is to gather information. If there is also a need to engage groups of people to gain buy-in to change, then a workshop format is likely to be best. Experience suggests that 15-20 people are about the right number for these workshops.

Whether you adopt an interview or workshop approach, you will need to ensure that the sample of people attending is representative. You need people who have a strategic perspective on what knowledge makes a difference in the industry and how investment in knowledge-based activities can help organizational performance. It is advisable to identify specific organizational groups or divisions which have their own clear purpose and outputs and work with each of these in turn, following this with an integrating review of all of the information collected to identify important knowledge flows across boundaries.

The interviews or workshops should be used to understand each flow in turn. There are three components to the gathering of information from each interviewee (or in a workshop):

- Collecting detailed information to describe the nature of each flow from the perspective of that interviewee (or the participants).
- The interviewee's (or participants') rating of the effectiveness of each flow, both in terms of current practice and desirable performance. Table 2.1 is a survey template to collect this data.
- The interviewee's (or participants') view of the enablers and blockages to each flow using the four questions shown on Figure 2.2.

There are no right or wrong answers in this approach. Not all flows will have a desirable rating of 7; it depends on the level of contribution each makes to organizational performance. The objective is to achieve consensus about the ratings for each knowledge flow. Significant differences between interviewees or within a workshop setting provide an opportunity to explore the reasons for the different perceptions: the four alignment factors provide the mechanism to understand the

Table 2.1: Template for a survey to collect information about the effectiveness of knowledge flows in the organization

	Low			Medium	High			Rating
	1	2	3	4	5	6	7	
1. I-I Knowledge flows between individuals in my organization.	Little knowledge sharing due to insecurity, politics etc.			Knowledge mainly shared with local trusted colleagues.			Widespread and active participation in mentoring, coaching, communities etc. demonstrating a high level of trust between people.	*Desirable Rating:* *Actual Rating:*
2. I-O Practices that ensure that the knowledge/ experience of individual employees flows to where it is needed internally.	Limited use made of mechanisms (like databases or communities) to access or share knowledge across the organization.			Local initiatives to spread individual knowledge becoming more evident. After-action reviews completed for major projects. Incomplete coordination.			Accessing and sharing knowledge is embedded in core processes and carried out as a matter of course.	*Desirable Rating:* *Actual Rating:*
3. I-E Knowledge flows from people employed by my organization to external customers/suppliers/ alliance companies (all classed as partners here).	Employees are not able to build relationships externally due to lack of time or poor processes.			Increasing evidence of employees forming relationships with external partners, but this is incompletely coordinated rather than part of the knowledge strategy of the business.			Employees are expected to form trusting relationships with key partners and this is supported through the knowledge strategy. Participation in professional bodies and networks likely to be common practice.	*Desirable Rating:* *Actual Rating:*

continued on next page...

Table 2.1 - Continued

	Low		Medium		High		Rating
	1	2 3	4	5 6	7		
4. O-O The systems, structures, and processes in my organization that help knowledge flow from one place to another.	Isolated examples of knowledge-sharing systems and process. No integration and much "reinventing the wheel".		Cultural initiatives starting to support infrastructure and process initiatives. Incomplete coordination though.		A fully integrated system with cultural initiatives supporting process and infrastructure investments.		*Desirable Rating:* *Actual Rating:*
5. O-I Practices that ensure that knowledge available in the organization improves the competence of individual employees.	Few supporting structures available to help individuals know what to do.		Some best practices and templates and other resources available for core activities. Incomplete coordination of investments in learning and development.		Developing employees is a business priority. Best practice guidance widely available and readily accessible. Learning encouraged, appropriate resources available.		*Desirable Rating:* *Actual Rating:*
6. O-E Systems and to make knowledge available to external customers/ suppliers/alliance companies (all partners here).	No support for customers/suppliers/ partners, e.g. by providing access to update, status, diagnostic, delivery etc. information.		Increasing evidence of facilities for external organizations to access and use essential information from within your business.		Your business model drives the enhancement of secure systems to allow external partners to access all necessary supply/diagnostic/status etc. information.		*Desirable Rating:* *Actual Rating:*

	Low		Medium			High		Rating
	1	2	3	4	5	6	7	
7. E-E Knowledge flows between other companies in my industry (including suppliers, customers, and competitors).	No significant conversations evident between players in the industry.			Ad hoc conversations and meaningful relationships becoming increasingly evident.			External relationships between players in the industry are vibrant and productive.	*Desirable Rating:* *Actual Rating:*
8. E-I Knowledge transfers from external customers/suppliers/ alliance companies (all classed as partners here) to individual employees in my organization who need it.	Individuals isolated from external partners (customer/ supplier or other partner) or professional knowledge networks.			Systems, processes, and resources increasingly available to allow some key individuals to learn from external partners or professional networks, but activities are incompletely coordinated.			External liaison roles have been created and are coordinated effectively. Employee development includes participation in external professional knowledge networks.	*Desirable Rating:* *Actual Rating:*
9. E-O Knowledge flows from customers/suppliers/ alliance companies (all classed as partners here) into the decision-making infrastructure of my organization.	No formal mechanisms exist to elicit or capture external feedback or use this to improve products, services, or processes.			Increasing evidence that feedback is collected from key partners and taken into account in new/improved products, services, and processes, although this is not a coordinated process.			External knowledge is actively sought and mechanisms are in place to feed this into improving products, services, and processes in a coordinated way.	*Desirable Rating:* *Actual Rating:*

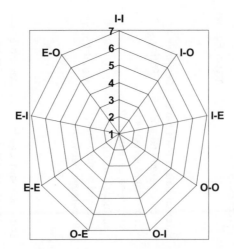

Figure 2.3: Plotting the knowledge flow ratings

sources of the differences of opinion. Once approximate agreement has been reached, then transfer your desirable and actual ratings for each knowledge flow for each part of the organization of interest onto a radar chart like that shown in Figure 2.3 by plotting each one against the appropriate axis and joining up the points.

The gap between desirable and actual ratings will be a useful pointer to areas where attention is required – the biggest gaps indicate the priorities. When all the knowledge flows work together the value creating potential is increased. If the pattern is different for each part of the organization, then look for opportunities to understand why some flows work well in one place and not in others (again, the four alignment factors should be the starting point) and whether experience and good practice can be transferred.

Real life stories

You might find it useful to benchmark your results against those of other organizations. When we used this survey with 26 large organizations from a wide range of sectors and industries, we found the following:

1. On average, the highest rated knowledge flow was that between individual employees (I-I). This was viewed as being significantly more effective than any of the other knowledge flows.
2. A cluster of five other knowledge flows received approximately the same ratings. The three flows relating to the internal structure of the organization and its support for knowledge flows to and from individual employees (O-I, I-O, O-O)

were rated above average in terms of their effectiveness. Similar ratings were given to the flow of knowledge from individual employees to external industry players – meaning partners, customers, suppliers etc. (I-E) – and then from these players back to the infrastructure of the organization (E-O).

3. The ratings for the effectiveness of the flows of knowledge from external partners to individual employees (E-I) and from the organization back to the outside world (O-E) were marginally, but significantly, lower.

4. The flow of knowledge from external relationships in the broadest sense into the decision-making processes of the organization (the E-O knowledge flow) is particularly interesting. In the defence sector "need to know" has historically shaped the actual and perceived importance of knowledge flows to and from external relationships. Hence the E-O knowledge flow was rated as low by a defence procurement organization, matched by a low rating for the O-E knowledge flow in a defence supplier organization (data collected in 2004 – the situation could well have changed today). In contrast, in high-technology organizations, the pace of change and the need to collaborate with partners to develop new technology, plus the level of customer intimacy needed for profitable innovation, meant that flows of knowledge from external relationships into the organization (E-O) were an area of relative strength.

5. Examining the statistical patterns in the data confirmed that the flow of knowledge between players in the industry (E-E) needs to be treated a little differently to the other knowledge flows. The nature of the E-E flow has to be interpreted as the product of industry dynamics, which determine the main pattern of knowledge flowing between players. Some industries are necessarily more transparent and collaborative than others. This interpretation was confirmed by separate investigation conducted to further explore the reasons behind all the ratings. It is likely that history and other factors will make this knowledge flow the most difficult for any one organization to influence. In fact, this external industry context may also shape the relative emphasis placed on all of the other knowledge flows.

Clearly all knowledge flows need not be equally strong or effective – their relative importance depends on the context.

Based on this observation, the two examples of alignment factors analysis, included here, have been chosen because, in our experience, they relate to the flows most likely to be challenging for many organizations. The first is based on published material from Buckman Laboratories in 2004,[3] which is a well-known Most Admired Knowledge Enterprise winner. Table 2.2 summarizes the alignment factors for the "I-E" knowledge flow, that is, "individual employees sharing their knowledge with external customers, suppliers and partners". Recognizing the importance of the flows across the boundary of the organization is a sign of Knowledge Management maturity and has clearly underpinned Buckman Laboratories' Knowledge Management successes.

Table 2.2: Alignment factors supporting the "I-E" knowledge flow at Buckman Laboratories

Motivation	The company set the goal that "everyone in the organization must actively support the needs of the customers by as much direct contact as possible. No one can just sit back and leave that to those who deal with customers every day."
Skills and Knowledge	All associates know how to participate in any discussion about the customer. People are trained to use the systems and empowered to use what is available. The Buckman Labs Learning Centre provides the means for individual employees to acquire the knowledge and skills they need – including typing skills and how to communicate in a networked organization.
Action Required	All associates have access to the same systems and are asked to be "effectively engaged on the front line". Employee online discussions about what this means concluded "it's about involvement, commitment, creativity, passion and ultimately the freedom to do everything we can to use all the knowledge we have to make sure that we have done our utmost to satisfy the customer in all areas".
Environment	Collaborative systems have been put in place to allow each associate access to the necessary knowledge to deliver value to customers.

Table 2.3: Alignment factors supporting the "E-E" knowledge flow at a mobile telephone operator (as of 2004)

Motivation	Synergies between technologies and how these affect lifestyle choices are believed to be the basis for developing future products and services. The organization therefore needs to support and encourage the public debate about how people want to live their lives in order to refine their role in providing solutions in the future.
Skills and Knowledge	Knowledge of how to establish and maintain effective relationships with other players in the industry is important as no one company can drive this debate alone.
Action Required	Stimulating public and industry debate requires many techniques to be adopted. Visionary leadership, public relations initiatives, and thought-leadership publications are elements of this.
Environment	The industry environment is relatively collaborative as it is driven by technology standards that need to be negotiated between leading players.

The second example is based on a mobile telephone network operator. Table 2.3 summarizes the alignment factors for the "E-E" knowledge flow, that is, "knowledge flows between other companies in the industry, including suppliers, customers and competitors". Influencing the knowledge flows within an industry is particularly important in dynamic and rapidly evolving situations such as communications technology development.

Top tips

✓ Depending on the nature of the organization, it may not be possible to treat all external relationships in the same way. Be willing to repeat the process for each kind of relationship in turn if necessary (suppliers, partners, customer, and "others").

✓ Use the nine knowledge flows to look for new sources of knowledge which may add value, rather than simply looking to improve the effectiveness of existing flows.

✓ Remember to integrate all nine flows after you have looked at them individually. They really can't be considered in isolation from each other as one creates the environment in which another takes place.

✓ Revisit the process regularly. This isn't a one-off event. The organizational context is dynamic and therefore the factors underpinning the effectiveness of each flow will be continually changing, as will the relative importance of each flow.

✓ Don't allow interviewees to put the highest rating as "desirable" against all nine flows. It is important to think through what really matters.

✓ Look for patterns across the flows (using the alignment factors as a guide). You may find repeated problems that can be resolved with a coherent intervention. Seek to influence these patterns for greatest impact.

✓ Don't rush thinking about the alignment factors. With some careful thought about what they really mean for each of the nine knowledge flows it is possible to design simple interventions with high impact.

✓ Don't be rigid about organizational boundaries – in today's networked organizations these can be fluid. Set the boundary that is appropriate for the situation you are trying to understand, but then apply it consistently.

The research and the team involved

This research was carried out in two phases during 2003 and 2004 by a working group of members of the Henley KM Forum. The aim was to find a way to integrate the different facets of a knowledge-based approach into a guiding framework so that organizations at various stages of maturity can:

- diagnose why their initiatives may not be working as effectively as they hoped;
- choose which knowledge-related initiatives to pay attention to next;
- take informed action to improve the business value from knowledge available to the organization.

This required both a broad conceptual framework as well as enough detail to allow users to drill down into the practical factors influencing effective performance and value generation. The resulting two-level model was designed to achieve this. Its use was evaluated through surveying the knowledge flows in 26 organizations, with telephone interviews being used to collect more detailed information about the reasons for highly rated flows. The final guidance was intended to be used as a diagnostic tool, the results of which require interpretation in the context of each organization. It was not intended to provide prescriptive guidance for any particular organization. The Project was co-championed by Dr Christine van Winkelen and Dr Jane McKenzie of Henley Business School, together with Lt Col Peter McGuigan of ES Land. The working group included representatives from:

Aegis	*Defence Procurement Agency*
ES Land	*Getronics*
GSK	*Orange*
QinetiQ	*RWE Innogy*
RWE Thames Water	*Unisys*

together with an invited associate: John Burrows (formerly Buckman Laboratories).

Final reflections from the research

We found that the extent to which the nine knowledge flows work smoothly and efficiently together and operate coherently in support of the organizational objectives is a reflection of the maturity of a knowledge-based organization. As awareness and a knowledge perspective develop within the organization, internal flows within knowledge domains tend to become effective first, then flows back and forth between the "individual" and "organizational" domains become more effective. It isn't until knowledge flows to and from external partners, suppliers, and customers are fully integrated with the other knowledge flows that full knowledge

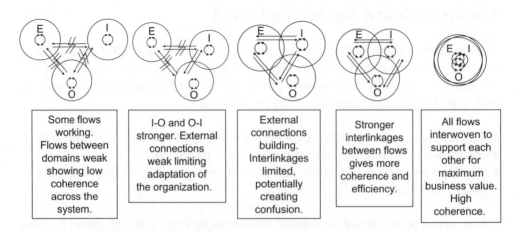

Some flows working. Flows between domains weak showing low coherence across the system.	I-O and O-I stronger. External connections weak limiting adaptation of the organization.	External connections building. Interlinkages limited, potentially creating confusion.	Stronger interlinkages between flows gives more coherence and efficiency.	All flows interwoven to support each other for maximum business value. High coherence.

Figure 2.4: Moving towards maturity as a knowledge-based organization

value can be released. This is illustrated in Figure 2.4. The process is highly dynamic as the organizational context changes.

Notes

1. Sveiby, K.-E. (2002) "Creating Knowledge Focused Strategies: Good and Bad Practices", Henley KM Forum 2nd Annual Conference, Henley Management College, UK. See also, Sveiby, K.-E. (2001) A Knowledge-based theory of the firm to guide strategy formulation, *Journal of Intellectual Capital*, 2(4), 344-358.
2. See for example: Bateson, G. (1972) *Steps to an Ecology of the Mind*, New York, Ballantine Books; and Dilts, R. (1990) *Changing Belief Systems with NLP*, Capitola CA: Meta Publications.
3. Buckman, R.H. (2004) *Building a Knowledge-Driven Organization*, McGraw Hill.

Section II

Enable operational effectiveness

By "operations" we mean the systems and processes that give an organization its ability to deliver against its purpose. In other words, the ways that goods or services are produced for an external customer, client, or user by transforming raw materials or knowledge into something they need. Some commercial organizations work on a cost leadership business model; they manage operational process costs so tightly that they can charge customers less than their competitors for much the same product or service. Even if the business model is to deliver sufficiently differentiated products or services for which customers are willing to pay a premium, few businesses can afford to neglect the cost of their operations. For public services, the political climate in most countries has been driving cost reductions in operational activities for many years.

What do we mean by operational effectiveness?

Operational effectiveness means optimally sourcing, transforming, and using resources to produce goods or services as cheaply as possible, whilst still maintaining quality, delivery, and other customer satisfaction, environmental, or governance objectives. Knowledge is a production resource; in the case of a service business such as consulting, it may be the main resource. However, even when production involves physical resources such as raw materials, knowledge associated with transforming material into final product is an important cost factor. It may be embedded into the operational systems so that the production process is as reliable and reproducible as possible. However, it may also be generated through ongoing learning about how to do things better.

Some organizations call their operational activities "front office" and the functions that support these "back office". Usually this reflects the fact that those in front office activities interact directly with external customers or users. Here we are focusing on the front office, rather than the back office support functions, because these are directly responsible for generating value in the organization and because they are subject to particular pressures which can make it more demanding to construct the business case for introducing knowledge initiatives.

A knowledge perspective is usually introduced into operational activities in an organization to reduce costs, increase speed, or improve quality (the key measures in an operational environment). However, it might also be intended to differentiate the service being offered to customers or to stimulate innovation. Typical objectives could therefore be to:

- ensure that everyone has access to the most up-to-date knowledge when they need it;
- embed processes that help capture learning from operational activities so it can be used either elsewhere or at a later date;
- ensure that good practices are identified and shared with others who could benefit from them;
- make visible people with particular knowledge for dealing with operational issues, customer requirements, or problems as quickly as possible and to the required standard.

Usually there is an emphasis on exploiting the knowledge available to the organization as effectively as possible, along with initiatives for incrementally improving the knowledge base to embed continuous learning about how to do things better. More radical innovation may be more difficult to achieve. If this is a priority for your organization, take a look at Section III and think about how to combine the recommendations with the ideas discussed in this section.

The challenge in offering advice to managers seeking to improve operational effectiveness (which probably means every manager with responsibility for operational activities) is that context matters. There are some principles that are common to all situations, in particular recognition of unique and valuable knowledge and reducing the high-level barriers to knowledge flows as discussed in Section I. However, beyond this, to design and implement knowledge initiatives you need to pay particular attention to the specifics of the situation.

How do you enable it?

The chapters in this section consider the implications of various different operational situations from a knowledge perspective.

The first chapter asks you to decide what aspects of operational activities drive value generation for the organization. The argument is that the operational activities are subtly different for a manufacturing business, a knowledge-based service organization such as a consulting firm, or an organization like water, gas, or banking, which connects users to services. Consequently improvement initiatives will have different priorities in each setting and the people involved will respond differently to them, due to the nature of their work, how it is managed and organized, and how they engage with it.

The second chapter similarly focuses on knowledge initiatives in yet another context, in this case various types of projects. Projects are the means through which many organizations deliver their products or services. Rather than treating all projects as the same, distinguishing them according to the level of risk involved introduces important knowledge considerations. Changes may be required throughout the project lifecycle, but to identify what knowledge initiatives can improve operational performance requires an understanding of the starting point and tailoring them to suit the planned path to the final outcome. The final chapter acknowledges that no organization can deliver in isolation. Most organizations have suppliers of one kind or another. Increasingly, many also work with one or more partners in alliances or consortia, in order to deliver something more complex in knowledge terms than they can achieve cost-effectively alone. Managing the knowledge flows associated with each type of external partnership in an appropriate way is therefore an essential aspect of operational effectiveness.

The pressure of delivery schedules affects all types of operational situation. All too often, these time pressures mean that those with operational responsibilities consider they haven't time for something as potentially intangible as knowledge or learning initiatives. The fact that knowledge initiatives may take some time to show real benefits can also make them difficult to prioritize in an operational environment. Yet, this is where they matter most because it is where an organization achieves what it exists to do. The research presented in these chapters was undertaken to identify what makes the most difference in a particular situation, as well as to consider how to implement initiatives in the most compelling ways for this demanding and time poor audience.

Finally, how people involved in operational activities are managed can hinder their involvement in learning and knowledge sharing. Incentive systems can drive competitive behaviours between different parts of the organization, or even between individuals; short-term delivery targets may be prioritized over longer term capability building. To create an environment where people care enough to use the best possible knowledge available in their work, and to help others to do so too, requires encouraging leadership behaviours and appropriate people management practices.

Key questions to ask yourself

As you start to use the ideas in the next three chapters ask:

- What is the best way to characterize the operational activities of your organization in terms of the value generating front line, the nature of projects, and the kind of external collaborations the organization is involved in? Different parts of the organization may be characterized in different ways. One size doesn't fit all between organizations, and neither does it within most large organizations.
- What is the business case for initiatives that improve learning and knowledge flows in operational activities in your organization? The objective is to make a real difference to what matters most, not to create "nice to have" add-ons.
- What are the opportunities to use the knowledge-related activities outlined in the rest of the book in the most appropriate way? In particular Section IV practices to improve learning and knowledge flows may be particularly useful, as might the Section VI discussions of embedding new ways of working and thinking into the organization.

Chapter 3

Snapshot

How can a knowledge perspective make a difference to performance at the front line of operations in an organization? The front line is where the activities occur which allow an organization to achieve its main purpose and generate value.

The research showed that how you go about introducing knowledge initiatives to the front line depends more than anything on how much discretion individual people there have to decide how to do their job.

If people have a lot of autonomy and discretion in their jobs, then you have to get their buy-in and commitment. Communication must be about building understanding of *why it matters*, as much as what needs to be done and how it could happen.

If people have less discretion and autonomy in their roles because the nature of their job dictates what happens when, then you can be more focused on action. Communication must be about *what needs to be done* and how it could happen, as well as why it matters.

Why this matters

"We're too busy for that!"

Have you ever heard your company's front line staff say that? In most businesses, the front line operates at a high speed. People are under intense time, cost, and performance pressures. Knowledge is often not valued, nor perceived to be part of the way to deliver what matters.

"Today's work today!"

Sales, deliveries, output, productivity, profit etc. – these are the important things at the front line. Knowledge initiatives need to make a difference here and now at the front line. Yet all too often they seem to be about long-term programmes, culture change initiatives, and technological infrastructures. Where is the relevance?

"What's in it for me?"

Even though knowledge-related initiatives have made progress in many businesses, frequently they do more for back office supporting functions than core business activities. Even when front line people think they are a good idea in theory, the benefits seem nebulous so they become a low priority.

Yet . . . the only place improving knowledge flows matters is at the front line of the business!

The front line is where the business interfaces with the customer, with suppliers, with partners. The whole "brain" of the organization must be at the disposal of people at the front line as they really do both create and use the intellectual resources of the business. If you have spent time thinking about knowledge and how to enable the business to be more effective, then you know that today simply working the physical (and human!) assets harder isn't enough. Instead, success comes from being smarter, more innovative, and having an engaged and customer-centric workforce.

Knowledge initiatives exist to develop the organization's brain and put it to work more effectively. They are about breaking out of the vicious spiral of "too much work, and too little time to think about how to work better".

What this means for your organization

"Our reward and recognition process incentivizes front-line knowledge-sharing. Has there been a post-project review? Have the lessons learned been identified? And have they been made available for others to share?"

Adrian Malone, whilst Head of Knowledge Management, Taylor Woodrow

The first place to start is to be clear about who is at the front line of your organization. For the purposes of this research, the front line means those people carrying out activities that are directly involved in fulfilling the purpose of the business.

You therefore need to select which of three value generation models[1] best describes your company's business, or at least the part you are interested in here, using Table 3.1 to help.

Creating an action plan

Once you have identified which model applies to you, go to the relevant section below to find out what to do next.

Table 3.1: Three value generation models of organizations

	Value Chain	Value Shop	Value Network
How value is generated	By transforming some forms of raw materials or parts into products that customers need, through the distribution of those products to the customers, and through the after-sales support provided. Management in value chain businesses fundamentally has a process bias because advantage comes from cost-efficient manufacturing, distribution, and support of products.	By identifying and solving customer or client problems. Customers pay for solutions, or effort spent on their problems. Marketing is largely relationship management and competitive advantage comes from improved reputation. Management in value shop businesses is people-oriented because the competence of people is the source of sustainable advantage.	By providing a networking service between clients or customers who are, or need to be, interdependent. Customers pay for both access to the network and for exchanges via the network. Management attention in value network businesses is focused on the type and distribution of customers.
Front line activities	Logistics, production, marketing and sales or after-sales service.	Finding customer problems, solving them, choosing between options, executing or implementing solutions, and evaluating progress.	Promoting the network or managing access contracts, providing the network service, and maintaining the network infrastructure.
Examples	Pharmaceutical and healthcare products manufacturers, car production manufacturers, consumer goods manufacturers.	Professional services firms, IT services providers, consultancy firms, R&D services firms, education services providers.	Water, gas and electricity utility firms, mobile telephone network operators, banks.

Value chain businesses

At the front line of your business:

- Time pressures are high.
- Fire fighting is often the priority to deal with quality or output issues.
- There is an ongoing pressure to optimize production efficiency.

Often jobholders tend to have lower discretion about how to organize their time and have to follow procedures carefully. Processes and procedures often control how work is done – but can also act as a barrier to understanding between different functions and business areas. The barriers to coordinating knowledge sharing between different manufacturing sites and between manufacturing and research and development sites can be particularly high.

A knowledge perspective makes a difference by ensuring that:

- learning from mistakes and sharing good practices reduces defects and improves quality;
- everyone knowing who knows what saves time;
- good ideas about how to do things better are found when people have time to talk about their work.

As people have less discretion and autonomy in their roles because the nature of their job dictates what happens when, then you need to focus on action. Communication must be about *what needs to be done* and how it could happen, as well as why it matters.

We were told that the following activities are most likely to be useful at the front line of value chain businesses. Tick the ones you are doing already: these

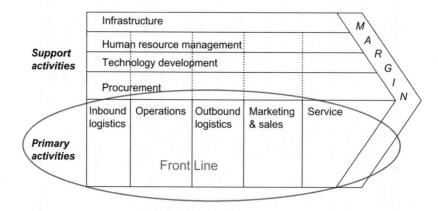

(from Stabell and Fjeldstad 1998)

Figure 3.1: The front line of value chain businesses

should be your starting point. Celebrate these successes – and amplify them across the business. The ones you haven't ticked could be next on your agenda.

Organizational processes to share existing knowledge

- Use commonly accepted vocabulary rather than specialized jargon to ensure knowledge systems are understood and used by everyone.
- Hold regular meetings and workshops for front line teams to share experiences and learning.
- Develop processes to capture knowledge from people leaving or moving to new roles.

Ways of organizing work

- Identify and flag experts within the organization and free up their time so they can operate across different teams and projects.
- Create time for knowledge activities, such as finding out good practices elsewhere.

Encourage people to care about their work and the needs of colleagues

- Build in time for learning and helping others.
- Make explicit what each group and individual is expected to contribute to the overall business objectives, so that everyone knows what others need in their jobs.
- Recognize and value those who show concern for the needs of others.

Establish the value and importance of better knowledge practices

- Make sure knowledge-sharing initiatives clearly support the business objectives that have been widely communicated.
- Provide adequate resources to support knowledge-sharing activities.
- Make sure that senior managers actively demonstrate their commitment to good knowledge practices.

Value shop businesses

At the front line of your business:

- Working to tight deadlines is common to deliver proposals or customer solutions.
- Commercial pressures are high to meet staff utilization and profitability targets.
- There can be a high sense of urgency to meet customer expectations.

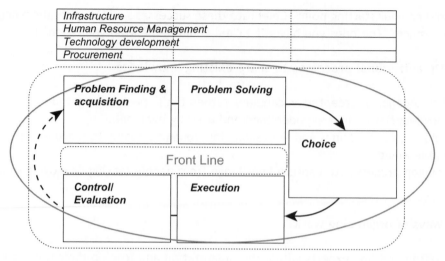

(from Stabell and Fjeldstad 1998)

Figure 3.2: The front line of value shop businesses

Often jobholders can have quite a lot of discretion as they need to be able to take into account many commercial considerations in reaching decisions. This means that the nature of the tasks being undertaken is relatively complex. Often close relationships are needed with a range of different colleagues in order to achieve objectives.

A knowledge perspective makes a difference by ensuring that:

- networks across the organization built from communities of practice and collaborative workspaces generate rapid solutions to customer problems;
- using technology to connect people to each other and to databases of current information and knowledge increases the speed of working, reduces re-work, and improves staff utilization;
- innovative solutions that generate new revenue streams come from connecting knowledge about different parts of the business.

As people have a lot of autonomy and discretion in their jobs, then you have to get their buy-in and commitment. Communication must be about building understanding of *why it matters*, as much as what needs to be done and how it could happen.

We were told that the following activities are most likely to be useful at the front line of value shop businesses. Tick the ones you are doing already:

> "With the front line, it's vital to make the benefits of knowledge-sharing very explicit – so that tapping into the resource becomes an intuitively obvious 'no brainer'."
>
> *Duncan Ogilvy, Knowledge Management Partner, Mills & Reeve*

these should be your starting point. Celebrate these successes – and amplify them across the business. The ones you haven't ticked could be next on your agenda.

Encourage a collaborative culture

- Encourage informal user groups and support more formal communities of practice.
- Hold teambuilding events and social events to foster networking.
- Organize breaks and social events for informal knowledge exchange.

Enable knowledge sharing through information and communications

- Provide technology tools that support information sharing and easy communication.
- Use software that supports collaborative document development and sharing.
- Provide a well-developed intranet with access for all the front line team.
- Provide sophisticated search engines that mean people don't need to know specialized taxonomies or terminology to find things.

Encourage people to care about their work and the needs of colleagues

- Train people in active listening techniques – hearing what people really say and mean.
- Make explicit what each group and individual is expected to contribute to the overall objectives, so that everyone knows what others need in their jobs.
- Make explicit how each group and individual is expected to contribute to the work of other groups and individuals so people can see where they fit in.
- Formally recognize and/or reward those who help others.

Establish the value and importance of better knowledge practices

- Make sure knowledge-sharing initiatives support the communicated business strategy.
- Regularly review all knowledge-sharing systems and processes to make sure they meet changing business and user needs.
- Make sure that senior managers actively demonstrate their commitment to good knowledge practices.
- Engage key stakeholders who understand knowledge-sharing practices and can help embed them into business processes.

Value network businesses

At the front line of your business (see Figure 3.3):

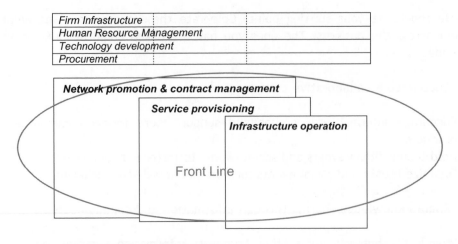

Firm Infrastructure		
Human Resource Management		
Technology development		
Procurement		

Network promotion & contract management

Service provisioning

Infrastructure operation

Front Line

(from Stabell and Fjeldstad 1998)

Figure 3.3: The front line in value network businesses

- There are often pressures from limited resources to maintain complex infrastructures cost-effectively.
- A rapid response is needed to minimize network "downtime" and resume service to customers.
- Customer interaction may be provided through call centres in which there are tight targets on call-throughput.
- Financial constraints often reduce the available options.

Often jobholders have lower discretion about how to organize their time and may have to follow procedures carefully due to regulatory constraints. Within a work team, relationships between colleagues may be relatively close. Barriers to knowledge flows within teams may be relatively low, but these barriers can seem higher when knowledge flows between different teams are considered.

A knowledge perspective makes a difference by ensuring that:

- learning from mistakes and network events prevents the repetition of errors and reduces costs and network downtime;
- capturing and sharing best practices reduces costs by improving efficiency;
- increased knowledge sharing between teams and groups generates ideas to contribute to continuous improvement targets.

As people have less discretion and autonomy in their roles because the nature of their job dictates what happens when, then you need to focus on action. Communication must be *about what needs to be done* and how it could happen, as well as why it matters.

We were told that the following activities are most likely to be useful at the front line of value network businesses. Tick the ones you are doing already: these should be your starting point. Celebrate these successes – and amplify them across the business. The ones you haven't ticked could be next on your agenda.

Ways of managing people

- Make knowledge sharing part of the performance appraisal process.
- Make good knowledge-sharing behaviours a selection criterion for recruitment.
- Provide training and coaching in knowledge-sharing skills.
- Use on-the-job training with expert colleagues to pass on experience.

Organizational processes to share existing knowledge

- Use a commonly accepted vocabulary rather than specialized jargon to ensure knowledge systems are understood and used by everyone.
- Hold regular meetings and workshops for front line teams to share experiences and learning with immediate and more dispersed colleagues.
- Reinforce the importance of using manuals and good practice guidance material.
- Develop processes to capture knowledge from people moving to new roles or leaving the organization.

Organizational processes to renew the operational knowledge base – looking internally within the business

- Use brainstorming and focus groups to generate new ideas.
- Encourage people to learn from experience.
- Include lessons learnt in formal reporting systems.
- Establish after-action review processes.

Real life stories

Pharmaceuticals (a value chain business)

A pharmaceuticals manufacturer operates plants on several continents. Staff working on the shop floor have no access to PCs, nor do they belong to inter-site communities of practice. They are expected to be aware of production improvement targets and to be actively committed to and involved in improvement activities specifically related to their product area.

Generally speaking, the roles are well defined and there is little multi-tasking required by individuals – yet cross-functional activities are needed to achieve the overall production improvements. Opportunities for improvement are most likely to come from identifying good ideas from other sites and transferring them into the local plant. However, language, time zone differences, national cultures, and technology issues all get in the way of communication and knowledge sharing between plants. Day-to-day pressures and fire fighting also tend to take priority over knowledge-sharing initiatives.

It has been found that the production operators don't want to have to spend a lot of time writing things down or reading a lot of documents. Providing opportunities to share their experiences through personal contact is particularly welcomed.

Production operators are encouraged make suggestions for continuous improvement – with the mantra "stealing with pride" to encourage them to draw on ideas from other plants. The following schemes/programmes have been found most useful: *Just Do It/Just Stop It/Steal of the Month/Stole with Pride schemes, Knowledge Café/Knowledge Camp events, etc.* The most successful examples of those site-specific schemes have been captured as KM good practices/success stories and their adoption is being monitored throughout the organization.

In some sites, small Knowledge Management teams representing all departments have been set up. These include one knowledge manager plus up to ten knowledge advocates or Infobrokers. Knowledge advocates from different departments champion, teach, or facilitate Knowledge Management tools and techniques in order to embed a knowledge-sharing culture into day-to-day departmental activities. This programme not only cascades KM down to shop-floor level, but also creates a healthy competitive environment between departments, for example identifying and adopting good practices in their departments.

IT Services (a value shop business)

> "What we've found is that sharing knowledge *within* front-line teams helps the process of sharing knowledge *between* front-line teams."
>
> *Jim Downie, knowledge management group, Unisys*

In the sales and delivery operation of a global IT services provider, employees have direct contact with clients, either developing new business, or delivering existing client engagements. The emphasis is on building relationships with clients, solving their problems and demonstrating high levels of consulting and services delivery skills.

Often people work in teams. They may be focused on, for example, sales, service delivery, or bid preparation. The tasks are varied, but tend to be relatively complex due to the speed of change in the competitive environment and the complexity of the client problems. Often individuals need to have high levels of specialized skills and they are expected to use their discretion in day-to-day decisions, within the overall performance and results framework of the business. To be successful, they need to establish close relationships with each other, as well as with people in the client organizations.

Barriers to communication and knowledge sharing can arise from team members being in different geographical locations and the fact that people are engaged on several projects at the same time. A range of technology solutions is used to facilitate more effective collaborative working. The main pressures on people come from the need to work to tight deadlines and to meet commercial objectives.

Shared values are essential so that people can use their discretion appropriately and considerable effort has been put into communicating and embedding these in the organization. Team meetings are particularly important as the basis for knowledge sharing. Team building and social events are used to help build relationships, and often these are related to customer events and specific business successes. They are also used to recognize exceptional individual achievements. It has been found that the stories describing what can be achieved reduce cynicism and build commitment. Coaching people and leading by example also help demonstrate what a collaborative approach to knowledge sharing can achieve.

Water utility provider (a value network business)

A global water utility provider supplies clean water and wastewater services to a highly populated area of the UK. The people who maintain the physical infrastructure of the water network are at the front line of the business.

The wastewater services involve managing sewage treatment works and the associated infrastructure of pipe work. Individual technicians have little or no direct contact with the users of the network. Their jobs are mostly routine when the infrastructure is running to plan; when non-standard events happen they must respond rapidly. Tight control over costs creates pressure on individuals because they have limited time to carry out all the required tasks.

Relationships between people in the same team are generally quite close, and most job-related communication happens directly between the team leader and the team. Relationships can be more distant between different teams and the organization is also relatively hierarchical.

Team leaders have access to electronic information via email, databases, and intranet sites. Field-based technicians use mobile technology for business critical data capture and transfer and for general communication. Each provincial site has a close verbal communications network and operations communications meetings are held regularly to keep field-based staff informed on local and wider business issues.

The organization recognizes that it needs to feed a cycle of continuous improvement. Learning that arises from events (e.g. problems with the network) is especially important due to the nature of the business. An event-learning database is one of the primary sources of information for the company's learning process. It enables both learning about specific events and trend analysis. The workflow process that sits within the database is designed to facilitate local learning as it enables managers to review events, to identify and analyse their root cause, then document learning points and actions to either prevent or minimize the same or similar events happening again. Tracking of the actions is carried out to ensure implementation. The database provides a documentation management function and a notification and reminder function to prompt and encourage process compliance.

An initiative is underway to capture and share the knowledge of individuals before they leave key roles, important for knowledge retention. The longer term objective is to enhance the formal business "exit process" to include guidelines for knowledge capture and retention supported by examples of good practice. By doing so the process is owned appropriately and becomes embedded through standard business practice. Individual performance development reviews already include an element of knowledge-sharing objectives.

Top tips

Time, money, and available effort – these are the issues that matter at the front line. You need to show how giving more attention to knowledge would save time, make money, and improve productivity . . . today!

The starting point is:

- Ask the front line what would be their project to improve things – then help them organize it and support them in doing it. Make knowledge initiatives at the front line completely user-centric.
- Build from what is already working and making a difference.
- Look for successes and use these as the stories to generate enthusiasm elsewhere.

There are three kinds of interventions you can make at the front line:

Mandate – you must do: this requires formal process embedding.
Encourage – it would be good to do: use of recognition and best practice examples. Make it easy to "do the right thing" by designing knowledge initiatives for usability.
Enable – opportunities that are up to you: don't be over-reliant on this approach working in the face of the contrary pressures that the front line is under.

Tell them straight – straight talking is the language of the front line.

The research and the team involved

This research was undertaken by a working group of companies within the Henley KM Forum. Data was collected through a standardized interview structure that knowledge managers could use with people at the front line of their businesses. In addition to discussing the nature of their role and the pressures facing them, the interview required these people to rank in order of usefulness nine categories of Knowledge Management activities and identify which of 81 individual Knowledge Management practices distributed across the categories were either making a difference, or which they viewed as most likely to make a difference, to their job performance. The role characteristics were assessed by the knowledge manager, usually in consultation with a front line team leader/manager. In this preliminary study, we collected data through 17 interviews spread approximately equally across the three value generation models. Ten different organizations were involved. The findings are based on identifying typical role characteristics and the highest ranked Knowledge Management categories.

The research was intended to help managers engage in productive dialogues with their own front line teams about how improved knowledge practices make a difference to the business. It was not intended to provide prescriptive advice for a particular business.

The Project was co-championed by Dr Christine van Winkelen of the Henley Knowledge Management Forum and Peter Hemmings of KN Associates (previously Thames Water).

Companies involved in the working group included:

Business Collaborator	*DLO Andover*
Getronics	*GlaxoSmithKline*
Metronet	*Orange*
QinetiQ	*RWE*
Thames Water	*Unisys*

Particular thanks are also due to the following organizations that provided additional case study material: HP Services and Henley Management College.

Final reflections from the research

This exploratory study indicates that there are similarities between front line operations in the three types of value generation model. In particular, front line employees in all three types of operation ranked "encouraging people to care about their work and the needs of colleagues" as relatively important in making a difference to performance. However, there are also indications that there are differences between the three types of front line operation and we suggest that these result in the need for managers to adopt distinct strategies if they are to embed a knowledge perspective in each type of front line operation:

- Value chain operations – focus attention on embedding better knowledge practices through the way work is organized. This also reflects the process orientation of managers in these organizations.

- Value shop operations – focus attention on embedding knowledge sharing through providing the means and motivation to support better collaborative working. This may involve capturing and sharing solutions to customer problems, as well as connecting people to directly share expertise.
- Value network operations – focus attention on embedding better knowledge practices through the way people are managed so that they are motivated to share knowledge about how to improve network performance or customer requirements (depending on their role).

These three models proved very useful in helping the working group members make sense of their experience from their own organizations, as compared with that of others in the group. The models created a common language to talk about similarities and differences. It should be noted that the most difficult organizations to fit into the model were public sector or ex-public sector organizations. The customer orientation and financial basis for defining "value" inherent in these models required some flexibility in interpretation in a public service environment. The findings presented here do incorporate findings from interviews with such organizations; however, it is recommended that public sector managers take particular care in adopting the guidance.

Notes

1. For more information about these three models see Stabell, C.B. and Fjeldstad, O.D. (1998) Configuring value for competitive advantage: on chains, shops and network, *Strategic Management Journal*, 19, 413-437. Figures 3.1, 3.2, and 3.3 have been reproduced from this journal with the permission of the publisher. See also Fjeldstad, O.D. and Haanes, K. (2001) Strategy tradeoffs in the knowledge and network economy, *Business Strategy Review*, 12(1), 1-10.

Chapter 4

Snapshot

Increasingly organizations structure all or part of their operations around projects. An examination of the enablers and blocks to knowledge flows both within and between projects shows that on the whole, projects have more in common with other operational environments than is often believed to be the case. Consequently, general approaches, tools, techniques, and thinking to improve the flow of knowledge around organizations can be applied to good effect in project environments. Project managers often offer the focus on short-term deliverables as opposed to long-term capability building as a justification for ignoring general knowledge-sharing practices. This concern can be addressed by arguments relating to the basis of value generation.

Understanding the type of project is an important consideration because it determines which particular knowledge practices are most likely to be helpful. By categorizing projects into one of four types, it is possible to select the knowledge practices that best match key project characteristics. One category of projects tends to benefit most from informal knowledge approaches while another needs more systematic and structured processes and tools. However, as projects tend to evolve from one type to another, this means that the knowledge approach will need to evolve too, which can be challenging both for the project manager and for managers focusing on improving performance from a knowledge perspective.

Why this matters

Organizations increasingly use projects to structure the integration of knowledge from multiple sources and produce a defined deliverable. Projects fit into more conventional hierarchical and bureaucratic functional organizational structures in different ways. Here we are focusing on two particular structures:[1]

1. *Project-based organizations* in which most activities happen within projects. Here the project rather than the functional dimensions of structures and processes are emphasized.

2. *Project-led organizations* in which some activities are organized through projects, but most of the work is delivered through conventional functional operational structures and processes.

In a conventional bureaucratic organizational structure, specialist functions such as marketing and research and development are extremely effective at developing and maintaining the organization's knowledge in particular domains. However, in its purest form, the project-based organization is a network of independent projects with little or no central control and therefore little opportunity to centralize organizational memory repositories or to coordinate knowledge flows across project silos. Increasingly too, successful organizations need to form alliances and federations to exploit their knowledge. For project-based organizations this creates yet another challenge: the management of knowledge between organizations.

In the past, people argued that the special nature of the project environment presented particular challenges for knowledge sharing in terms of both the need to share and learn *between* projects, and the need to create, share, and use knowledge *within* projects. Several factors were considered to make knowledge sharing difficult, effectively blocking knowledge flows around the organization.[2]

- Often, projects are unique and novel. This can lead project teams to believe the knowledge they need is also unique and novel, with the result that "wheels are reinvented" and mistakes repeated.
- Projects are transient. Team members disband at the end of a project and move on to new work. This means that new relationships have to be formed at the start of each project, which might increase barriers to learning from the experience of others.
- Traditionally, projects are closely controlled to make sure they are completed on time, on budget, and to the required quality. This tightly controlled environment is unlikely to create conditions conducive to the creation of new knowledge.

Although all these factors are undoubtedly true, the second phase of the research we are drawing on here suggested that this is no different to many other organizational contexts. Even in long-lived organizations, today's workforce is highly mobile. Many teams and relationships between groups and even organizations are transient. Additionally, the tension between immediate task and performance demands and the need to create new knowledge and build longer term capability is found in all organizations with output-based performance measurement systems. This means that concentrating on the differences between projects and other organizational contexts is misleading.

The belief that project environments are different can lead managers to ignore a wide variety of good knowledge-sharing practices. In both project and non-project working, knowledge needs to flow between individuals, organizations, and the outside world. The model of knowledge flows and enablers considered in

Chapter 2 can be just as applicable to a project environment as any other type of organizational structure. Nevertheless, an analysis of the specific knowledge needs of different types of projects can make it easier to select the most appropriate approaches from the wide range of knowledge-related practices that are available.

What this means for your organization

A useful starting point is to classify the projects in your organization. One way of doing this is to use a model which distinguishes project types,[3] classifying them against two dimensions: how well defined are the goals of the projects, and how well designed are the methods of achieving these goals? This gives a two-by-two matrix that describes four types of projects as shown in Figure 4.1.

1. *Goals and methods are well defined*: projects such as constructing a conventional building or bridge in which it is possible to move quickly from planning to action.
2. *Goals are well defined but methods are not*: projects such as developing a drug to address a specific ailment or creating a new environmentally friendly car without knowing the approach or the components to be used. Such projects are typically managed using milestones that represent components of the eventual product.
3. *Methods are well defined but goals are not*: usually information technology projects designed to implement systems in the organization. These projects are managed using milestones representing completion of lifecycle stages.

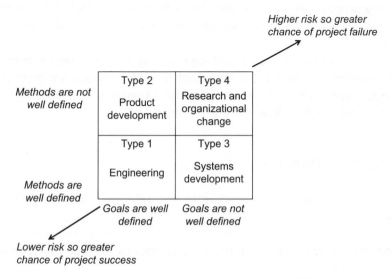

Figure 4.1: The goals and methods matrix[3,4]

Table 4.1: Categories of knowledge practices

Organizational practices	Informal knowledge systems	e.g. social spaces; non-billable time
	Information technology systems	e.g. project extranets; data mining
	Human resources	e.g. training and coaching in knowledge behaviours and skills; incentives for knowledge sharing
	External relationships	e.g. benchmarking against competitors; membership of external networks
	Organizational practices	e.g. senior responsibility for knowledge and learning; well-defined project management processes with embedded knowledge practices
Project practices	e.g. project checklists; shared diaries; project reviews; lessons learnt sessions	

4. *Goals and methods are not well defined*: typically "blue sky" projects, such as the early stages of organizational change, or pure research. The focus is on mission definition, team building, and refinement of objectives.

Different management styles are needed for each project type. Projects pass through different quadrants of the matrix as they progress from initiation through to finalization and closeout. Projects can start as any type, but tend to move into the Type 1 quadrant in their later stages because this is the best way to manage the delivery process. As a result the most effective approaches for encouraging knowledge flows will need to change too. Different techniques will assume greater relevance over time.

There are a wide variety of knowledge-sharing practices that can be used to enable knowledge to flow, so it is important to identify which are most useful for each project type. Table 4.1 shows six useful categories of knowledge practices that enable knowledge to flow more effectively.

Creating an action plan

Some knowledge practices are valuable regardless of the project type. In particular:

- Making sure the entire project team has access to documents, drawings, and plans databases.
- Establishing project reviews at appropriate points.

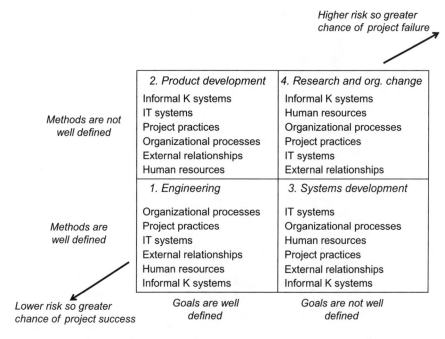

Figure 4.2: Mapping practice categories to project type[4]

After that, the starting point is to identify the project type and then use Figure 4.2 to determine the most useful categories of practices to enable knowledge to flow.

Some general observations are:

- In general, more informal approaches to managing knowledge, such as social activities and other non-billable activities, are most valuable when methods are not well defined.
- When goals are not well defined, people management practices such as training or coaching in knowledge-sharing behaviours or incentives for knowledge sharing are more valued. This is because it is important to engage people and discover their needs when goals are unclear.
- A more structured process approach to managing knowledge is needed by the time the project is a Type 1 project (goals and methods well defined).
- Moving from the top half of the matrix (where methods are not well defined) to the bottom half (where they are) is likely to present the biggest challenge as a major shift is needed from informal to more structured practices.

Evolving the practices and approaches as the project itself evolves will deliver the most value to the current project, as well as future ones.

Next we will look at each type of project in turn.

Projects where the goals and methods are well defined

> At architectural and interior design firm Simons Design, a new headquarters building has purposely seen the creation of a "knowledge café" – a staff restaurant and coffee shop where employees are encouraged to sit and talk, and trade experiences and insights. "By design, it's the only place in the building where people can get a coffee – there are no 'mini-kitchens' or drinks machines anywhere."
>
> "It's impossible to over-state the importance of face-to-face contact and discussion – and in a project-based business like ours, where by definition people are focused on the projects that they are working on, we have to deliberately engineer opportunities for that to happen."
>
> *Steve Major, Managing Director, Simons Design*

The two most useful categories are organizational processes and project practices. In particular this means adopting relatively structured approaches to encouraging knowledge to flow, whilst balancing the need to establish relationships and trust. Useful practices can include:

- holding regular meetings at which project managers can share experiences and learning;
- holding problem-sharing sessions or project clinics;
- organizing social events at which informal knowledge sharing can take place. This is needed to support relationship building within this relatively structured project environment.

In contrast, it is not helpful to make knowledge sharing an explicit "add on" to project activities or to provide specific incentives for idea generation. If knowledge sharing isn't embedded in the working process, then the process needs to be revised.

Projects where the goals are well defined, but the methods are not

> "It's absolutely vital that knowledge management is embedded into our day-to-day activities. When we work on a bid, we want to make sure that every scrap of reusable information has been harvested."
>
> *Alma Kucera, whilst UK & Ireland Head of Knowledge Management, HP Services*

Here collaboration tools and processes are needed to identify people in the organization involved in the project who may have encountered similar problems before. Technology plays an important role in connecting people and allowing shared working, while ways of stimulating creative thinking are also needed.

Projects where the methods are well defined but the goals are not

Project goals will be refined through effective consultation processes, which rely in building trust and good relationships. So, for these projects, concentrate on people related knowledge practices. Useful practices include:

- setting up mentoring schemes;
- providing access to intranet and internet forums to build communities and relationships;
- training facilitators who can help establish productive conversations between different groups to stimulate knowledge sharing and creativity.

Projects where both the goals and the methods are poorly defined

Priorities for these projects include:

- providing the means to identify experts within the organization, and freeing up the time of experts so that they can contribute across projects;
- making use of supplier and partner knowledge to challenge current thinking and introduce new ideas;
- holding regular meetings and seminars for project managers so they can share experiences and learning;
- organizing opportunities for informal knowledge sharing to stimulate creative thinking and make connections across projects.

Real life stories

These cases were selected because they represent organizations with predominantly Type 1, 2, and 4 projects respectively.[4]

Thames Water

Thames Water is the largest water company in the UK, serving 23% of the population. Worldwide, there are 20,000 employees and 70 million customers in 44 countries. Thames was bought by the German multi-utility business RWE. The projects in Thames Water's UK capital works programme, worth £400m a year, are predominantly Type 1 projects (goals and methods both well defined).

Strong organizational processes are balanced by a focus on people. KM has been successfully applied through such practices as:

- the launch of an intranet;
- the launch of knowledge communities that use collaborative working technology, "own" documentation and processes on behalf of the company, and meet regularly to help people build relationships;

- a "who's who" directory so that people can quickly find colleagues with particular skills and experience.

The KM Team is responsible for the library function and the business performance management function. This allows an integrated approach to capturing, applying, and updating documentation and processes. Knowledge Management is also integrated into the system of measures for business improvement, which increases its visibility and ensures consistent results.

HP Services

Hewlett Packard has a turnover of about $72 billion and employs 140,000 people worldwide. The company is organized around four core businesses: imaging and printing, personal systems, enterprise systems, and HP services. Consulting and Integration sits within the Enterprise Systems Group and aims to be a "locomotive" that "pulls the business forward" by helping customers who know where they want to get to in terms of the functionality of new enterprise IT infrastructure, but do not necessarily know how to achieve this. In the goals and methods matrix, Consulting and Integration projects are Type 2 (goals well defined, methods not well defined).

HP Consulting has developed a knowledge strategy that incorporates a project-oriented information repository as just one of a number of IT-based tools that facilitate effective Knowledge Management. Acting as a library that is searchable by approximately a dozen project characteristics – including customer, type of project, countries, and technologies involved – the aim is to store every scrap of reusable material. Looking for lessons learnt, and identifying potentially reusable material, is a formal part of the project "shutdown" procedures. The knowledge strategy includes:

- an information repository system, the technology foundation for the collaborative workspace, contribution repository, and solution store, which together form the basis of collaborative working in the company;
- the creation and effective adoption of formal global communities of practice and communities of interest, with involvement of some experts from outside;
- the adoption of worldwide standards in team-based collaboration, including with customers and partners;
- improving access to experts in the company through "ask the expert" and submissions to knowledge repositories.

Arup R&D

Arup was founded in 1946 and employs 7,000 people worldwide. The company offers expertise in all aspects of the built environment and sets out to differentiate itself on the basis of innovation and creativity in designs and solutions. Well-known projects have included the Sydney Opera House and the Millennium Bridge in London. There is a strong culture of empowerment across the company, which was driven by the founder Ove Arup.

Within R&D at Arup, many of the projects undertaken initially have few well-defined goals or methods – placing them in Type 4 of the goals and methods matrix. To achieve results, Arup R&D focuses on:

- communities, cafés, and other social spaces to encourage informal knowledge sharing;
- finding the right person through an in-house yellow pages system;
- external networking and participating in professional institutions;
- giving people permission to fail without a climate of blame and a willingness to take risks;
- projects, brainstorming, discussion – virtually and actually – and exploitation of all other opportunities to meet to share ideas and solve problems.

Top tips

At the beginning of this chapter it was argued that on the whole project environments are not that different to many other types of organizational contexts in terms of what is needed to enable knowledge to flow effectively. However, the research did show that there was some evidence that the tension between project delivery and making time for knowledge sharing is perceived as a particular block to knowledge flows (effectively short-term and project-focused demands supersede a longer term and wider organizational perspective). Examples of the concerns of project participants can include:

- not having time to do knowledge sharing properly;
- needing to account for time on time sheets;
- project delivery targets being the only things that are recognized as performance;
- project processes limiting knowledge-sharing practices;
- being too busy to attend training.

To help address these concerns, suggested responses were created by a team of knowledge managers as shown in Table 4.2.

The research and the team involved

This research was carried out in two phases, one during 2002 and 2003 and the second during 2009 by working groups of members of the Henley KM Forum.

Table 4.2: Possible management responses to concerns about KM practices

Project management concern	Management response to introduce a knowledge perspective
KM will slow my project down and cost money.	If it does, then you shouldn't go near it! KM doesn't always require money, or even significant chunks of time, but what if it stopped you reinventing a solution already in existence – or you repeated someone else's mistake? You might find that you can't afford *not* to do KM!
I have no time or budget planned in to do KM.	Then start with something simple and natural, like a 10-minute After Action Review with your team, or a Peer Assist with representatives from other projects to help you shape your own. You'll be surprised how willing others are to share their experience when you ask them.
The purpose of a project is to produce specific deliverables on time and to budget, not to do KM.	I couldn't agree more. KM doesn't have a purpose in its own right. I prefer to think of it as a set of improvement tools and techniques, some of which will help you produce your deliverables on time and to budget. Tell me a bit more about your deliverables, and I'll help with some suggestions about where some of my tools and techniques might help.
I'm too busy putting project management processes and standards in place to worry about KM.	Maybe there's a way to embed KM in your standards and processes rather than adding another layer of requirements. It's fine to do KM by stealth. What matters is that it improves the quality, speed, or value of what you do. Try showing me some of the processes and standards you're working on, and I'll see if I can give you some ideas as to where KM tools and techniques might make a difference, without creating a burden.
All projects are unique, so knowledge is unique to a project, and therefore no-one will understand knowledge from other projects.	Well, at the level of specific detail, that may be true – but I would challenge that there will be some principles and learning points which are relevant to other projects. If you're considering the lessons from a project, it helps to have a "customer" in mind (an internal customer for the learning, not an external customer). What sort of questions might they ask you if they heard about the success of your project? What would your advice be to them to ensure that their project was able to repeat that success? When we think in those terms, then it's easier to find the principles and guidelines which *are* relevant to other projects.

In the first phase, two focus groups of knowledge managers were used to populate six categories with 71 specific Knowledge Management practices. This was used to develop a questionnaire that was completed by 12 organizations covering 15 projects representing all four project types in the goals and methods matrix. This allowed the prioritization of the practice categories in relation to each project type.

In the second phase, case studies of four organizations were undertaken. Two were project-based organizations and two were project-led organizations. They represented both the public and private sector. In each organization studied, a workshop was held with representatives from the project management and Knowledge Management communities to examine key knowledge flows and what enabled and blocked them. This was compared with the pattern of responses from 27 organizational members of the Henley KM Forum representing a wide variety of sectors and industries described in Chapter 2.

These research activities were intended to help managers identify useful practices for their organization to set priorities for introducing Knowledge Management practices to projects to improve their performance. They were not intended to provide prescriptive advice for a particular business.

Dr Judy Payne, a member of the KM Forum team and Visiting Fellow at Henley Business School, led both phases of the research. In the first phase, the member co-champion was Tony Sheehan of Arup. In the second phase Martin Fisher of the NHS West Midlands was the member co-champion and Dr Steve Simister of Henley Business School also acted as an academic co-champion. Working group members included representatives from the following organizations:

Phase 1

Abbey National	*Armstrong Pumps*
Balfour Beatty	*Bovis Lend Lease*
Cluttons	*DPA*
EC Harris	*Ericsson*
ES Land	*HECM*
HR Wallingford	*Metronet Rail BCV*
MWH	*Orange*
PRP Architects	*Thames Water*
Unisys	

together with invited associate: John Burrows (formerly Buckman Laboratories).

Phase 2

Audit Commission	*Balfour Beatty*
BG Group	*Cadbury plc*
HM Treasury	*MOD*
Office of the Parliamentary and	*OGC*
* Health Service Ombudsman*	

QinetiQ   *The British Council*
Unisys

together with invited associate: Chris Collison (Knowledgeable Ltd).

Final reflections from the research

Most of the enablers and blockers of knowledge sharing in the project organizations studied in the second phase of this research are clearly related to organizational factors that affect the motivation, skills and knowledge needed, action required, and general knowledge-sharing environment as explored in Chapter 2. This provides support for the argument that learning from projects is shaped largely by the ongoing learning activities of the wider organizational context.[5] In knowledge terms, project environments seem to have more similarities with than differences to other operational environments. This is good news for the project management community because it means that it can tap into the Knowledge Management tools, techniques, and thinking that have developed over the past 20 years.

Notes

1. Hobday, M. (2000) The project-based organization: an ideal form for managing complex projects and systems? *Research Policy*, 26, 689-710.
2. See for example: Turner, J.R. (1993) *The Handbook of Project-based Management*, McGraw Hill; Prencipe, A. and Tell, F. (2001) Inter-project learning: processes and outcomes of knowledge codification in project-based firms, *Research Policy*, 30: 1373-1394; Sydow, J., Lindkvist, L., and DeFillippi, R. (2004) Project-based organizations, embeddedness and repositories of knowledge: editorial, *Organization Studies*, 25(9), 1475-1489; Lampel, J., Scarborough, H., and Macmillan, S. (2008) Managing through projects in knowledge-based environments, *Long Range Planning*, 41, 7-16.
3. Turner, J.R. and Cochrane, R.A. (1993) "The goals and methods matrix: coping with projects for which the goals and/or methods of achieving them are ill-defined", *International Journal of Project Management*, 11(2).
4. All case studies were prepared in 2003. These case studies and Figures 4.1 and 4.2 were first published in Truch, E. (ed.) (2004) *Leveraging Corporate Knowledge*, Gower Publishing Ltd. Reproduced with the permission of the publisher.
5. See for example: Scarborough, H., Swan, J., Laurent, S., Bresnen, M., Edelman, L., and Newell, S. (2004) Project-based learning and the role of learning boundaries, *Organization Studies*, 25(9), 1579-1600; Scarborough, H., Bresnen, M., Edelman, L.F., Laurent, S., Newell, S., and Swan, J. (2004) The processes of project-based learning, *Management Learning*, 35(4), 491-506.

Chapter 5

Snapshot

Any form of partnership depends on knowledge sharing to achieve its potential and deliver the anticipated value. However, different types of partnership rely on different mechanisms to facilitate the process. Three categories of inter-organizational collaborative relationships are covered here: supplier/buyer arrangements, alliances, and consortia. A number of practices that will help improve knowledge flows in each relationship category are identified. In supplier relationships the focus is on *what* knowledge is available and delivers value. Processes, standards, and technology are important to support mainly explicit knowledge flows. In alliances the knowledge focus is on *who* to contact as well as *what* knowledge is available. Connecting people at many levels and showing what can be achieved by sharing success stories are both important to identify opportunities to deliver business together. Finally, in consortia the focus is on *what* knowledge should be made available as well as what exists and *how* it can be mobilized. Facilitating connections between people is important, and standards, processes, and collaborative working technology allow different knowledge bases to be integrated efficiently. Attention needs to be paid to briefing people about what knowledge should be shared and what must be protected.

It is individuals that make partnerships work well. The values and skills needed by critical people involved in the three categories of relationships are also identified.

Developing the organizational capability to work collaboratively in partnerships is essential in an increasingly networked world. Learning from current collaborations to ensure future successes means developing processes to capture learning about relationship management and supporting structures like communities of practice so that relationship managers can improve their performance.

Why this matters

No business organization can operate in isolation. Every organization, whatever its mission and purpose, must interact with others to achieve its goals. Whatever the form of the relationships between organizations, the intention is to increase flexibility and add value, whilst managing risk.

> "There's a huge amount to be gained from sharing knowledge with other organizations: we gain from sharing their insights and expertise – and they, in turn, benefit from the knowledge residing in our organization."
>
> Claire Fallon, Head of Knowledge Sharing and Collaborative Working, Arts Council

The relationships might involve outsourcing non-core activities to reduce fixed costs, or could involve long-term relationships with strategic partners to develop shared capabilities that create more opportunities for all those involved. Supply chain partnerships offer the opportunity to work together to save costs, reduce errors, or save time, while speculative partnerships can stimulate the creative thinking that leads to new products or services. Partnerships can also spread the risk in new ventures.

In Chapter 2 we saw that key value adding knowledge flows to external organizations need to be integrated to create an effective knowledge strategy. It was argued that the full value of internal knowledge initiatives cannot be fully realized unless external knowledge flows are integrated too.

Even when investing time and resources in partnerships may seem to offer high potential value for the organization, at an operational level it can be a challenge to ensure that the relationship delivers the returns anticipated. To some extent, this is because it depends on individual effort to make the relationship work, but another challenge is that the most valuable knowledge is always that which is most difficult to put into words (called tacit knowledge). This is the accumulation of years of learning and experience and leads to what are sometimes called intuitive responses – quick but accurate assessments of issues and options. When people from different organizations start to work together it can be difficult to share this kind of knowledge (assuming it is appropriate to do so within the remit of the partnership arrangement). The lack of shared experience and sometimes different terminology and ways of describing situations makes sharing this knowledge more difficult. The effort that needs to be placed on developing communication and establishing the trusting personal relationships needed for tacit knowledge exchange may be considerably more than had been envisaged. In addition the collective tacit knowledge about how things are done in each organizational setting unconsciously colours assumptions about what action to take.

Adopting a knowledge perspective can improve the performance of collaborative partnerships, as long as appropriate approaches are adopted for each type of relationship.

What this means for your organization

Organizing the diverse range of inter-organizational relationships into categories highlights the knowledge priorities required to get the best from each situation.

The organizational arrangements and the skills and values needed by individuals involved affect which knowledge initiatives will be most helpful. We have focused on three categories of relationships here:

1. *Supplier* – a supply chain relationship that exists for business improvement. The organization serves its customers by transacting with a partner to draw on expertise that is embedded in the supplier's product or service.

Few businesses can retain in-house the capability to undertake all of the activities needed to create the products or services delivered to customers. For example, partly assembled component modules may be purchased, or internal services to keep the business running may be outsourced. Increasingly organizations are identifying which activities they can and should retain in-house, and which they should purchase from outside. When significant business activities are purchased or outsourced through this kind of collaboration, then there may be a longer term investment in aligning how the organizations work together.

Key characteristics are:

- A contract determines the specific basis for the relationship. The contract may specify quantities or the basis for procurement of unknown future quantities of business.
- The purchaser owns the relationship with the final customer.
- It is relatively easy to define the value being delivered to each party by the relationship.
- Dispute resolution procedures are clearly defined.
- The relationship is managed through an explicit set of processes and rules. For longer term contracts, close relationships are likely to develop between key individuals in the two organizations. These allow for disputes to be resolved on an informal basis. However, formal methods exist and can be used.
- Decisions about the duration and commercial basis of the relationship are often centralized, though individuals in various parts of the purchaser organization may interact with the supplier in accordance with the contract.

2. *Alliance* – a relationship between two firms that exists because it extends the business opportunities of each without the need for expensive new knowledge development. The two organizations have complementary expertise and work closely together to deliver products or services to customers.

Neither business alone can meet the needs of customers on a competitive basis. The skills and expertise of both organizations need to be integrated to create or deliver the product or service.

Key characteristics are:

- A partnership agreement can provide a broad framework for the collaboration. Each specific piece of work together may then be covered by a contract.
- One party is likely to own the relationship with the customer; the involvement of the other party may not even be visible to the customer.

- Opportunities to deliver business together may be identified opportunistically or through joint strategic planning.
- Both parties are relatively certain that value will be delivered from the partnership, though the extent of the value could be unpredictable.
- The partners have established formal or informal mechanisms to assess each other's performance.
- The decisions about exactly which business opportunities to pursue together are often decentralized.
- Individuals in one organization form relationships with their counterparts in the partner organization. Typically, in large organizations there are complex patterns of connections between people in the two firms. These are likely to exist at many different levels, in different business divisions, in different country operations etc. This provides a flexible and adaptable means of working together to meet the needs of different types of customers. People from both organizations could be co-located on a client's premises, or spend a large amount of time on each other's premises. In the extreme, groups of people from both organizations may be jointly branded under a new identity to deliver a specific piece of work together.
- In the largest alliances, an alliance manager for each organization is in place and represents the capabilities of the organizations to each other, tracks the performance of the partnership, and also sells the benefits of the partnership back into their own organizations to sustain enthusiasm and commitment. Each alliance manager often works through a virtual team of involved individuals from across his/her own business.

3. *Consortium* – a relationship between several organizations that exists because it extends the business opportunities of each without the need for expensive new knowledge development. The organizations combine their expertise to provide products or services to customers.

Alone, none of the businesses involved can fulfil the needs of customers on a competitive basis. The customer also recognizes that the skills and expertise of several organizations need to be integrated to create or deliver the product or service and requires them to work together to achieve this.

Key characteristics include:

- A contract determines the specific basis for the creation of the consortium. A partnership agreement may possibly emerge regarding future work together, though this is not a requirement.
- The consortium is likely to be given a name or other form of identification.
- The consortium is visible to the customer.
- One party is likely to own the relationship with the customer, though the customer sets targets based on the collective performance of all consortium members.

- All parties are relatively certain that value will be delivered from the consortium for each specific customer engagement. There may be uncertainty about future collaborations.
- Consortium members involved in delivering one contract together may be direct competitors in a different situation.
- Individuals in one organization form relationships with their counterparts in the partner organizations. Typically, in large organizations there are complex patterns of connections between people in the firms. These are likely to exist at many different levels, in different business divisions, in different country operations etc. People from several organizations in the consortium could be co-located on a client's premises.
- The consortium is likely to be led by a senior project or programme manager, who is likely to be highly skilled at negotiation and project management techniques. Collective decisions may be achieved through workshops. Clear procedures are in place to resolve disputes. The scale of the partnership means that relatively structured (and even formal) management processes are needed.

In general, there is a different basis for each kind of relationship, with contracts and formal arrangements being explicitly used for some more than others. Figure 5.1 illustrates the general situation where supplier relationships tend to have a more explicit basis for aspects of knowledge in the relationship than certain types of alliances.

Even though relationships are established between organizations, most thrive and make a difference because people with the right knowledge, skills, and motivation make it work. Sometimes these people might have the formal title of relationship manager and their sole responsibility is to create connections and ensure that value is delivered to all parties involved. However, often the people who make relationships work have other priorities and responsibilities; they may need help to appreciate the importance of the relationship to the organization and the value that should be expected from it.

Promoting the reasons why the relationship matters and sharing success stories can make a difference in a number of ways, including allowing other parts of the organization to see the value that can be achieved and prompting them to look for opportunities to benefit from the organization's investment in the relationship. An additional benefit of sharing success stories can be maintaining the visibility of

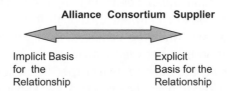

Alliance Consortium Supplier

Implicit Basis for the Relationship

Explicit Basis for the Relationship

Figure 5.1: The extent of the formality of different categories of relationships

those involved back in their own organization even if they are deeply embedded in the relationship to the extent of spending most of their time on partners' premises.

Creating an action plan

Key actions vary according to the type of collaborative relationship. We shall look at each in turn.

Supplier/buyer partnerships

Generally, there is no intention by the purchaser to absorb the supplier's knowledge; instead the decision is to purchase it for specific purposes. Consequently, interactions may be based largely on information exchange, rather than more contextual knowledge exchange. The efficiency of information exchange can be increased by coordinating business processes, such as providing electronic access to forecasts of requirements and through adopting transparent procurement performance criteria. Longer term contracts may involve the supplier co-locating on the purchaser's premises in some way; this will encourage understanding and increase the speed of responsiveness to changes.

There is also a knowledge implication within the purchaser organization: those using the contract with the supplier may be distributed around the business and need to be able to communicate their experience to a central coordination point.

The focus of knowledge-related initiatives to improve day-to-day operation of the supply agreement needs to be on *what* knowledge is available, as shown in Table 5.1.

More strategically, mechanisms to share planning and forecasting information with the supplier should be developed. These may be electronic or based on regular meetings. Collaborative capability depends on the ability to learn from the way one supplier relationship is operating to make other similar ones more effective.

Alliances

Access to the partner's knowledge is required to identify, design, or deliver the product or service that meets the customer needs. However, the knowledge bases of the organizations remain independent and separate. Each does not need to absorb the detail of the other's knowledge, though it is necessary to understand the capability each has and what the combined business opportunities are. The multiple levels of relationships between individuals in the two organizations are crucial to effective knowledge flows to deliver specific pieces of business together. The alliance managers need to have the skills to act as knowledge brokers to ensure that joint successes are shared and leveraged across the businesses to sustain momentum and commitment.

Table 5.1: Practices to improve knowledge flows in supplier relationships

People-based initiatives	Process-based initiatives	Technology-based initiatives
• For some large and distributed organizations, a community of practice model may be useful to link together individuals who all engage with the same supplier, or set of suppliers. Sharing experiences and needs may be a powerful way of improving the performance of the agreement. • Training in the commercial and legal implications of contractual arrangements with suppliers should be widely available within the purchaser organization.	• The collection of supplier performance data should be integrated into workflow processes, rather than being an additional burden. • Facilitating "lessons learnt" reviews during the life of the contract provides the basis for ongoing improvement. Reviews should incorporate discussions about agreed performance measures, as well as broader issues about how to work together more effectively.	• Systems need to be created within the organization to share with all relevant parties the agreed basis for working with the supplier. Guidance should be clear and concise and include information about who to go to for help and assistance. Intranet technology can be useful as the basis for sharing factual information about the supply contract within the organization. Extranet or internet technology can be used to allow rapid access to, for example, supplier technical product information.

The focus of knowledge-related initiatives to improve day-to-day operation of the alliance needs to be on *who* to contact and *what* knowledge is available, as shown in Table 5.2.

More strategically, it is helpful to maintain a joint scorecard to monitor the performance of the alliance and include learning how to work well together within this. Incentive structures can be vital for engaging the interest and commitment of individuals within the organization to the partnership. For example you might make delivering successful business through the partnership part of individual and team incentive programmes. It is also helpful to include something to encourage people to communicate the basis of this success with others so that it can be adopted elsewhere.

Consortia

Consortia largely have the same objective as alliances, but the relationship process is complicated by the need to integrate several knowledge domains held by different organizations. Access to all partners' knowledge is required to identify, design, or deliver the product or service that meets the customer needs. At the outset it is important to gain clarity about roles and mutual expectations of

Table 5.2: Practices to improve knowledge flows in alliances

People-based initiatives	Process-based initiatives	Technology-based initiatives
• Communication throughout the network of individuals within the organization interacting with the alliance partner needs to be frequent and timely. Regular conference calls, web conferencing, email briefings, intranet postings etc. all need to be used. Workshops should also be used to allow people to meet and build an internal network of relationships. • The pattern of relationships between many individuals is essential to the effective performance of this type of partnership. Techniques like social network analysis to map the pattern of connections between people involved in the alliance can be used to identify crucial individuals, and identify opportunities for improvement or areas of risk.	• Compelling stories of joint successes are essential to sustain commitment between the partners. They also engage people within the organization by demonstrating how the partnership allows them to deliver their business objectives more effectively. • Facilitating "lessons learnt" reviews following significant joint pieces of business provides the basis for ongoing improvement.	• Key individuals involved in the relationship may spend a considerable proportion of their time on the partner's premises (this should be encouraged as it improves relationships and enhances knowledge sharing). Communications technology should be provided to enable them to work effectively and have access to all relevant information sources. Simple ways of feeding back issues and opportunities relating to the partnership need to be created – portal technology provides one way, regular audio conferences another. • Intranet and extranet technology can be used to capture and share information about how to work together most effectively. Templates, modules, briefings etc. can be captured and shared. Virtual collaboration tools can support joint proposal preparation and problem solving.

contributions. These agreements must be revisited regularly. The knowledge bases of the organizations remain independent and separate as each does not need to absorb the detail of the other's knowledge. Each party will continue to use their knowledge in competitive situations outside the consortium. Good ideas or practices developed through the consortium contract are likely to be fed back into the individual organizations for them to use elsewhere (possibly even in future competitive scenarios).

The focus of knowledge-related initiatives to improve day-to-day operation of the consortium needs to be on *what* knowledge is available and *how* it can be mobilized, as shown in Table 5.3. These priorities are slightly different to those of alliances because connecting several areas of expertise across multiple organizations carries more risk of mistakes. Such mistakes can undermine confidence and trust in the partnership. A high level of project management skills is therefore essential. Similarly, decision-making involves more players and reaching a consensus can take time and benefit from excellent negotiation skills.

Table 5.3: Practices to improve knowledge flows in consortia

People-based initiatives	Process-based initiatives	Technology-based initiatives
■ Communication throughout the network of individuals within the organization who interact with partners in the consortium needs to be frequent and timely. Regular conference calls, web conferencing, email briefings, intranet postings etc. all need to be used. In addition to concentrating on the operational issues needed to deliver the specific contract, time and attention should be given to capturing information and knowledge that will be useful to the organization in carrying out future business (this may be technical or commercial). ■ Individuals joining the project teams need to be trained or coached about how the partnership works, how to behave with partners, and what knowledge it is appropriate to share and which remains the intellectual property of his/her employing organization.	■ Compelling stories of contract milestone successes are essential to sustain commitment and goodwill between the partners. Managers need to identify, capture, and disseminate these success stories. ■ Facilitating "lessons learnt" reviews during and following participation in consortia provides the basis for ongoing improvement by the organization in understanding how to operate within such consortia. ■ People participating in the consortium need to feel a sense of belonging. Distinct consortia branding can make people feel part of something coherent. However it is also important to ensure they can maintain their links back to their main employer.	■ Intranet and extranet technology can be used to capture and share information needed to deliver the contract. Virtual collaboration tools can support joint proposal preparation and problem solving. ■ Key individuals involved in the relationship may spend a considerable proportion of their time on client or partner premises (this should be encouraged as it improves relationships and enhances knowledge sharing). Communications technology should be provided to enable them to work effectively and have access to all relevant information sources. Simple ways of feeding back issues and opportunities relating to the consortium need to be created – portal technology provides one way, regular audio conferences another.

More strategically, incentive structures are key to engaging the interest and commitment of all the firms in the consortium to making it more effective. Performance measures that track the performance of the whole project (team), not the individual companies, drive collaborative behaviours. Open book accounting within specific projects has been shown to be very effective in building trust and reducing disputes. Collaborative capability depends on the ability to learn from the way one partnership is operating to make other similar ones more effective.

Individual managers' values, skills, and behaviours make a difference to relationship performance

In these three relationship categories, knowledge types have different levels of importance and alternative structural arrangements are required to carry the knowledge flows. The purposes of the relationships vary in terms of risk and of the organization's ability to predefine its outcomes. In combination, these differences mean that the individuals involved in each type of inter-firm relationship will rely on different skills and behaviours to get things done; what they believe is important will also differ. Table 5.4 compares the various personal characteristics that relationship managers either demonstrated, or explicitly viewed as important, in those involved in the relationships that they were responsible for.

Table 5.4: Values and skills of individuals as key enablers of inter-firm relationships

	Supplier	Alliance	Consortium
Values of the Individual			
Commitment to mutual win-win solutions	Low	High	High
Transparency and openness	Low	Based on trust, moderately high	Moderate, based on trust
Willingness to take a risk	Low	Moderate at alliance manager level	Low to moderate
Tolerance for uncertainty	Low	Moderate	Moderate
Self confidence and humility	Low	High	High
Skills Needed by the Individual			
Legal contracting skills	High	Low	Low
Internal and external selling skills	Moderate	High	High
Facilitation skills	Low	Low	Moderate
Project management skills	High	High	High
Communications and listening skills	Moderate	High	High
Negotiating skills	High	Low	High
Networking skills	Low	High	High

It is possible to train people in the necessary skills for each type of relationship, though often organizations select people who already have the necessary values or skills for the most important or senior roles.

Real life stories

The three examples selected represent the benefits of a collaborative approach to partnerships in relation to supply management, alliances, and consortia respectively.

Suppliers in the construction industry

Managing suppliers in major construction projects puts the buyer in a difficult position. Major projects can last several years. As the site contractor, the buyer will have committed to a tightly defined agreement with a client in terms of price and time to deliver. In order to fulfil that agreement, the contractor needs a high degree of confidence that any relationship with a particular supplier will be durable and capable of meeting the specified outcomes. This inevitably leads to considerable investment of time and effort to define contractual performance criteria formally. This can become adversarial if not well managed.

One specific example relates to the process used by a construction contractor during an eight-year relationship to manage a refurbishment of a large public building whilst it was still in daily use. Although there was a contract in place, it had quickly become very much a document of last resort, and personal relationships had much more influence on the way the supply relationships operated.

Various factors were key to success. The first was getting everyone together in the same office, an unusual thing to do in an industry where mistrust between subcontractor and contractor means that contractual obligations often dominate the communication processes. The project manager for this contract encouraged subcontractors to be present at weekly client meetings and to attend Monday morning operational meetings to review the previous week's progress and plan for the coming week. Conversations took place about cost issues and time constraints. Problems were openly shared and disputes were settled locally rather than through designated escalation routes.

The second key factor was to encourage people to enjoy what they were doing and jointly identify with the project outcome. The project manager did not adopt a directive and confrontational style of project management. Instead, he focused on being fair-minded, having a positive attitude, and keeping people informed. Teams celebrated successes and the cross-organizational social relationships that emerged as a result of these activities bolstered ongoing knowledge-sharing activities to the benefit of the project.

The only formal measurement mechanism within the contractor's own organization was a monthly one-page summary of project status in a standard format produced by the project manager for the business directors. This helped the business keep track of the priorities in the project, manage the risk, and forecast resource needs.

Alliances – mobile phone operators

Even when two organizations need one another equally in order to fully satisfy a customer need, each tends to get different commercial benefits from the relationship. This "marriage" of interests creates a need for persuasion and influence as the basis for the relationship, rather than orderly processes and managed control.

A relationship manager in one large mobile phone operator commented that in this fast-moving industry, only a limited number of partners look promising, so attention tends to focus on the top ten firms with complementary knowledge and skills. Initially the proposal for a relationship often comes from the CEO level as a result of discussions about the potential commercial benefits of cementing a relationship. The pros and cons of the partnership will be considered internally (in this instance through a "Partnership Engagement Framework") so that everyone knows what is at stake. But the relationship stands or falls on whether the individuals expected to make it happen can get on with one another.

Each organization will have different priorities, customs, and behaviours. Whilst making money and reducing risk, time, and cost will be commonly agreed priorities, other differences may not be so easy to reconcile, particularly where, for example, brand identities are strong or operating cultures are incompatible. Frustrations often arise as a result of conflicting cultural values. So, for example, an organization that values friendliness, doing favours, achieving quick wins, and nimble decision-making finds it hard to work with partners who value formality, processes and procedures, long-term planning, and bureaucracy. If the pain of working with these frustrations outweighs the commercial rewards, then the relationship may survive in the short term, but founder in the long term.

Trust in the relationship builds as a result of good experiences. The relationship manager's job is to work with their opposite number to get inside the "mind" of the partner organization, keep communication flowing, monitor the status of the relationship, publicize successes, and generally find opportunities to get even closer. In this role, influencing, communicating, and networking skills are as important as the technical knowledge needed to recognize a good opportunity to extend the relationship. Expectation management is key, as well as being able to prioritize appropriately to build trust in the long run and keep people focused on the end goal. These relationships needed a lot of maintenance in terms of regular open communication and frequent face-to-face and social conversations.

Water engineering consortia

In water engineering, several domains of costly expertise need to be brought to bear on complex problems. The case organization was engaged in several regional consortia in which the clients were local water companies who worked closely with each other and one or more other contractors under a long-term umbrella agreement. This provided stability and predictability for the contractors and innovation and integrated solutions for the client.

Having a specific name for each consortium gave it an identity. This acted as a rallying point for employees seconded to the project and gave them the sense of belonging to a special group, when they were away from the home office.

Generally, a long-term contract defined the principles for a specific consortium project, defining the scope and required expertise. However, each project or work package was given separate approval by the client, in negotiation with the other partners. One advantage of this long-term relationship structure is the luxury of time to agree common measures that monitor key performance indicators for all partnership activities. This focuses attention on common issues and minimizes confusion as to what is important.

There is an obvious need for knowledge sharing between consortium members in this sort of arrangement, but crucially the various company employees seconded to the consortium also need links back to expertise within their own firms. Intranet technology was used extensively as a means of facilitating access to vital corporate knowledge bases for employees working in consortium projects. Company newsletters, monthly briefings, and project overviews were essential to give people a view of the full range of business activities. Critically the partners also each needed internal mechanisms to gather the lessons learnt about how to work more efficiently in future consortia. This needed a strong knowledge champion.

Working on the client's site is a commonly accepted way to facilitate knowledge sharing between specialist engineers, project managers, and design experts. Most of the detailed decision-making associated with each project or work package is made in joint meetings and workshops.

Top tips

"Speed of response and the overall timescale are critical. Sharing knowledge too late is almost as bad as not sharing knowledge at all."

Garry Sanderson, Director of Knowledge and Technical Services, MWH

✓ Relationships are always between individuals, even when there is a partnership agreement between organizations. Organizations must support individuals in forming and sustaining these relationships. This includes trusting and empowering them to make the relationships successful.

✓ Adversarial relationships between firms wastes resources. Too much effort is put into managing the contract rather than jointly delivering the customer solution.

✓ Sharing success stories resulting from the partnership within the organization and with the partner(s) is crucial to generate ongoing awareness and commitment. Managers adopting a knowledge perspective can make a real difference here.

✓ Different approaches to managing inter-firm relationships are appropriate in different situations. The knowledge approach needs to be matched to the scenario.

✓ Although the partnerships crucially depend on the relationships between the individuals involved, it is possible to learn from one scenario and transfer that experience to improve the performance of partnerships based on similar scenarios.

✓ A knowledge perspective is a very useful way to understanding how to manage a portfolio of different types of inter-firm relationship more effectively.

A strategic approach to collaborative partnerships involves developing the organization's relationship management capability. Understanding what is working well and amplifying successes by sharing learning and experience is at the heart of this. In large organizations, a community of practice for relationship managers may be able to take responsibility for developing and sharing this knowledge base.

The research and the team involved

This research was carried out during 2004 and 2005 by working groups of members of the Henley KM Forum. Following a review of the literature, 12 relationship managers from eight organizations representing the three categories of relationships (suppliers, alliances, and consortia) were interviewed. The basis of the interview was an exploration of what they considered made the inter-firm relationships they were involved in successful, what knowledge needed to flow between partners, and how better knowledge practices could make a difference to the value delivered from the relationships. The research activities were intended help managers identify useful practices for their organization. It was not intended to provide prescriptive advice for a particular business.

Professor Jane McKenzie, a member of Faculty at Henley Business School, and Dr Christine van Winkelen from the KM Forum team and Visiting Fellow at Henley Business School were the academic co-champions for this research. The member co-champion was Ibrahim Gogus of Oracle. Maria Solitander from the Hanken School of Management in Helsinki also provided valuable input to the research. Working group members included representatives from the following organizations:

Balfour Beatty	*Business Collaborator*
Cadbury Schweppes	*DLO Andover*
Getronics	*Henley Business School*
MWH	*Orange*

PRP   *Taylor Woodrow*
Unisys

together with invited associate: John Burrows (formerly Buckman Laboratories).

Final reflections from the research

Categorizing the range of relationships that we encountered through the research interviews provided a useful basis for reflecting on and differentiating the knowledge priorities of each. This allowed us to identify the organizational arrangements and individual skills and values that make a difference to performance in each category (the structural and human capital needed to make the relationship capital effective). The research presented in Chapter 2 has suggested that while increased effectiveness comes from the progressive capacity to align all three forms of intellectual capital, many firms struggle to integrate this external knowledge with the internal knowledge. Our intention has been to offer managers preliminary guidance in this area.

Whatever the category of relationship, the organization's collaborative capability will be developed through facilitating the review and learning processes that transfer knowledge about one collaborative relationship to make another even more successful.

Section III

Stimulate innovation

Chapter 6 – Building knowledge enabled innovation capability
Chapter 7 – Retaining and developing expertise

It has been said that modern organizations need to innovate or die. Certainly, in the long term, few organizations thrive without maintaining a constant stream of innovation. It's part of the dynamics of surviving in a global knowledge economy.

What do we mean by innovation?

You might describe it as a previously unknown or unrecognized way to fill a gap in our capacity to handle some part of our world. The result could be a better way of doing or achieving something or a mechanism which overcomes some frustration or inconvenience. It could be a radical disruptive innovation that brings into question many of the most cherished assumptions about how we go about familiar practices, for example, the motor car, electricity, or digital technology which were all disruptive innovations in their time. Or it could be an improvement to existing ways of doing something, for example, text messaging which now allows asynchronous communication on the move. However the source is almost always a connection between two previously unconnected pieces of existing knowledge. Very rarely is the source something completely unknown to anyone, although fundamental research does sporadically throw up some truly valuable new knowledge that becomes the root of many new innovations, for example decoding the structure of DNA or mapping the human genome.

In between the knowledge connections and the innovation that results from them, we need processes to test how robust and practical an idea is. If it's going to be a viable commercial proposition, we also need mechanisms to assess how relevant the idea is for fixing other people's frustrations or enhancing their ability to achieve something.

Innovation relies on knowledge combinations and these come from the mix and depth of expertise in an organization. Deep expertise can take many forms; some is related to the application of technical knowledge, but in other cases it might be knowing how to get things done in the organization. In the war for talent, many organizations are concerned about losing the critical expertise that makes the difference to their business. Maintaining the innovative capacity of the organization means devoting time to making expert thinking visible so that others can learn from it, as well as using continuity tools to mitigate the risk of loss. Embedding learning as part of the organizational culture helps to institutionalize the foundations for both expertise development and innovation.

How do you stimulate it?

If you want to encourage innovation there are three obvious conclusions you might draw from the previous paragraph.

(a) The more knowledge you can access, the more opportunity there is to make new and relevant connections.
(b) The more you can learn about *potential* (not just existing) customer interests the more likely you can apply that knowledge to make their life simpler, easier, faster, cheaper, more convenient, or less frustrating, and the more likely your new business proposition will be successful.
(c) One way to get from a) to b) is to put in place processes that stimulate knowledge connections by increasing expertise held within the organization and making it more accessible. Another equally important condition is developing the organizational capacity to learn constantly through both internal and external collaboration.

Most organizations already place considerable emphasis on internal collaboration. When we think of organizations as institutions providing products or services rooted in know-how that sets them apart from others, it's natural to focus attention on making the most of that distinction. Performance improvement efforts work to:

- prevent hard-won expertise remaining stuck in silos, projects, or people's heads because then it is underutilized;

- increase opportunities for re-use;
- reduce wastage when people leave.

Internal collaboration is vital for spreading meaningful knowledge beyond its immediate application. Learning develops through different types of purposeful collaborative conversations and is recycled for continuous improvement via the same route. Improving the quality of conversations is a process in itself which is covered in Section VI, where we think about making change stick, but it is also relevant here.

External collaboration is equally important for sustainable performance for two reasons. The first is an issue of value creation. However much your organization knows, there will always be another organization that could contribute a piece of knowledge needed to make your original idea workable and do it faster, more cost-effectively, or with more creative flair than you can. The way to access that knowledge is partnership, but collaborating across boundaries presents more challenges than internal collaboration as we have seen in previous sections. The second is that you may well overlook commercial opportunities if you are not well connected with the constantly changing knowledge landscape that exists beyond the boundaries of how you currently define your organization's reach.

How do you make it a habit?

In the long term, institutionalizing innovation capacity depends on developing a climate in which learning from different sources becomes an everyday occurrence and creative thinking is the norm. Of course a sense of purpose is helpful to guide the direction, but it shouldn't be too specific or it will filter out too much innovation potential. The key is to get to a point where everyone is open to the possibility of learning and imagining how to work differently, whilst still understanding what makes the organization distinctive compared to others. Time and the tools to facilitate thinking are essential for this activity.

There are many tools and organizational processes available that make it easier for people to learn from other experts, from external sources, in communities, and in their own thinking time through practice and simulation. Yet, however many of these procedures and opportunities you put in place, the ambient climate will affect whether people use them. If learning is not valued, if experimentation and managed risk taking aren't encouraged, if people don't trust one another or aren't given the time to think, have conversations to share experiences, and try out tentative developmental steps, innovation will not flourish.

As you will deduce from the various examples and case studies in this section, each organization will stimulate innovation in a way that suits their business priorities.

Key questions to ask yourself

As you start using the ideas in the next two chapters ask:

- What is an appropriate balance of effort to invest in increasing the potential to recognize new opportunities and in getting greater value from the knowledge you have already developed?
- What are the critical triggers to develop a suitable climate to cultivate learning as a natural part of your organization's ecology?
- Where do your existing processes inhibit or amplify the opportunity to connect people and ideas and to think productively together?

Chapter 6

Snapshot

To succeed in the twenty-first century, organizations need to create and respond to opportunities, develop new products and services, adapt and change – in other words, they have to innovate. The capability to manage the processes that enable this needs to be refined by managers. Knowledge enabled innovation is an organizational capability that takes time and effort to develop. We look at what this involves, how to go about understanding an organization's current strengths and weaknesses in this area, and what can be done to build the capability over time.

Six factors together create the organizational capability for knowledge enabled innovation: effective internal and external collaboration, developing a learning organization with the tools in place to re-use knowledge, learning from successful innovation, and recognizing opportunities for innovation. All six must co-exist and work together if this capability is to be maintained and developed.

Evaluating how well your organization performs in these areas is a useful starting point. Here a framework is proposed to help you do this in a structured fashion. If one part of the organization is better than another on any one of the factors, then managing a peer learning process can help build the capability of the whole organization.

Why this matters

Change provides opportunities for learning, which stimulates us to make different connections between what we know about already and to think of new and better solutions. This cycle is illustrated in Figure 6.1.[1] Collaboration-based management practices are a major driver for innovation. This is because collaboration facilitates the transfer of knowledge to those who can make the new connections that lead to the creation of knowledge and potentially to innovation.

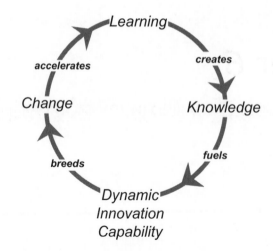

Figure 6.1: The knowledge enabled innovation cycle

What this means for your organization

Building the organizational capability to manage these processes well takes considered effort over a period of time. The starting point is to understand the organization's current strengths and weaknesses, then to pinpoint where there are ready opportunities for improvement.

There are six factors that together create the organizational capability of knowledge enabled innovation. They all reinforce one another, which means that it is important to approach capability development in an integrated and holistic way.

Internal collaboration

This involves putting in place mechanisms that help people connect with others across the structural boundaries, functional specialisms, technical disciplines etc. within the organization, as well as establishing a culture that is supportive of collaboration.

> "People on site are always creating clever solutions. We need them to recognise these as innovations and share them with the organization. We created a physical environment to promote exchange of information, with open-plan workspaces and a knowledge cafe. The more we can get people to meet informally, the more they will share information."
>
> *Steve Major, Managing Director, Simons Design*

External collaboration

This involves providing ways to support relationship building between internal people and other "partners" (in the widest sense) across the external boundaries of the organization; then it is important to transfer the knowledge generated in those relationships to others elsewhere in the organization and integrate it with internal knowledge.

Re-using existing knowledge

This involves establishing mechanisms for people to capture the knowledge they have gained in the course of carrying out the organization's business (be that as individuals, teams, projects etc.) and then providing access for other people to re-use it at a different time and place.

Creating a learning organization

This means creating an organizational climate that is responsive to and welcoming of change. Flexibility and adaptability are the norm and people expect to find new and better solutions within their jobs and to be able to implement these.

Learning from innovation activity

This is about providing processes and systems to build the organization's capability to be more efficient and effective when it innovates.

Recognizing opportunities to innovate

"We are developing a learning organization with a number of initiatives. We developed 'baton passing' to pass learning on in a structured way. It's an activity-based workshop run with people who have been working on a project and people who are new to the area. It's a structure for making their tacit knowledge more explicit."

Wendy Jordan, Commissioning Consultant, Innovation, British Council

This is about creating an organizational climate in which innovation is recognized as important and in which involving others both in evaluating opportunities and in shaping the innovation is the norm.

Creating an environment that supports creativity and innovation involves:

- a leadership style that is courageous and encouraging;
- a sense of direction and purpose in the organization;
- a culture of experimentation;
- a culture of trust and openness;
- an engaged and committed workforce who are stimulated and challenged by their work;
- appropriate IT support: managing information, explicit knowledge, and connecting people;
- Time allowed for learning, knowledge sharing, and conversation.

Creating an action plan

A maturity model for the six factors that make up the organizational capability of "knowledge enabled innovation" allows you to assess the strengths and weaknesses of different parts of your organization and facilitate knowledge sharing between them. The peer learning process is a very effective way to build organizational capability. The maturity model is shown in Table 6.1.

The steps you could follow to use this maturity model are:

1. Identify a group of people representing different parts of your organization (different teams, activities, or functions). At least six is desirable, 10-12 is probably the maximum. Invite them to a 1.5-2-hour workshop.
2. At the start of the workshop give everyone a copy of the model and talk through what the six factor headings mean so everyone has a similar understanding.
3. Ask them each to rate their team/group/activity (as appropriate) for each factor according to the 1 to 5 level definitions.
4. Then ask people to identify where they would want to get to on each factor within the next 12 months (identify the gap between the current and desirable rating).
5. Ask them to pick two priority areas that they think would make the most difference if they were to move from where they are to where they want to be within 12 months.
6. Collect the information and use a flipchart to represent who has what rating (the River Diagram shown in Figure 6.2 can be a useful way of showing the overall picture). Add in the desired ratings and what the priorities for improvement are (maybe in a different colour).
7. Look at who is strong at each factor and who wants to improve on it. Connect these people so they can discuss what the strong group is doing and how the weaker group can learn from this. These "peer assist" conversations should ideally be started at the workshop, then encouragement given for them to continue afterwards.

More details about how to use an extended version of this approach are available in the book *Learning to Fly*.[2] You may also choose to introduce a company or programme view at the end if you have other options to offer people who want to make improvements on particular factors.

Some hints and tips for getting the most from the peer learning process:

- Encourage people to start at the bottom (maturity level 1) and work up, rather than the top and work down when they are deciding how to rate their part of the organization.
- You may decide that 12 months is too short a timeframe for improvements in your organization. More than three years is unlikely to be helpful though.

Table 6.1: Knowledge enabled innovation maturity model

	Recognizing high-value opportunities to innovate	Re-using knowledge	Internal collaboration	External collaboration	Learning from innovation activities	Building a learning organization
5	Recognized process for opportunity capture and evaluation. Culture of open-mindedness to new approaches and knowledge sharing to find solutions is expected. Local teams routinely review opportunities to see what they can add to generate new solutions. Processes and tools are in place to support this. Problem owners expect to involve others. Incentive systems support this.	Widespread adoption of the available knowledge capture and sharing processes and technologies. A mature Information Management approach is evident. People actively search the repositories provided and re-use the information captured in them, contacting the originator when appropriate.	A wide range of collaborative tools and technologies are used. Widespread participation in organization-wide networks based around key knowledge domains independent of hierarchy. Collaboration is recognized and demonstrated as a natural approach to problem solving and a necessary part of innovation. Widespread recognition of the value of others' knowledge.	Capability to collaborate with a wide variety of external organizations, including competitors. Partners involved in innovation activities. Relationship management viewed as a core competence and ways of improving it are actively sought. Range of measures adopted to assess relationship effectiveness. Mechanisms adopted to support calculated risk-taking in working with partners.	Learning from innovation is routine. Getting better at innovation is regarded as important and a variety of measures are used to track performance. People proactively seek to learn how to improve the efficiency and effectiveness of innovation.	Continuous and dynamic learning is completely embedded in daily work practices. The capacity to turn learning into innovative practices is widespread and well understood. Inspiration, empowerment, and ideas generation are widespread at every level within a change-oriented culture.

continued on next page…

Table 6.1 - *Continued*

	Recognizing high-value opportunities to innovate	Re-using knowledge	Internal collaboration	External collaboration	Learning from innovation activities	Building a learning organization
4	Most teams have adopted processes to capture and evaluate opportunities. Most problem owners try to involve others to find innovative solutions and processes and tools exist to help them do this. The benefits of an open-minded approach are largely recognized and people in most parts of the group proactively seek to contribute their insights and ideas.	All available knowledge capture and sharing processes and technology enablers have been adopted. Knowledge sharing is evident across most internal boundaries. Knowledge re-use is expected as normal behaviour and has proactive management support.	There is a strategic approach to collaboration. Management recognize that working outside of boundaries improves problem solving and innovation. Most people use collaborative tools and technologies. Most people participate in networks that reach across the organization, connecting with other people to solve problems, learn, and innovate.	Active collaboration with a wide range of external organizations. There is a strategic approach to relationship management and efforts to continuously improve relationship management capability are evident. Processes and procedures to involve partners in innovation activities and manage risk have been largely adopted.	A range of practices is in place to learn from innovation activities (including piloting and prototyping). A number of measures to track innovation performance have been adopted by most of the group.	A variety of mechanisms has been adopted to support, capture and codify learning from activities and these are being widely used. A continuous improvement culture is largely evident. Ideas about how to do things in a very different way are largely welcomed, with most people understanding how to progress these.

	Recognizing high-value opportunities to innovate	Re-using knowledge	Internal collaboration	External collaboration	Learning from innovation activities	Building a learning organization
3	Many teams have adopted processes to capture and evaluate opportunities and have set up cross-team communication mechanisms to seek wider input to generate innovative solutions. Evidence of an open-minded approach to generating solutions in many places. Management support for this way of working is evident.	Processes and systems for capturing and sharing explicit knowledge have largely been adopted. Many examples of the knowledge sharing taking place locally between the group and with other parts of the organization. Formal and informal management processes support knowledge re-use.	Active collaboration with others across the organization to solve problems and generate innovative solutions. Many people participate in dynamic networks based on important knowledge areas and these involve many parts of the organization and bridge hierarchical levels. A range of collaborative tools and technologies is available and used.	Effective relationship management to support external collaboration is recognized as a strategic benefit to the group. Collaboration is mainly within the supply chain. There is an organized approach to involving partners in innovation activities and to risk assessment. A number of measures to evaluate relationship effectiveness have been adopted.	People are learning from innovation activities and recognize their value, including the use of piloting and prototyping. The impact of innovation activities is evaluated using a number of measures.	Processes and practices to learn from daily activities have largely been adopted. People recognize what is done well and what needs to be improved, have plans for improvement and a willingness to change. Many examples of the connection between learning and innovation are recognized and built upon.

continued on next page...

Table 6.1 - *Continued*

	Recognizing high-value opportunities to innovate	Re-using knowledge	Internal collaboration	External collaboration	Learning from innovation activities	Building a learning organization
2	A few teams have adopted processes to capture and evaluate opportunities. Some people participate in self-help forums to generate wider input for more innovative solutions. An open-minded approach to finding solutions exists in a few cases.	Some processes and technology enablers are being used to support knowledge sharing and re-use. Knowledge re-use is welcomed by some managers, but is communicated through informal rather than formal means.	Some collaborative tools are in place, but used sporadically. Some people participate in dynamic networks and a number of these bridge hierarchical levels. Some local teams look beyond their own boundaries (and even into the wider organization) to solve problems and generate innovative solutions.	Some relationships are recognized as beneficial and receive management attention. Some processes are being trialled to support a more structured approach to learning from external collaboration and to involve partners in innovation activities. Measures to evaluate the effectiveness of collaboration activities are being considered.	Some mechanisms have been adopted to learn from innovation. A few examples of successful piloting and prototyping initiatives exist.	Some mechanisms have been developed to support, capture, and codify learning from everyday activities and these are being used in a few places. Some teams are receptive to change. The connection between learning and innovation is understood by some.

	Recognizing high-value opportunities to innovate	Re-using knowledge	Internal collaboration	External collaboration	Learning from innovation activities	Building a learning organization
1	No single recognized process or approach for capturing and evaluating opportunities. Local teams are largely focused on their own specialisms and activities and don't actively seek to contribute elsewhere. Incentives, processes, and tools are of limited help. Little recognition of the need for an open-minded approach.	Lack of a systematic approach for capturing and sharing knowledge means that knowledge re-use is ad hoc. Ways of supporting knowledge sharing across organizational boundaries rarely used. Knowledge re-use is not part of the culture.	Basic tools and technologies to support collaboration have been adopted by a few people. Little collaboration beyond the immediate team, focus is on local ways of working and the task at hand. Few people participate in networks outside their own level. Little recognition of the value of collaboration.	External collaboration is limited to those relationships initiated through personal contacts. No formal relationship management activity so collaborative activities are not connected. No structured processes to assess risk. Partners rarely involved in innovation.	Few mechanisms in place to learn from innovations. Piloting and prototyping uncommon and learning from experimentation is not developed. Outcomes of innovations are not fully evaluated.	Learning exists in pockets, with individual heroic efforts driving change. Learning happens locally, but is not always connected and acted upon more widely. There is a limited recognition that the culture needs to be more change friendly.

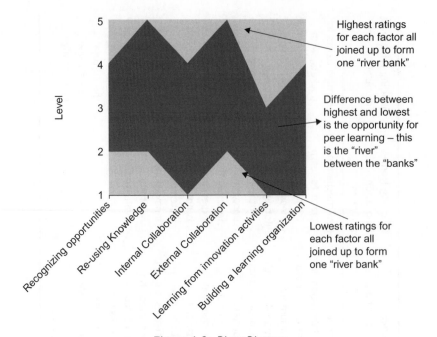

Figure 6.2: River Diagram

- There will be a lot of discussion about what the six factors mean for your organization. This is fine, as long as everyone understands and agrees with the final interpretation.
- The most value will be gained if you can repeat this process to track progress over time. This should be a productive learning process though, rather than a control and performance measurement process. A learning approach encourages collaborative conversations and peer learning, bringing all parts of the organization up to their highest desirable levels.
- The discussion is the most useful part of this process – allow time for it and encourage it.

Real life stories

HighTech

This case study particularly illustrates collaboration and knowledge re-use.

HighTech is a multi-national organization that has established its brand image around its capacity to be innovative. The Knowledge Management team in the part of the organization that designs and delivers solutions for customers has prioritized knowledge re-use initiatives. Their key communication message is that knowledge re-use will release more time for people to be innovative.

A matrix of communities of practice facilitates knowledge sharing and collaboration. Regular events bring people together from across the whole organization to provide knowledge updates about products and solutions, as well as to support social interactions and networking. Customers and partners are included in these events.

Explicit knowledge is captured in a structured way in repositories. Metrics are used to track and report on the contribution of knowledge and its re-use.

The culture is one of mutual respect and trust. Knowledge sharing is valued and this is included in performance feedback systems, as well as employee time recording processes. The Knowledge Management team has the active support of senior management.

Prof-Design

This case study particularly illustrates re-using knowledge and learning from innovation activities.

Prof-Design is a mid-sized architectural design partnership with several offices across the UK. The creative strength of the organization is particularly enhanced by its participation in various design competitions. Several teams within the organization can find themselves competing against each other in the same competition as they participate in different consortia with external partners. This internal competition is viewed as healthy and productive.

The culture is one in which individuals particularly value peer recognition for their design skills and a coaching style of management is seen as most appropriate to support and encourage individual creativity. Each office tends to specialize in a particular aspect of design and, increasingly, complex projects require collaboration between them.

Knowledge Management initiatives are concentrating on improving the management of explicit knowledge resources through improved database technology and developing a process to learn more effectively from design reviews and feed this learning into future projects.

Construction-Design

This case study particularly illustrates building a learning organization and external collaboration.

This privately owned group of companies can deliver all aspects of construction: the focus here was the design company. Generally, incremental innovation predominates. However a recent radical innovation project, which achieved significant savings for a key customer and led to the establishment of a new business internally, has challenged the organization's view of its own capabilities.

The general approach to business is to work in partnership with key customers, adopting a consultancy and advisory approach. After-action reviews are carried out at the end of projects together with the customer and partners in the project to see what should be captured as best practice and what should be carried forward into future projects. The internal view is that the relationship with the customer benefits from this continuous improvement mindset.

The culture of the organization is relatively open and trusting with organizational values being openly discussed. An internal conversation across the organization about what they are passionate about as a business has surfaced a primary passion for relationships – achieving customer satisfaction through a "trusted advisor" role. The Group is interested in innovation that leads to better customer relationships and better delivery. Where they see opportunities to be innovative, the organization actively seek opportunities to work with investors who will value this approach.

Charity

This case study particularly illustrates managing innovation and collaboration.

Charity is a large UK-based charity. The organization raises funds for scientific research that is undertaken both by researchers based in external institutions and by its own fully-funded research institutes. The importance of fund raising to the organization means that it is essential that it maintain its reputation for being authoritative and trusted.

Considerable attention is given to measuring the quality of the scientific innovation that has been funded. A sophisticated approach has been refined over ten years to track the outputs (for example, quality of publications and patents), as well as the value of those outputs in terms of the outcomes that they generate and their impact on both donors and end users. Efforts are also being made to find out from successful scientific researchers what have been the key influences on them and what fuelled their thinking and creativity.

More widely, message board technology has been used to make new ideas visible across the organization and support collaboration between disparate groups of scientists. Charity seeks to be innovative in its approach to fund raising and marketing and a team within the Development department explicitly experiments and "plays" with creative ideas.

The Knowledge Management team is working to facilitate knowledge flows across various internal boundaries of the organization and the funded institutions. A network of knowledge activists supports this.

R&D Co

This case study particularly illustrates collaboration and recognizing opportunities to innovate.

R&D Co is a scientific research establishment in which radical innovation is largely the purpose of the business generating 70% of revenue, with incremental innovation generating the remaining 30%. Enablers of innovation are considered to include the shared physical office spaces for working, team-based collaborative-working technology, and a carefully designed content management system for finished documents. External partners (suppliers, contractors etc.) are given limited access to parts of this. Technology also supports employees in identifying who knows what through a "people finder" application, which rates the relative match of the individual with the topic of interest. The success of these systems is evaluated in terms of the level of use and verbal feedback from users.

Communities based around common technology or scientific discipline interests are supported by the organization. These are intended to facilitate interactions and collaboration beyond the immediate work teams. The organization subscribes to many external resources (such as libraries and databases) to maintain the knowledge base of the organization and to stimulate ideas generation.

The scientists and engineers who make up a large part of the workforce of the organization are motivated to contribute to an expertise database because it contributes to their reputation and the perception of their capability. The culture generally avoids the trap of "not invented here". People are willing to build on previous work. External publications or contributions to the expertise database form explicit targets within the performance management system in some parts of the organization.

Learning about innovation management has become more conscious within the organization. Specific initiatives have been put in place to ensure consistency around core commercial processes. History and the level of expertise that has been built up over time has created a culture in which people take pride in what they do and the organization actively seeks to solve "the impossible problems" that cannot be solved elsewhere.

Top tips

One of the main benefits of the maturity model is that it improves the quality of conversations about issues that otherwise can be difficult to articulate. The framework creates a common language within the organization, as well as a basis for objective assessment. Therefore, it is essential to make time for these conversations and to get a wide variety of people involved.

Research elsewhere has shown that blockages to innovation include:

- Not having enough people trained in innovation management: Do you have training courses, development, and coaching opportunities to ensure that you have such skills in your organization?
- Inability to translate innovations from one environment to another: Can one part of the organization use ideas that have been generated elsewhere? Does someone have responsibility for facilitating the translation process more effectively?
- Failing to learn from previous new product or service development: Is there an evaluation process to find out what went well and what could be improved? How is this learning captured and what ensures that it can be used by different people at a different time and in a different part of the organization?

The research and the team involved

This project was carried out by a working group of knowledge managers from member organizations of the Henley KM Forum. Public, private, and third sector organizations were included. Expert advisers and academics also participated. Phase 1 of the project took place between September 2006 and May 2007 to explore the issues associated with Knowledge Management and innovation. Phase 2 took place between August and December 2007 to identify approaches to building organizations capability. Data was collected through a survey of 13 examples of innovation in 9 organizations followed by telephone interviews to develop detailed case studies in 5 of these; an extensive review of the academic and practitioner literature was also carried out. The intention was to help knowledge managers engage in productive dialogues with colleagues in various functions about how knowledge enabled innovation could make a difference to the business. It is not intended to provide prescriptive advice for a particular business.

The Project was co-championed by Professor George Tovstiga and Dr Christine van Winkelen of Henley Business School and Michael Craven of the Architecture Centre Network in Phase 1 and Wendy Jordan of The British Council in Phase 2. Working group members included representatives from:

Audit Commission	AWE
Cancer Research UK	HP Services
Mills & Reeve	MOD
MWH	National School of Government
Permira Advisers	PRP Architects
QinetiQ	Simons Group
Unisys	Vodafone Group

Advisers and participants in the project also included: Chris Collison of Knowledgeable Ltd and Richard Potter (previously of QinetiQ).

Final reflections from the research

Knowledge Management and innovation management are complementary disciplines. The maturity model is effectively a set of *leading indicators* showing potential future performance (rather than actual delivered performance). Capability building is known to be a long-term process. In contrast, output measures such as the proportion of revenue generated by new products are *lagging indicators* which show the results from previous investments. There will always be a delay between investments in capability building initiatives and evidence of improved performance. Organizations track output measures to find out whether the time and effort invested has been productive in the long run. It can be argued that even when performance (as measured by output indicators) is currently high, tracking both leading and lagging indicators is necessary to ensure that the capability building elements are still in place and the high performance will be sustained.

By adopting a knowledge-based, capability building perspective on innovation, it is possible to provide an integrated approach for measuring performance. This involves three steps:

1. Use the maturity model as a scorecard to track performance in capability building.
2. Identify the key stakeholders of the organization (those who influence strategic or operational decisions in relation to innovation) and measure their satisfaction with the organization's innovation performance.
3. Agree and track specific measures of the outputs of both incremental and radical innovation activities, organizing them around the outputs valued by key stakeholder groups to optimize overall value generation.

Notes

1. George Tovstiga, who co-championed this research, developed this model in the book Birchall, D. and Tovstiga, G. (2005) *Capabilities for Strategic Advantage: Leading through Technological Innovation*, Hampshire: Palgrave Macmillan.
2. For more information about working with maturity models and using them for peer learning, see Collison, C. and Parcell, G. (2004) *Learning to Fly*, 2nd edn, Chichester: Capstone Publishing Ltd.

Chapter 7

Snapshot

Many organizations are concerned about losing professional expertise. Here, three broad approaches for retaining and developing expertise are described that complement each other, together with a wide range of associated practices and techniques.

Two of the approaches focus on facilitating the handover of knowledge from individuals. The first is about maintaining continuity for the business by supporting knowledge sharing in a variety of ways at the time the expert is leaving. The second concentrates on retaining and deepening expertise by helping experts make visible their own thinking processes, as well as encouraging them to provide colleagues with opportunities for deliberate practice and reflective learning.

The third approach takes a longer term perspective and considers how to develop a learning culture. Here the emphasis is on thoroughly integrating knowledge sharing and expertise development into the business model of the organization.

Why this matters

With rapidly growing global competition for professional workers and a generation of baby boomers about to retire, many organizations are concerned about losing professional expertise. The knowledge and expertise of experienced staff are critical to organizations particularly in challenging business circumstances because expertise, by definition, is about knowing how to handle the more difficult problems in a field.

For some organizations, the threat of knowledge loss they face at an organizational level is replicated on a departmental level. The rotation of managerial and technical staff and repeated reorganizations disrupt the "natural" networks through which staff traditionally learnt from each other.

Efforts to retain existing expertise tend to be introduced to manage risk. A good starting point is to identify when the organization is over-reliant on key individuals.

Additionally, initiatives that focus on the development of deeper expertise could be introduced internally for a number of strategic reasons:

- To improve operational efficiency: a way of being able to do higher quality work more quickly and efficiently.
- To increase the body of knowledge in the organization by helping experts to learn more and others to learn more from them. This will stimulate innovation.

What this means for your organization

Facilitating knowledge handovers from individuals

Good planning can predict some departures. Even then, there may still be a need to recover useful knowledge and insight near to the expert's departure time. Sometimes this involves a handover to a successor as the expert retires or moves to another position. At other times, the handover is not to a specific successor but into the organization more generally.

Two aspects of expert practice need to be considered separately when planning a handover between individuals to retain expertise. The first of these is the knowledge of the departing experts.[1] This includes:

- *technical knowledge* of their domain, such as emerging directions in their field, promising technology, the operation of tools, machinery, analytic processes, theory regarding the interaction, causes, and characteristics of the knowledge of their domain, etc.
- *organizational knowledge* of who is involved in decisions, relationships between departments, resources within and outside their company;
- *analytic knowledge* of the theories, frameworks, and guidelines that help with everyday work.

This kind of knowledge is best passed on through what we are calling "continuity tools"; approaches to facilitate knowledge handover when someone leaves a role. In planning initiatives to improve the individual knowledge handover using continuity tools, it is useful to think through the following questions:

1. What are the "at risk" knowledge and skills? Not all knowledge is equally important to the business.
2. How critical is the loss of that knowledge?
3. Who are the users of this knowledge and what is the information they will need?
4. What is your intent? Do you need to capture knowledge the successor will need? Do you need to get experts to teach others how they diagnose and solve technical problems?
5. How difficult are the skills learners will need to develop? How much practice and customization will be necessary?
6. What expertise sharing approach will be the most natural fit with your culture?

7. How many different approaches could you pilot?
8. What support will you need from the organization to pilot the approaches?
9. What do you need to do to prepare the departing expert so they focus on the right content?

The second dimension of expert practice is relevant both for initiatives to retain existing expertise and to develop deeper or new areas of expertise. This goes to the heart of the concept of expertise itself. It is the ability to analyse and solve problems, make connections, and identify opportunities within the field. This is much more intuitive and, unlike many aspects of knowledge, it is extremely difficult to capture and document. Although expertise takes knowledge to perform, it also requires skill and personal experience developed through work in the field and/or deliberate practice.

Deep expertise is passed on through what we have called "thinking tools" – approaches that expose already competent practitioners in their field to the thinking processes of experts. This is illustrated in Figure 7.1. There are two main ways that an expert can develop their professional colleagues:

- A set of activities that are undertaken to support deliberate practice and reflective learning. The expert engages the learner in a dialogue about discipline problems, how the learner would approach them, and guides them in developing solutions, challenging the learner to think.
- Experts share how they themselves approached discipline problems so the learner can glimpse the field through the expert's eyes. Here, templates and tools may be used to guide the learner's thinking processes.

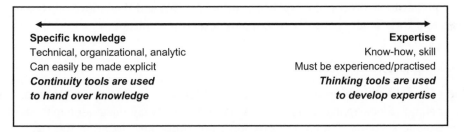

Specific knowledge	Expertise
Technical, organizational, analytic	Know-how, skill
Can easily be made explicit	Must be experienced/practised
Continuity tools are used	*Thinking tools are used*
to hand over knowledge	*to develop expertise*

Figure 7.1: Relating continuity tools and thinking tools to knowledge retention

Developing a learning culture

Rather than concentrating efforts on handing over knowledge from individuals, an alternative approach is to focus on integrating knowledge and expertise development into the way a business is run. Organizational approaches involve a combination of:

- senior management prioritizing the development of individual and organizational knowledge;

- engaging employees in developing knowledge and expertise;
- assigning specific responsibility for developing knowledge and expertise;
- building trusting relationships between staff on which learning can be based.

In exploring the developing of a learning culture some useful questions to ask are:

1. Where is your organization now? How big a shift would it take to develop a culture of learning?
2. At what level are you contemplating this shift? Departmental? Divisional? Organizational? Where does the current leadership stand in relation to that shift? What about middle management?
3. Are there some core values of the organization that are already aligned with this shift?
4. What will motivate staff to really engage (more than through the performance appraisal)? What problems will this solve for staff?
5. How important is it to make this shift? Your personal vision? A mission critical shift? Where in between?
6. What approaches to engaging people would make seeking help and sharing knowledge feel natural and important to people's daily work?
7. What would help your organization to connect experts and learning practitioners?

Creating an action plan

We will first look at how to introduce continuity tools and then move on to thinking tools and then finally consider developing a learning culture.

Retaining knowledge: continuity tools

One of the disruptive problems when experts leave is picking up the threads they left behind. Since many organizations have a variety of document management and storage systems, finding information from their files, locating the right passwords, maintaining contacts, knowing the hidden tricks of using certain physical or analytic tools, maintaining relationships with associations, suppliers, and external organizations all can become unexpectedly problematic when the expert leaves. The loss of this knowledge can disrupt business continuity.

On an organizational level, the same problem can occur. When a large number of experts in a skill group leave at once, the organization can be left with a critical hole in its capabilities.

On an individual level, many organizations have tried capturing experts' knowledge through video or audio tape interviews. However, most organizations, even ones using a sophisticated search tool, find that those interviews are rarely used by remaining staff. Alternatives they find far more useful included career or skills frameworks. Organizations can analyse the skill profiles of departing and remaining staff and use the career framework to anticipate skills gaps. They can also be used to understand critical skill areas in the organization.

"We used a variety of tools from this project. We had a senior individual moving on, so we developed a relationship map of his key contacts. We also held a Question Time piece, a technical exchange focused on particular topics and a session around operational and process knowledge. We are also starting work on improving knowledge retention on a day-to-day basis, so this isn't just addressed when people leave."

Sindy Grewal, Head of Knowledge, Audit Commission

Exit interviews are also highly valuable when they are done well. These can involve a series of interviews covering key processes, bodies of knowledge, contacts, tools, tips, associations, and databases. The specialists involved then produce a summary for the new job holder. While this is time consuming, those who conducted these exercises found them highly useful.

Expert seminars also have a role. The departing member of staff, together with a skilled facilitator, can hold seminars for remaining staff on key topics.

Transferring expertise: thinking tools

Deliberate practice and reflective learning

In the words of various experts:

"You have to give them time to think it through. How do you get key learning points across? Sometimes you have to state the obvious; sometimes you need to stand back; sometimes you have to directly impart knowledge. But you need to take time out for that process."

"Don't give too much information at once. Rather than sitting down at the start of a job and going through it all, talk about what the outcome needs to be and where to start, then let the learner have a go and ask questions as they do so."

"Ask what happened, how did it go, what's the big picture, what are the principles underlying it."

"Ask questions of the learner about how they would go about things, and then hand back the task to the learner to follow through."

Deliberate practice is a time set aside for improving performance – a reflective time for the learner to try new things, refine and develop their understanding. It is also the time in which the expert can show the learner different ways to perform specific aspects of their craft.

Expertise grows out of experts' experience. By encountering similar problems and opportunities over the course of their career, experts develop the ability to recognize patterns in the types, causes, and consequences of the normal problems in their field and the ability to extrapolate from those problems to exceptional ones. From seeing the outcome of their decisions, they are able to distinguish effective from less effective responses. Experience and feedback are critical components of expertise development. Through this repetitive experience experts develop the ability to recognize patterns in the situations they encounter, expand their options for action, and develop their judgment in selecting an approach. Experts' pattern recognition abilities often become so intuitive they don't know how they determine what is happening in the situation or decide what to do.

Experts can support their colleagues in developing their expertise in a number of ways.

- Set aside time for deliberate practice.
  - Expose the learner to new situations, having ongoing discussions about what is happening in each.
  - Make time for extensive reflective conversations about key events and meetings (formal or informal).
- Ask, don't tell.
  - Teach the learners how to diagnose and solve discipline problems by part-formulating the problem and describing the desired outcome, rather than giving all the answers about how to get there.
  - Invite the learner to think through issues, rather than instructing them.
- Challenge assumptions (feedback).
  - Ask the learner what they need to think about in this situation and then challenge them repeatedly about their assumptions.
  - Work with the learner to frame the right question that gets to the heart of the matter.
- Explore the basic principles and the context (understanding).
  - Work with the learner to identify the basic principles that help them diagnose the situation and determine an appropriate solution.
  - Consider the big picture – what is the context that the learner has to bear in mind?
- Explore alternatives (repetition).
  - Look at the issue from different perspectives with the learner.
  - Explore the impact of different circumstances and scenarios on the options available.
  - Invite the learner to try different solutions, to think through varied options.

Making thinking processes visible

Seeing experts "in action" also helps the learner to develop their expertise, particularly when the learner has thought through the same issues in their own practice session. Seeing how the expert addressed those issues, especially in real life situations, helps the learner calibrate their own emerging approach. Approaches that can be helpful include:

> "MWH's world-renowned expert on Pipelines was nearing retirement and we needed to ensure that his knowledge was transferred. An engineer worked alongside him for the five years before his retirement, sharing knowledge and getting an in-depth understanding of his expertise. She is now a world-renowned expert herself and, importantly, she is now passing her knowledge on to a new group of engineers."
>
> *Sarah Grimwood, E-A Knowledge Manager, MWH*

- *Shadowing:* This involves attending meetings with the expert to see him or her review a situation and develop a course of action. It can usefully be integrated within other coaching or mentoring activities.
- *Case presentations:* Design reviews in engineering and architecture environments and case reviews in a medical and social care context are common and are all based on professional review by peers. The same principles can be translated to a business context by looking for projects or situations to engage learners in a discussion and provide a basis for the expert to express their thinking.
- *Sharing work in progress:* Experts who openly share drafts of their work in progress, and expect others in the team to do the same, demonstrate how thinking is developing over time. Offering and expecting open and honest feedback supports a culture of reflective practice.
- *Simulations:* Simulations can capture the thinking processes of experts and allow learners to experiment with alternatives.
- *Challenging tasks:* A powerful way for learners to develop their expertise is to actually try out their understanding of a situation and implement a course of action. Working together on real and challenging tasks was an approach adopted by many experts in developing others. However, the risk generated by learning from real tasks was also acknowledged and the expert remains responsible for "stopping mistakes from going out the door".
- *Frameworks:* Various approaches can be used to guide learners' thinking as they explore the domain. Spreadsheets which set up various options, checklists of key questions, and templates that lay out important considerations can all be helpful.

Developing a learning culture

- *Senior management focus:* For leaders in many organizations, learning and developing knowledge are incidental to the core operations of the organization. However, in the organizations that have made learning and developing expertise part of the way things get done, senior managers are more than supportive. They have made it part of their own leadership practice.
- *Engage employees in developing knowledge:* This is much more than encouraging staff to share and connect. It involves establishing regular mechanisms that bring knowledge to bear on operations. To incorporate developing, sharing, and reusing knowledge, these mechanisms themselves need to be part of everyday

> "It's a question of identifying where critical knowledge lies and putting in a plan for strategic knowledge transfer. It is not something that can be achieved in a one-hour knowledge download. A lot of organizations already have tools such as communities of practice, which are one of the most natural ways of transferring knowledge. Others make a virtue of their alumni."
>
> *Chris Collison, Author and Consultant*

work, for example incorporating knowledge gap assessments into project planning, or extending the remit of communities of practice to include responsibility for answering technical questions, developing careers, and updating procedures.

- *Assign specific responsibility for developing knowledge and expertise:* Organizations that have built knowledge sharing into the culture also make knowledge sharing a real responsibility of staff. The obvious way to develop this sense of responsibility is through career development and performance management systems which need to be designed to include responsibility for knowledge sharing.

- *Build strong relationships between experts and learners:* Useful approaches include:

- Traditional apprenticeship
- Buddy system mentoring
- Individual coaching
- Expert team coaching
- Two-way mentoring.

All of these build relationships through ongoing, regular contact between experienced staff and those learning from them.

Real life stories[2]

Using continuity tools: Knowledge handover process at a group of oil, gas, and petrochemical companies

This story is in the form of an interview with the knowledge manager regarding the organization's Knowledge Retention Programme (KRP).

What does the company do?

We are a worldwide group of oil, gas, and petrochemical companies with interests in biofuels, wind and solar power and hydrogen. We help meet global energy demand in economically, environmentally, and socially responsible ways.

What does this process do?

KRP is a process to capture, package, and share the knowledge of departing staff in a way that is useful to successors and other experts. We interview staff about their work, work processes, developments in their field, where information is located, websites, their networks both within and outside the company, trade associations, pretty much everything needed to maintain continuity between the current job holder and their successor. At the same time KRP is used to share key learnings with a wider audience of experts, to make sure critical knowledge is embedded and re-used in the organization.

KRP focuses on the knowledge that matters. We don't let the staff member rattle on with war stories. We probe for useful information. To ensure that we focus on important knowledge we prioritize the topic areas with the departing staff member's manager. We elicit the knowledge that will provide continuity for the business in general, and for the successor to start with a smooth transition.

KRP packages information for the user. One of the big problems with knowledge capture is its re-use. We don't just transcribe the discussions. We write a report for the successor and fellow experts that covers key issues they will need to know. So the user's point of view is very much embedded in KRP, not only in the report, but in the questions we ask as well. For improved company-wide sharing the outcome of KRP is put on the company Wiki, and further dissemination takes place through "lunch and learn" sessions and corporate academies.

KRP is adaptable. We use various different versions of this tool. One is for staff in a job change where we know who their successor will be. This is "KRP Light". We invite the successors to participate in these discussions. Having the successor in the room asking questions helps. When conducting KRP for a retiring expert, we invite peers and other experts to participate in the debrief.

How long are KRP interviews?

These interviews are very comprehensive. There are between two and six two-hour interviews depending on the individual and the topics. The first interview is to get oriented, identify the areas to focus on. The rest are deep dives into key topics.

Can anyone conduct these interviews?

No, they require very specific skills. We conduct KRP Facilitator training sessions, which we update with the latest learning from the KRP sessions across the world. We also have a KRP Facilitator network to exchange the latest learnings.

Do you have feedback from successors on the value of the reports?

We collect customer feedback after each KRP programme and six months later to find out what value the KRP programme has been.

Any advice you could give a KM colleague to help them conduct good debrief sessions?

Keep the process simple so that people understand what you are doing. Limit expert involvement to a minimum by introducing a trained facilitator. And have a process in place to focus on the really critical knowledge.

Using thinking tools: Expertise retention and development using thinking tools

Several mini-stories illustrate how the approaches to make expert thinking visible can be put into practice:

Case presentations

A public sector organization is responsible for investigating complaint cases. A manual was prepared on how to approach cases, but it was found that this seemed to stop people thinking about the specifics of each case. The manual was removed and just an outline of broad principles retained. This ended up reducing consistency in decisions across the organization. The solution turned out to be guidance on managing case work together with Open Forum discussions on cases. All the relevant facts are presented and discussions cover whether to take on the case, recommendations, outcomes, decisions on redress etc. The expert investigator who tends to take on the most complex cases makes a point of taking these to the Open Forum as this is a way others can learn about how she approaches these. She also encourages others to use the Forum to clarify thinking – going through the process of preparing the presentation is valuable in itself. The Forum sessions are recorded so that others can view them later too.

Masterclasses

An organization set up a series of discussions in which experts and learners could collectively think through a discipline problem. A facilitator helped the experts articulate cues, avenues of thought, assumptions, and the potential courses of action they consider. The facilitator also asked learners to think through their own assessment of the situation and the courses of action they would consider. A lively discussion between experts and learners helps them see how the experts would approach the problem and helps the learners think through other possible action using the experts' insights. It can be helpful to work in small groups of six to eight learners who can benefit from each other's insights. This also reduces the time commitment for the expert.

Simulations

An organization responsible for auditing the activities of banks needed to ensure that its bank examiners could handle a variety of situations. Expert examiners

oversaw the creation of a set of simulations used within a broader training programme and incorporated highly structured coaching support. The examiner's role
was analysed and eight key milestones in the bank examination process were identified. Simulations were developed for each milestone, with the difficult experiences that an examiner could encounter being the target. Each simulation was
built to give people feedback on the decision route they are pursuing as they work
through the simulation, with links to resources to help understand aspects in more
depth. It allowed the learner to deliberately experiment with what would be
involved in pursuing different courses of action. The simulations were developed
in-house using commercial software, allowing them to be readily modified in the
future. They followed a simple layout:

- a video of the situation (in which experienced examiners role-play bank staff);
- multiple choice courses of action;
- scoring of the action choice;
- further video of the bank staff reaction to that action;
- coaching buttons that give audio descriptions of why each action was a good or
  poor choice;
- clickable coaching on the player's choices.

While a simulation seems like a large investment for expertise training, the bank
estimates that the development and delivery cost of this simulation, when distributed over the population of people who have participated, is very similar to that
of a conventional training session.

Developing a learning organization: a culture of sharing knowledge at Fluor Corporation

This story is in the form of an interview with leaders of Fluor's Knowledge
Management initiatives.

What does Fluor do?

Fluor is an international company providing engineering, procurement, construction, maintenance, and project management services worldwide to the oil and gas,
power, chemicals, mining, life sciences, and other capital-intensive industries.
Fluor designs, builds, and maintains many of the world's most complex and challenging capital projects.

Currently, every market and geographic region that Fluor serves is in a tremen-
dous growth mode. Fluor is experiencing the largest growth mode in the history of
its company. Many projects are over $1 billion, and there is currently a huge
backlog of projects. For example, more than 1,000 new employees joined Fluor's
Houston office in 2007; Manila and New Delhi have grown by 250% with other offices
experiencing similar growth.

What makes sharing knowledge and developing expertise vital to the organization?

Knowledge sharing is a business imperative. The globally competitive business market drove the need for knowledge sharing and collaboration across organization and geographic boundaries. Fluor often has several different offices working on pieces of the same project, and often executes multi-party projects with competitors as joint venture partners. Fluor also needs the ability to tap into experts anywhere in the world. The overall strategic direction for knowledge retention, sharing, and collaboration tightly links with Fluor's business environment.

Fluor responded to this challenge by establishing knowledge communities in each of its major functional areas. Launching its formal KM strategy in 1999, Fluor now has 43 communities of practice covering all major functional groups and several support services. Almost 100% of the targeted workforce is involved in one or more communities, sharing knowledge globally, enabling work processes, and bringing new people up to speed quickly. Fluor's Knowledge Management system has over 25,000 active members who download 400 knowledge objects daily, submit 350 new or updated knowledge objects each week, and submit 300 questions and answers each week in the forums. Over 30,000 knowledge objects and over 9,000 forums are read each week. Anyone anywhere in the world can ask a question to our knowledge forums and expect a prompt answer. Our knowledge forums are very active, with over 13,000 submissions and 500,000 reads in 2007. Most questions are technical.

Because Fluor operates globally, there was also a strong need to develop consistent business processes and tools. Fluor uses knowledge communities and its *Knowledge OnLine*SM technology platform to support global execution of project work (instead of moving people around). Fluor uses the term knowledge communities instead of communities of practice because the term fits better for their organization. Fluor's current challenge isn't the loss of knowledge, but the need to use standard processes (e.g. project management processes) and collaborative technologies (e.g. *Knowledge OnLine*) to transfer knowledge, especially to new hires.

Knowledge sharing appears to be "baked in" to your culture – please tell me about it.

KM is ingrained right from the start. Emphasizing the importance of knowledge sharing and global access to expertise begins during recruitment and new hire orientation. New hires quickly learn that knowledge communities are the way to connect to knowledge and expertise.

Fluor encourages knowledge-sharing behaviours across the organization. Any employee can join one or more knowledge communities, and can post a question or answer a question in Knowledge OnLine. By joining a knowledge community, employees have opportunities for career advancement, and subject matter experts gain enterprise-wide recognition. Additionally, Fluor integrates knowledge-sharing objectives into every employee's annual performance appraisal to ensure that Knowledge Management is an instilled value in the organization.

Fluor's knowledge retention and transfer processes are also integrated with the employment lifecycle at Fluor. For example, its knowledge retention and transfer processes are highlighted in its recruitment activities. On their first day, every employee worldwide is directed to a company and functional community-based orientation process that emphasizes knowledge-sharing behaviours. Every function within the company has a documented career path which includes necessary experience, training, skills, and expected knowledge-sharing behaviours. Information on these career paths can be found in the online community space.

How is the importance of sharing knowledge communicated throughout the organization?

Fluor has always benefited from strong executive support for our Knowledge Management activities. An integral part of Fluor's Knowledge Management strategy has been effective communication. Fluor utilizes several communication principles to ensure effective and timely communications. Fluor believes it is important to leverage all the communication channels within the organization and proactively look for opportunities to communicate about Knowledge Management.

Fluor has numerous communication strategies in place in support of knowledge retention and transfer. These include new hire orientation, global teleconferences, department meetings, lunch-and-learn sessions, and online community front page success stories which change every two to three days. Fluor's most successful communication campaign is the annual *Knowvember* campaign which began in 2002. Employees are encouraged to submit success stories to the campaign throughout the year. The success stories are shared in Knowledge OnLine. In addition, we have a peer recognition campaign, *KM Pacesetters*, where individuals can nominate employees for their knowledge-sharing behaviours. The winners are recognized as part of our *Knowvember* celebration.

Top tips

✓ Retaining knowledge does not necessarily need a corporate programme to be in place; as it is individually focused, it can be piloted in a relatively low-key, low investment way.

✓ A knowledge audit can be used to set priorities and may be useful to help identify areas of expertise that have not yet been recognized as such and which could disappear before the organization has realized it has them. It may also identify areas in which the organization has an emerging competitive advantage and the expertise related to them.

✓ In certain types of organization the nature of the business model is that the individuals do the work rather than groups, so the organization does rely on individuals. However, where this doesn't apply, a learning culture that genuinely builds knowledge into how work gets done creates a context that encourages sharing of deep expertise. It means the departure of employees, however quick or unexpected, does not risk the loss of essential knowledge for the business.

The research and the team involved

This research was carried out in two phases between 2007 and 2009 by working groups of members of the Henley KM Forum. In the first phase, a broad review of approaches to retaining and developing expertise was undertaken. Altogether 29 organizations participated in this research, 13 from within the Forum and 16 from outside. Information about company approaches was collected through interviews with those engaged in the knowledge retention and development activities of the organization. Both public and private sector organizations were included.

In the second phase, a more focused study of expert thinking processes and how this relates to KM programmes was undertaken. Data was collected through interviews with experts, most of whom were employed in working group member organizations, though some were identified through external contacts. Telephone interviews were used to collect the data (21 interviews were undertaken) and an extensive review of the academic and practitioner literature was also carried out. Those interviewed were selected as both experts in their field and good at developing others.

The research activities were intended to help knowledge managers to integrate a focus on expertise development into KM programmes more effectively. They were not intended to provide prescriptive advice for a particular business.

Dr Richard McDermott of McDermott Consulting and a Visiting Academic Fellow at Henley Business School led the research in conjunction with Dr Christine van Winkelen of Henley Business School. Sarah Grimwood from MWH was the practitioner co-champion of the second phase. Working group members across the two phases of the research included representatives from:

Audit Commission	*AWE*
BT	*Cadbury Schweppes*
The Carbon Trust	*Department of Health*
GCHQ	*Hewlett Packard*
HM Treasury	*Hyder Consulting*
MWH	*Oracle*
Parliamentary and Health Services Ombudsmen	*PRP Architects*
QinetiQ	*Taylor Woodrow*
Unisys	

together with invited associates:

Chris Collison	*Cranfield University, RMCS*
Debbie Lawley	*Knowledgable Ltd*
Roger Darby	*Stretch Learning*
Tim Andrews	*Willow Transformations*

Organizations outside the working group that participated in the study included:

Boeing	*The Federal Reserve Bank of Cleveland*
Fluor Corporation	*IBM*
Jet Propulsion Laboratory	*Mindtree*
NASA	*Northrop Grumman*
Sandia National Labs	*Shell Oil*
Tennessee Valley Authority	*Unilever*
US Army Battle Command	*Wipro*
Xerox	

Final reflections from the research

Links with other knowledge initiatives are the easiest way to bring a focus to expertise development. This includes extending the remit of communities of practice to support professional development; developing collaborative working technology and establishing briefing sessions to share work-in-progress; and including information about who experts are and how to find their checklists and templates on the intranet.

However, including an emphasis on expertise development within broader Knowledge Management programmes could represent a shift in two important ways:

1. From predominantly paying attention to *organizational learning*, to also being involved in *individual development* which is likely to involve strengthening connections with other functions and initiatives, such as training and development. The potential challenges involved in bridging these functional boundaries are considered in Chapter 8 .
2. From paying attention to capturing and sharing the *thoughts* generated by experts (as knowledge outputs), to paying attention to *the thinking processes* they are using and how these develop. New approaches and "tools" will be needed, from exploring how to craft more insightful questions, to understanding how to have more effective conversations. See Chapter 17 for recommendations to improve the quality of conversations.

Notes

1. See also "Learning the Master's Art: How to Preserve the Real Expertise of Retiring Staff" by Richard McDermott (submitted for publication).
2. These cases were prepared during 2007 and 2008. Reproduced with permission.

Section IV

Increase learning capacity

Learning is something that we can tend to take for granted because it is part of how we become who we are. From our home life and from our education as children, through further education then professional development and training in the workplace, to our wider interests and activities we develop skills, abilities, points of view, ways of thinking, habits, and preferences that shape what we do, how we see ourselves, and how others see us. Yet, new technologies have revolutionized how we connect with sources of knowledge that we can learn from, both digital and personal. The knowledge content available to us is growing at an ever-increasing rate. Learning relevant knowledge and how to work and live in an ever-changing world are challenges we all face.

It is an even bigger challenge for organizations, because the scale is magnified and the risks and opportunities are greater. Learning how to perform current activities better, learning about new ways of doing things, and even learning how to learn more efficiently have never been more important if organizations are to survive and thrive.

What do we mean by learning capacity?

By learning capacity we mean the ways in which individuals (and organizations as collections of individuals) are able to recognize, absorb, and use knowledge. Knowledge is both the input and output of learning. The knowledge that flows around an organization stimulates, provides the raw material for, and transfers the benefits of learning. Increasing learning capacity also means getting better at the process of learning itself.

Increasing learning capacity improves operational effectiveness because it provides the basis for continuous improvement activities, which incrementally refine processes and practices. Re-using knowledge (learning from the activities of others) saves time and money and allows the intelligence of people in the organization to be directed at solving new problems rather than old ones. Learning capacity is also the basis for stimulating innovation by giving people access to new knowledge which challenges existing thinking.

Chapter 11 views the organization as a learning system of nested levels with individuals at the centre, reaching out to the groups they belong to, the organization, and then spreading to inter-organizational learning. The efficiency and effectiveness of knowledge flows within and across these levels are the basis of the efficiency and effectiveness of an organization's learning system. This is a similar idea conceptually to the nine critical knowledge flows between individuals, the infrastructure of the organization, and the outside world identified in Chapter 2. Developing an organization's learning system requires a more strategic approach to assessing these knowledge flows (which was covered in Section I) as well as specific attention to the principles and mechanisms involved in learning. One additional consideration which seems to create tension in some organizations is the division of responsibility for aspects of learning. Different departments may work to improve individual learning and development, organizational learning, competitor intelligence, etc. But if the efforts of each function are not aligned it can send conflicting messages and waste resources. We explore how to align the learning processes in Chapter 8.

How do you increase it?

It can be helpful to start by thinking about what learning involves. The way that knowledge is created in our minds through the process of learning has been the subject of philosophical debate for millennia. There are different schools of thought on this.[1] For example, there is the view that data, information, and explicit knowledge are something that we can all acquire in the same way so that we all make increasingly accurate and identical views of the world, effectively all building the same knowledge base. Another view is that what the same thing means depends on our unique starting point and therefore differs for each of us. In this view, knowledge is not an abstract thing to be collected, but is a process of interpretation. This process happens at each level of the social system, be that in the head of an individual, or the group or organization he or she belongs to.

Although these schools of thought are somewhat contradictory, both are in evidence in the way that organizations approach learning. When the individual is treated as a relatively passive recipient of knowledge, perhaps with technology being used to convey it to them, then the first school of thought is implicitly being adopted. However, when their active involvement and engagement with the knowledge content is required, then the second is evident. Chapter 8 explores the need to join up learning initiatives in different ways depending on the extent to which the individual is viewed as a passive recipient or an active participant in learning.

Even in the case of explicit knowledge (knowledge that can readily be put into words) different systems of meaning making inevitably result in different constructions, interpretations, and application by different people. Hence, attempting to capture such knowledge, for example in Electronic Document and Records Management Systems (EDRMS) has inevitable limitations. Chapter 9 considers how to bring a knowledge perspective to such systems, rather than simply treating them as information repositories.

Tacit knowledge cannot easily be put into words and therefore is inherently more difficult to transfer between individuals. It takes time and effort to develop, is potentially more valuable to the organization because of this, and is highly dependent on the systems of meaning making involved. Within an area of shared work practice, a system of meaning is communicated through a common language that allows knowledge to develop and be embedded in the practice. Knowledge can leak from organizations when practices are shared with outsiders; yet it can stick in certain places within organizations because communication is ineffective or technical mastery is complex.[2] Communities of practice are one approach to improving knowledge flows even to the point that tacit knowledge may be exchanged. Chapter 10 looks at how to create the conditions that support these knowledge flows, as well as the organizational conditions that can sustain the resources and commitment needed to make these work.

The social structure of an organization leads to the emergence of shared values and a collective sense of identity. Dominant logic is an emergent property.[3] This is the collective tacit knowledge about what is acceptable and how things should be done. It becomes a form of shorthand that speeds decision-making and creates a kind of equilibrium in the organization. However, the longer the organization has been in equilibrium, the harder it is to unlearn the dominant logic and develop new ways of doing things when the conditions have changed. Looking outside the organization to find new ways of thinking about challenging issues is one way of building this kind of learning capacity. Chapter 11 explores how to get the most out of participating in external collaborations intended specifically for learning.

The four approaches to building learning capacity covered in this section generate value in an organization by developing human, structural (also called

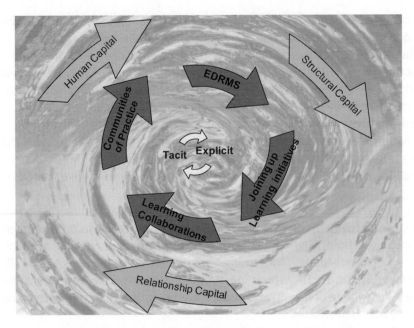

Figure IV.1: Generating intellectual capital through increasing knowledge flows to build learning capacity

organizational), and relationship capital through increasing knowledge flows as illustrated in Figure IV.1. Clearly, these are not the only ways to increase individual or organizational learning. Several different approaches are covered in other chapters of this book, for example:

- Peer learning is described in relation to the use of maturity models in Chapters 6, 9, and 12.
- Learning in different kinds of project environments is considered in Chapter 4.
- Learning to make better decisions by individuals and collectively across the organization is explored in Chapter 12.
- Learning to improve the innovation capability of the organization is examined in Chapter 6.
- Learning how to improve knowledge sharing through more effective conversation is outlined in Chapter 17.

Key questions to ask yourself

As you start to use the ideas in the next four chapters ask:

- Who is responsible for taking a strategic perspective on learning in the organization?

- Which long-term investments in building organizational learning capacity are needed to create a more sustainable future? How can managers and leaders best support these?
- Is the balance of attention being given to different kinds of learning and accessing different kinds of knowledge appropriate for the pace of change in your industry or external environment?
- Which approaches to learning will make the most difference most quickly? How will increasing the flow of knowledge speed this up? How can you show some "quick wins" to build interest and sustain momentum?

Notes

1. The influence of how knowledge is viewed on organizational approaches to managing knowledge has been discussed extensively. See for example: Easterby-Smith, M. (1997) Disciplines of organizational learning: contributions and critiques, *Human Relations*, 50, 1085–1113; Easterby-Smith, M. and Araujo, L. (1999) "Organizational learning: current debates and opportunities", in Easterby-Smith, M., Burgoyne, J., and Araujo, L. (eds), *Organizational Learning and the Learning Organization: Developments in Theory and Practice*, London: Sage; Burgoyne, J. (2002) "Learning theory and the construction of self: what kinds of people do we create through the theories of learning that we apply to their development?" in Pearn, M. (ed.), *Individual Differences and Development in Organizations*, Chichester: John Wiley and Sons Ltd.

2. See for example: Wenger, E. (1998) *Communities of Practice: Learning, Meaning and Identity*, Cambridge, Cambridge University Press; Brown, J. and Duguid, P. (2001) Knowledge and organization: A social-practice perspective, *Organizational Science*, 12, 198–213; Szulanski, G. (1996) Exploring internal stickiness: Impediments to the transfer of best practice within the firm, *Strategic Management Journal*, 17, 27–43.

3. A useful overview is available in Bettis, R. and Prahalad, C. (1995) The dominant logic: retrospective and extension, *Strategic Management Journal*, 16, 5–14.

Chapter 8

Snapshot

Many organizations are striving to become a "learning organization", one that continuously learns to improve performance. However, developing the capability to learn effectively from the experience of people going about the organization's business, successes and mistakes along the way and from the vast array of stakeholders with an interest and involvement in today's organizations is a constant challenge. One important practical consideration is how do the different functions responsible for aspects of learning coordinate and integrate their activities? For example Knowledge Management tends to focus on initiatives that generate organizational level learning, whilst human resources functions tend to have a responsibility for individual employee learning. A consistent set of principles and strategies streamlines the overall learning efforts and ensures they are as effective as possible – "joining up" learning helps build the capability to become a learning organization.

Looking at the learning processes that underpin both individual and organizational learning highlights ways in which the human resources/training and development and Knowledge Management functions can collaborate and, in the process, deliver truly joined-up learning. A set of strategic principles, a set of specific proposals to integrate initiatives across the "employee lifecycle", and a health check to diagnose the organizational receptivity to change are all included here.

Why this matters

The knowledge we already have is the basis for whether we recognize new knowledge as important or valuable, as well as our ability to make sense of that knowledge and apply it. For organizations, this absorptive capacity[1] is significantly affected by the breadth of the knowledge of individuals within the organization. Consequently supporting individuals' learning and knowledge development to keep pace with developments in their fields is very important. The other important factor that determines an organization's absorptive capacity is the number of ways in which the potential of new knowledge can be transformed into operational value – this can be achieved through a range of organizational learning mechanisms.

In practical terms, this is directly linked to the idea of creating a learning organization. As Charles Handy said "The learning organisation can mean two things. It can mean an organisation which learns and/or an organisation which encourages learning in its people. It should mean both."

However, we also know that professional groups tend to end up sharing a common language around a topic or task with their own colleagues. Knowledge managers and human resources managers are functional groups that have developed specialist knowledge around organizational learning and individual learning respectively. Other research has shown that this impacts the learning capability of the organization as:

> "It therefore can be difficult to bridge internal boundaries and integrate the contributions of different groups to organizational learning because of contrasts in the technologies they offer, and the goals they attach, to the process."[2]

A successful partnership between KM and HR combining individual and organizational learning will create greater value for the business by presenting managers and employees with a clearly "joined-up" approach. However, in many organizations, learning-related processes and activities happen in relative isolation from one another, possibly for the reason that different professional disciplines are adopting different perspectives and priorities. Moving forward from this position requires management commitment to three principles:

> "It's more important to do the right thing, rather than worry about who did it, or who takes the credit for doing it."
>
> *Graham O'Connell, Head of Organisational Learning and Standards, National School of Government*

- Joining up learning-related processes and activities generates value for the organization.
- Different kinds of learning-related processes and activities need to be joined-up in different ways.
- Active engagement and dialogue between people involved in learning in different functional areas is the best way to achieve this joined-up approach.

What this means for your organization

The starting point is to think about what is being learnt.

Individual learning: Individuals learn and acquire knowledge in different ways. Figure 8.1 offers a useful spectrum that asks you to think about whether a specific

Passive Reception............Mixed................Active Learning

Figure 8.1: Spectrum of learning activities according to the level of engagement of the learner[3]

learning activity requires the individual to learn passively by being provided with information and guided through it, or actively by engaging with a real issue and thinking through the implications. Or is it through a process in which active learning and passive learning are mixed? Many individually focused learning activities and processes could be initiated by line managers, human resources, training, or other employee development functions.

> "Capturing the knowledge that has been gained from a project is one thing – learning the lessons embedded in that knowledge is quite another."
>
> *Martin Fowkes, whilst Knowledge Manager at Taylor Woodrow*

Organizational learning: Here one important consideration is whether learning involves explicit or tacit knowledge. Explicit knowledge is knowledge that has been codified into words, pictures, or other digital media that make it easily transferable. In contrast, tacit knowledge is knowledge that cannot easily be put into words. Initiatives aimed at improving organization-wide learning of explicit knowledge, for instance, might be thought of in terms of technologies such as databases or processes to capture and share lessons learnt. A focus on improving organization-wide exchange of tacit knowledge might see the development of communities of practice to connect people with relevant experience.

These distinctions matter because they help to crystallize what the priorities are and where the opportunities lie for responsible functions to collaborate. Mapping all of the individual and organizational learning initiatives in your organizations against these dimensions can provide a basis for identifying opportunities to integrate activities effectively. This is illustrated in Figure 8.2.

Creating an action plan

Moving forward involves adopting both a strategic framework and then identifying practical opportunities to integrate specific learning activities.

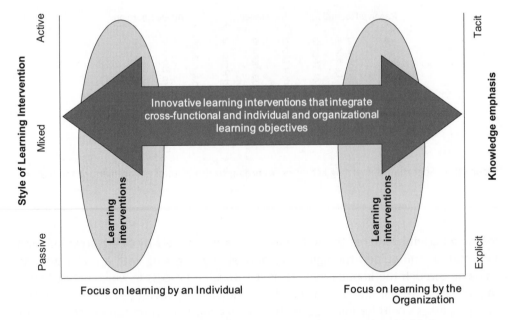

Figure 8.2: Identifying opportunities to integrate learning-related initiatives

Developing a strategic framework for learning

A strategic framework can be used to bring together different functions and departments involved in learning initiatives and processes. Elements of a strategic framework include:

- Agreeing a set of principles encompassing learning and people-based knowledge initiatives.
- Acknowledging different practices will be used in different functions, but that there need to be common drivers and strategic objectives. For example, jointly focusing on enabling business teams to be successful, rather than on functional activities.
- Embedding a consistent learning strategy into the design of the organization through role definitions, performance management, and reward systems.
- Undertaking joint cross-functional *learning needs* analysis, rather than training needs analysis, with the goal of developing organizational capability, as well as individual competence.
- Agreeing the role of managers in integrating and cascading learning approaches.
- Creating the conditions to allow opportunistic interventions, as well as top down holistic approaches (all linked by the agreed principles).

It is also important to decide whether to achieve alignment and an integrated approach via compliance (that is, top down instruction) or the development of a common strategy by the functions involved. In both cases, clear objectives and metrics for learning in the organization will determine what receives attention.

Practical opportunities to integrate learning activities

There are many opportunities to foster closer collaboration between functions responsible for thinking about people management and those responsible for thinking about Knowledge Management. You could use the list below as a starting point for discussions in your organization once you have mapped all of your learning related activities onto a diagram like Figure 8.2.

1. Employee leaver/transfer processes linked to knowledge capture and transfer initiatives.
2. Communities of practice used as a vehicle to support mentoring programmes.
3. Personal and organizational development initiatives to generate better quality productive conversations between people.
4. Formal courses and e-learning reinforced through activities in communities of practice.
5. Communities of practice providing experience and expertise to shape the design and delivery of formal training and e-learning courses.
6. Induction process enabling and encouraging new hires to join communities of practice and including training in knowledge-sharing behaviours, the use of collaborative tools etc.
7. Knowledge-sharing/management principles included in management development.
8. Learning from after action project and event reviews fed into induction and training design (courses and e-learning).
9. New hires complete yellow pages/people finder type information during induction.
10. Participants in conferences/standards meetings etc. provide briefings and seminars as part of continuous professional development initiatives.
11. Intranet portal used in a coherent way to distribute information, good practices, policies etc. as well as links to experts. HR learning management/e-learning systems combined with the intranet/knowledge portal of the company.

Several of the proposals to integrate learning activities and processes can be mapped on to the employee lifecycle, which can be helpful in recognizing opportunities for functional specialists and other managers to work together more closely as shown in Figure 8.3.

There are also barriers to effectively integrating learning activities. A cross-functional discussion about these issues is important:

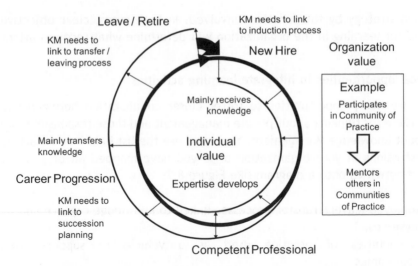

Figure 8.3: Relating knowledge initiatives to the employee lifecycle

> "Because there's no tension, we can actually interact very well – which makes a big difference."
>
> *Lucy Miller, learning from experience manager, Ministry of Defence*

- The current trend to e-learning as the preferred method of training delivery pushes learning towards the "passive" mode and can reduce the productive conversations that may allow tacit knowledge to be exchanged. This impacts the individual learning potential, as well as the organizational learning potential by limiting feedback loops.
- There is often a lack of mechanisms for different functions to know what respective priorities are and opportunities (and time) to communicate regularly with each other to identify areas of common interest.
- A culture may prevail in which functional managers do not feel that they have the remit to change the way learning is managed. Anything working in opposition to the prevailing culture is unlikely to be effective in the short term and a more productive approach may be to change processes and systems within the existing culture.

Real life stories[4]

Generating a strategic framework for learning – mobile phone operator

KM and HR colleagues developed a strategic framework to encompass individual and organizational learning in a global mobile telephone network operator. A virtual management team supported by a community of practice for everyone involved in learning was created to take forward the implementation of the strategic framework. The strategy was intended to deliver benefits by integrating the best prac-tices in traditional training and knowledge building into improved working methods and incorporating these into the way the organization learns.

Specifically it ensured that:

- Learning and knowledge development activity would be directed at improving business performance.
- A climate would be created that supported employees learning, sharing, and building knowledge in alignment with the strategy.
- Varied methods for learning and knowledge building would be employed which were coherent and appropriate.
- Learning would be put close to the job, with an emphasis on customer-facing staff, ensuring practices were shared, validated, and adopted across the organization.
- Managers and leaders would be champions and role models for learning.
- The learning function would be a flexible, professional, and influential partner to the business.
- The know-how of employees would be fully utilized to enable business growth.

Using communities of practice as the basis for integrating individual and organizational learning – pharmaceuticals firm

The strategy of the manufacturing business of a global pharmaceuticals firm drove their knowledge strategy bias towards exploiting existing knowledge to improve efficiency: "we are always working on making our valuable knowledge explicit". Communities of practice were their main mechanism to integrate learning activi-ties. The various functional areas were responsible for individual learning interven-tions to support the adoption of good practices and the KM function concentrated on the development of organizational competency and capability in specifically identified areas of knowledge focus. Communities of practice became the place where these two aspects connected by generating content and feedback and sup-porting the standardization of approaches.

Adopting an integrated approach – QinetiQ

QinetiQ is a provider of technical services, which employs scientists and engineers from many disciplines. The strategic orientation of the business requires there to be an emphasis on knowledge creation, making collaboration and connections between people in different parts of the business a priority. Whilst recognizing the boundary between individual learning and organizational learning, HR people acknowledged responsibility for collective learning and therefore helped to create some of the "bridges" between the two "levels" of learning.

Active learning activities and processes

A substantial part of the role of the top technical people (Fellows and Senior Fellows) was to maintain and develop "capability". They were judged (and judged themselves) very much on the basis of the value of their team (its expertise, its reputation, and the demand for its services). Thus the organizational learning element was actually built into these individual roles. Fellows were at the pinnacle of the "Career development map" for technical people and were appointed and reviewed by a peer review process (internal and external) that was organized by HR. For the technical community, the bridge was therefore already built-in. One could also make a similar case for many functional groups, as the head had to maintain a professional capability.

Mixed active/passive learning activities and processes

Most senior managers in QinetiQ had a collective "staff engagement" target. It recognized the fact that knowledge workers are volunteers and focused on helping people to see (believe and feel) that "we are all in this together". It therefore provided a strong link between individual and collective competence and encouraged senior managers to speak and act in ways that reinforced that message. Another example was that HR set up and provided plenty of encouragement for a community for new graduates. It had two important functions: a support network for new hires to help settle them in (housing, meeting others, how do I . . .?) and it created a pan-organizational network addressing social, technical, and business issues. Individuals had to get funding from their local managers to participate and so they had to demonstrate value from their projects. In so doing, they were building a great deal of personal and collective know-how on how to "make things happen".

Passive learning activities and processes

"Review and improve" was built into all management processes in order to feed lessons learnt back into the way people are trained and into the help and guidance material provided as part of the business management system. This was a standard part of the quality model and the key element was the diligence with which the review is done and the effort put into extracting the generic lessons.

Top tips

A basic "health check" can help to identify how easy – or difficult – it will be to deliver truly joined-up learning. Ask yourself the following questions:

- Is the learning agenda driven from the top of the organization?
- Is there a common strategy and business case for learning, reaching across functional divides?

- Is learning regarded as important to the way that the organization operates – and do people feel encouraged to learn, and to contribute to the learning of the organization?
- Are managers held accountable for learning?
- Is there a track record of Knowledge Management and human resources people working together?

If every answer is "yes", then joined-up learning is a real opportunity waiting to be grasped. If only some questions can be answered with a "yes", then there are still untapped opportunities. But if every answer is "no", then the chances of getting full value from learning investments need careful evaluation and the starting point needs to be a strategic conversation about what learning means for the organization.

The research and the team involved

This research was carried out during 2005 and 2006 by a working group of members of the Henley KM Forum. Survey data from ten organizations represented a comprehensive review of planned learning interventions in a cross-section of private and public sector organizations. Additionally, the survey asked for examples of current integrated approaches to learning that bridged individual and organizational learning, as well as requiring cross-functional involvement, where they existed. An expert panel of 12 knowledge managers and six human resources managers then evaluated the integrated approaches identified, proposed new ones based on the individual and organizational learning initiatives collated through the survey, and explored the issues associated with implementing them. This was exploratory research intended to help knowledge managers engage in productive dialogues with colleagues, in particular in the Human Resources, Training and Development, and Organizational Development functions, about how to join up learning initiatives most productively. It was not intended to provide prescriptive advice for a particular business.

The Project was co-championed by Dr Christine van Winkelen of Henley Business School and Peter Hall of Orange. Working group members included representatives from:

Defence Procurement Agency   *GlaxoSmithKline*
Henley Business School   *Metronet Rail SSL*
Ministry of Defence   *National School of Government*
Nissan Technical Centre Europe   *Orange*
PRP Architects   *QinetiQ*
Simons Group   *Thames Water*
Unisys

together with invited associates: Dr Roger Darby of Cranfield University, Peter Hemmings of KN Associates, and Debbie Lawley of Willow Transformations.

Final reflections from the research

Political and power realities are different in every organization. Bridging functional divides to collaborate with colleagues interested in learning was clearly a political challenge in several of the organizations studied in this research. Different frames of reference, goals, and objectives and the general mindsets developed by different functions make any kind of cross-boundary learning challenging; there is no reason to expect anything different from the various functions involved in learning-related activities in an organization. Fostering mutual respect and knowledge exchange, encouraging the habits of cooperation, and fostering a sense of community shifts the patterns of behaviour in the organization and encourages the emergence of cooperation as the norm. This requires a long-term perspective that may be more possible in some organizations than others.

Notes

1. See for example Cohen, W.M. and Levinthal, D. (1990) Absorptive Capacity. A new perspective on learning and innovation, *Administrative Science Quarterly*, 35, 128-153, or Zahra, S.A. and George, G. (2002) Absorptive capacity: A review, reconceptualisation and extension, *Academy of Management Review*, 27, 185-203.
2. Child, J. and Heavens, S.J. (2003) "The social constitution of organizations and its implications for organizational learning", in Dierkes, M., Berthoin Antal, A., Child, J., and Nonaka, I. (eds), *Handbook of Organizational Learning and Knowledge*, Oxford University Press, Oxford, 308-326.
3. Leonard, D. and Swap, W. (2004) Deep smarts, *Harvard Business Review*, 82(9), 88-97.
4. These cases were prepared during 2005 and 2006. Reproduced with permission.

Chapter 9

Snapshot

Electronic document and record management systems (EDRMS) are increasingly seen as a way to effectively and efficiently store vast arrays of documents. From the perspective of improving access to knowledge in the organization, such information repositories are clearly potentially valuable in supporting better knowledge flows. Yet, the promise that such systems offer is often not fulfilled. By pinpointing precisely where value typically lies and identifying proven ways to extract it, the return on the investment in electronic document management can be significantly improved.

Intelligent EDRMS use means linking the technical ability to store, locate, and connect information with processes and approaches that tap into the unstructured knowledge in people's heads. This provides essential context and meaning to a situation and is a source of real value to the organization.

We found three potential sources of value generation from the effective EDRMS: compliance, competitiveness, and collaboration. Although, for most organizations, one of these is likely to be the primary value driver, all three need attention. The key is to determine an appropriate balance for your context. Implementing EDRMS needs to be viewed as a significant change programme. The factors that are known to underpin the flow of knowledge (motivation, skills and abilities, actions and the environment) point to the issues to be addressed through the change programme. In all cases, training, communication, and leadership are particularly important. Additionally adjusting work practices and building in learning mechanisms to evolve the system as conditions change are also essential. These factors are all captured in a maturity model to help establish a peer learning approach to delivering knowledge value from an EDRMS.

Why this matters

Why do they need to make me use (the system)? It must be because it's not much good. If it was any use I would use it anyway. Why do they have to force me to use it? They haven't convinced people of the value of the system.

This was the jaded response of one EDRMS user.

Millions of pounds and thousands of hours have been invested in the development and implementation of electronic document and records management systems (EDRMS). They promise seamless and effective Information Management that will lead to huge return on investment from efficiency and effectiveness gains. The reality for many companies is rather different. EDRMS are effective as repositories and often produce some efficiency savings but all too often they do not form part of the productive, active knowledge flows that helps businesses innovate, flourish, and grow in the way many managers hope.

Bringing a knowledge perspective into the implementation offers the potential of greater value generation. However, it needs individuals to be actively engaged with the system, rather than simply instructed to use it. We came to describe this as a requirement for "intelligent usage", which is evident when individuals are thinking about how to use the system to make better decisions in their own jobs, as well as what the possible knowledge needs of others might be in the future.

What this means for your organization

"For us, the benefits revolve around collaboration and competitiveness. We're sharing knowledge around the organization – and we're saving time, money and paper."
Cathy Blake, whilst Head of Knowledge Management at PRP Architects

In an EDRMS, "documents" is a broad description that includes audio files, video files, textual-based files, spreadsheets, photographs, CAD drawings, and PDF files, amongst others. In overall business terms, documents can also include non-digital media such as paper, microfiche, film, and video tape – all of which can now be scanned and incorporated into an EDRMS as digital files. Here, we use the term document interchangeably with the term record, although we recognize that there is an important distinction to be made in some situations.

There are three main ways in which EDRMS can be used to improve organizational performance: compliance, collaboration, and competitiveness.

- Compliance is about governance, auditability, and control.
- Collaboration is about improving connectivity and communication between people.
- Competitiveness is about organizational efficiency improvements.

Although there is likely to be a main purpose for your system, paying appropriate attention to all three "Cs" will mean that it can generate even more value for your organization. Our strongest recommendation from the research was that you need to understand what each of the Cs means in your organization, what the balance needs to be between them, and then design your system and implementa-

Table 9.1: Sources of value from an EDRMS

Compliance	Collaboration	Competitiveness
▪ Reduced approval stages due to increased confidence in/visibility of the process. ▪ Reduced time to produce policy/guidance due to less duplication of work. ▪ Auditable decision-making process and visibility of rationale. ▪ Reduced regulatory burden by streamlining electronic access to guidance and approval process.	▪ Improved innovation/new product development to keep business on leading edge. ▪ Added value to products/services offered to consumers leads to increased/secured sales. ▪ More business won through producing better quality proposals more quickly. ▪ Quicker and more informed decision-making. ▪ Quicker policy/document production.	▪ Reputation improved and more business won by faster and more flexible proposal preparation process. ▪ Cost saving from less waste of production materials. ▪ Cost and time-saving from re-using supplier evaluation criteria. ▪ Cost saving from less paper being used and stored. ▪ Cost saving from the reduction of re-work due to poor information.

tion plan accordingly. Table 9.1 expands on the potential sources of value from each of the three "Cs".

Compliance: Organizations using an EDRMS to support compliance with external regulatory requirements or internal standards tend to use it to collate information from various sources into an organized structure. Parallel preparation and reviewing is used to produce new documents. This means that there tends to be increased confidence in decisions because the thinking that led to the decision is more visible, decisions can be made based on up-to-date information, and the transparency of the process improves individual and organizational learning for the future.

Collaboration: Organizations using the EDRMS to encourage collaboration tend to use the system to support collaborative working on documents and to encourage people to search the repository to discover who had worked on topics of interest in the past, then to contact them for more detail. In some cases, the system is also made accessible to customers to support closer working relationships. As a consequence of improving collaboration through using the system, knowledge flows more freely across organizational boundaries, increasing understanding of how the various activities of the business fit together and allowing faster decision-making.

Competitiveness: Organizations seeking to improve their efficiency (competitiveness) through the EDRMS tend to encourage users to re-use rather than re-develop materials. This requires that information be stored in a consistent way so that it can be found by others at a later date, despite possibly having a different purpose to that of the originator. Efficiency gains come from the re-use of previous experience and effort. The additional benefit of having organized and accessible information is that decision-making is improved by having a greater evidence base to draw on, reducing the need for individual judgement and thereby reducing risk.

Creating an action plan

Imagining knowledge as a life-giving fluid flowing around the organizational arteries is a useful metaphor. To successfully deliver results, it has to flow efficiently and deliver effective nourishment from where it's created to where it's needed. Technology, processes, and people either enhance or block the flow. Implementation involves concentrating on how you can enhance the flow of knowledge into the "reservoir" of the EDRMS and then on to another user. Building on work that looked at how to enable more effective flows of knowledge around organizations (see Chapter 2 for more details) you can ask a series of key questions to better understand this process:

- Is there the right environment for the EDRMS?
- Does the EDRMS facilitate the right actions by users?
- Do people have the right skills and knowledge to use such a system?
- Are people motivated to use the system?
- Are people aware of the knowledge potential and business benefits of using the system?

It is important to recognize that EDRMS implementation is a major change management project and should be treated as such. The reality is that often organizations are relatively fragmented, rather than single joined up structures. There can be a resistance to change as a result of either excessive stability in the past, or fatigue from never-ending change. Culture change always takes more time than you would expect. We have identified five important factors that need to be developed together in a holistic and integrated way to underpin effective implementation.

> "IT is only part of the solution. It's important to put in the right culture as well, in order to get 'buy in'."
>
> *Andrew Sinclair-Thomson whilst Assistant Director at the Department of Trade and Industry's knowledge management unit*

Leadership: Leaders must demonstrate how specific use of the system makes a difference to what matters in their part of the organization. The leadership style that may be most effective is:

- Work with others to create a vision and direction.
- Help others see why things need changing and why there's no going back.
- Share the overall plan of what has to be done.
- Give people space to do what needs to happen, within business goals.
- Seek to change how things get done, not just what gets done.

Training: There is a spectrum of expertise amongst users, even when the system has been in place for a while:

Power user/expert user/super user: font of knowledge in how to use the system.
Specialist user: expert in using the system for a particular purpose.
Everyday or regular user: can use the common functionality of the system.
Laggard: doesn't have the skills needed to use it properly.
Resistor: thinks "filing is not my job" and gives it to someone else to do.

The reality is that a lack of knowledge and skill about how to use the system produces laggards. Many systems are not easy to use to start with. One user said: "You know, when I think I've grasped it, I then have a few days without using it and I've lost it, I have to re-educate myself."

- Usability and end-user requirements must be at forefront of the design process. Make sure the system is as simple as possible to use.
- Training needs significant attention – more than you imagine. Be creative in the ways that people can learn how to use the system and get support when they have problems. Manuals are not sufficient – people are reluctant to use them. Train local super users who are interested and willing to help others. Extensive and comprehensive training programme and materials are needed (including floor-walking helpers, games, surgeries, and best practice guides).
- Ensure an adequate level of computer literacy (the current level may be lower than you imagine).

Communication: Knowing that the system is there, how it can be used, and the difference it can make in achieving organizational objectives contributes positively to EDRMS usage levels. Clear and consistent communication is important. When we heard one system referred to as an electronic filing system in an organizational communication, we were not at all surprised to hear one interviewee saying that he does not use the system very much because "filing is not my job".

To move forward:

- Promote the benefits of the system regularly and often, until well after the initial launch.
- Celebrate success stories where the system has been used to improve business performance.
- Manage expectations; do not raise them too high, keep them realistic.

> "It's important to recognize that the technology is only a means to the end, and not an end in itself."
>
> Nicholas Silburn, Research Fellow, Henley Business School

Changing the way work is carried out: You also need to think about how the system relates to working practices and other initiatives. An EDRMS requires a critical mass of people to use it before it can be successful. A culture change is required: a shift from paper to electronic working and publishing work-in-progress instead of keeping it private. Getting the most from an EDRMS means a different way of working and thinking for most people, which takes time and effort to achieve.

- "Join up" collaboration initiatives by relating the EDRMS implementation to work and business processes and cultural change.
- Consider how to move to running the organization on real-time information from the system, rather than emailed and personally stored information.
- Decide which documents and records support knowledge processes that have the most value to the organization and try to remain focused on these.

Building in mechanisms for feedback and improvement: It is likely that the value delivered by the EDRMS will gradually be eroded if it is not updated to reflect feedback from users, as well as to respond to changes needed by the business. Mechanisms to manage the system on an ongoing basis are essential to sustaining value generation.

- Ensure that the system can evolve as the business changes.
- Put users at the centre of the development process.

Self-assessment using a maturity model

A maturity model for the three factors that ensure that you achieve value from the system and the five factors that enable it to be used effectively allows you to assess the strengths and weaknesses of different parts of your organization and facilitate knowledge sharing between them. The two parts of the maturity model are shown in Tables 9.2 and 9.3. Using this as part of a peer learning process is a very effective way to build organizational capability. The steps you could follow to use this maturity model are as follows:

1. Identify a group of people representing different parts of your organization (different teams, activities, or functions). At least six would be good, 10-12 is probably the maximum. Invite them to a 1.5-2 hour workshop.
2. At the start of the workshop give everyone a copy of the model and talk through what the eight factor headings mean so everyone has a similar understanding.
3. Ask them each to rate their team/group/activity (as appropriate) for each factor according to the 1 to 5 level definitions.
4. Then ask people to identify where they would want to get to on each factor within the next few months (identify the gap between the current and desirable rating).
5. Ask them to pick the two priority areas they think would make the most differ- ence if they were to move from where they are to where they want to be within that time.
6. Collect the information and use a flipchart to represent who has what rating (the River Diagram shown in Figure 9.1 can be a useful way of showing the

overall picture). Add in the desired ratings and what the priorities for improvement are (maybe in a different colour).
7. Look at who is strong at each factor and who wants to improve on it. Connect
these people so they can discuss what the strong group is doing and how the
weaker group can learn from this. These "peer assist" conversations should
ideally be started at the workshop, then encouragement given for them to
continue afterwards.

Table 9.2: EDRMS maturity model part 1: delivering value

	Collaboration & Sharing	Capture & Re-use	Compliance & Governance
5	Individuals across the organization expect to work collaboratively, openly sharing work-in-progress, as well as completed materials. People now regard the systems as "the first place to look" to find out who to work with on tasks. The organization has a fully integrated collaborative working strategy that includes use of the systems.	The systems are used to create, capture, and re-use information and knowledge to support and maximize individual and organizational performance. People now regard the systems as "the first place to look" for previous or related examples before creating something new.	The systems are used to develop and store good practice/guidance/ approval documents. Visibility of how decisions were reached in developing these documents using the systems has resulted in widespread understanding of how to access and contribute to them. People fully comply with document management policies, facilitating auditing and quality control processes.
4	Most users are saving early drafts of materials and inviting comments and contributions. People are searching the systems for similar work to find collaborators with appropriate expertise. Examples of substantial savings through collaborating using the systems have been recognized.	Most people use the systems to capture and re-use information and knowledge. There is a good level of understanding of how to store information so that others can find it. Examples of substantial improvements in efficiency through using the systems have been recognized.	Most people use the good practice/guidance/ approval documents in the systems on a regular basis and know how to contribute to improving them. There are examples of substantial savings from improved decision-making through better access to and understanding of the guidance and approval documents. Most people comply with document management policies.

continued on next page...

Table 9.2 - *Continued*

	Collaboration & Sharing	Capture & Re-use	Compliance & Governance
3	People are regularly collaborating on documents that involve multiple contributors. There is a clear policy on openness that is largely adhered to. There are many good examples of collaborative working using shared systems improving performance.	Many people are using the shared systems to capture and share knowledge, particularly in teams and communities, less evidently across other organizational boundaries. Conventions on naming and tagging are accepted and largely used to help others re-use materials. There are many good examples of improved efficiency from using the systems.	Many people regularly use the shared systems to access good practice/ guidance/approval documents. Some contribute to their development and the system's functionality is largely used to manage the document lifecycle. There are many good examples of faster and better decisions being made as a result of the systems being used to access current guidance and approval materials.
2	Some people are beginning to store early drafts of materials in the shared systems. There is some evidence of collaborative working to produce materials using the systems. There is patchy acceptance of the benefits of working in this way.	Some people recognize that knowledge is a corporate asset. Local teams are beginning to realize the value of capturing and re-using knowledge. There is patchy understanding of how activities could be undertaken more efficiently using the systems.	Some people access good practice/guidance/ approval documents using the shared systems. Few know how to contribute to their development and limited use is made of the system's functionality to manage the documents throughout their lifecycle. Some people comply with broadly adequate Information Management policies.
1	People expect to work individually. There is ad hoc collaborative working and the systems are only rarely used to find others who have worked on similar topics or to jointly prepare materials.	Knowledge is mainly viewed as a personal asset. People expect to work individually and have developed their own ways to store and re-use information. Some records are captured locally, allowing limited re-use.	A few good practice/ guidance/approval documents are held within the shared system and there is some awareness that these exist. There is limited compliance with the Information Management policies that do exist (basic version control and audit trail mechanisms).

Table 9.3: EDRMS maturity model part 2: making it work

	Leadership	Developing skills	Communication	Changing the way we work	Feedback & Improvement
5	All leaders across the organization are driving new forms of intelligent use of the systems by challenging people to improve, asking the right questions and praising/ rewarding the right behaviours.	All users are competent in using the systems to manage and exploit information appropriate to their roles. Attention is paid to improving skills and many opportunities are available to develop further.	Communication about the systems is creative, regularly updated, and uses multiple channels. Awareness gathers its own momentum, as enthusiastic users become advocates.	The systems are used to change the way people work. Workflow functionality and real-time working with documents on the systems have been adopted wherever possible. There is a widespread willingness to use the systems innovatively.	The systems are continually improved to meet changing business needs. Users and systems developers are in constant dialogue to ensure that the systems evolve in the most appropriate ways.
4	Most leaders are committed to intelligent use of the systems. They reinforce the right behaviour by acting as role models. They set expectations through a shared vision of the opportunities and benefits.	Most users are competent at using the systems. Users are actively encouraged to develop their skills in using the systems and there are a number of different ways available for them to do this.	Communication about the systems uses a range of channels. It is timely, accurate, reliable, and comprehensive. Success stories are shared in a proactive and motivating way.	Most users are visibly changing the way that they work. Real-time working with documents (rather than with local copies) is the norm. Opportunities to use the systems to improve individual and group performance are actively sought.	Most users provide feedback to systems-developers about their on-going needs from the systems.

continued on next page...

Table 9.3 - *Continued*

	Leadership	Developing skills	Communication	Changing the way we work	Feedback & Improvement
3	There are many committed leaders across the organization who lead by example. They cultivate innovative use of the shared systems and share a vision in which some benefits and opportunities are clearly articulated, others need refining.	Many people make basic use of the shared systems available, but few fully exploit the potential they offer. Opportunities exist for people to develop their skills in a variety of ways best suited to their learning styles.	Communication is frequent and provides a useful way of updating people about the shared systems. It includes some success stories about the benefits people have found from using the systems.	Many users are demonstrating that they understand how the shared systems can be used to improve the way that they work by finding new ways to use them. Real-time working on documents (rather than with local copies) is becoming commonplace.	A feedback mechanism between users and systems developers is in place. Users are encouraged to use it and many do.

	Leadership	Developing skills	Communication	Changing the way we work	Feedback & Improvement
2	There are some committed leaders across the organization. A shared vision of the benefits and opportunities of the systems is beginning to be articulated, though with limited consistency.	Some people understand the value of the shared systems to their jobs and feel confident to make limited use of the systems functions. Basic introductory training is available to all and uptake is encouraged.	Communication is undertaken using more than one channel. Not all communications messages are clear and consistent. It is not widely seen by all potential users.	Some users are using limited functionality of shared systems to change the way that they work. There are some local examples of teams using real-time working on documents (rather than with local copies).	A basic feedback mechanism is in place to allow users to pass on their needs to systems developers. There is little active encouragement to use it, but some people do.
1	A few leaders act as champions advocating use of shared systems. There is inconsistency in the way the vision of the benefits and opportunities presented by the systems is articulated.	Few users understand the potential benefits of using the shared systems and much available functionality is rarely used. Training is minimal, or is rarely taken up if it is available.	Communication materials are updated infrequently. Messages are sometimes unclear. Not many users receive the communications.	People expect to continue working in the same way and see no reason to change as a result of the introduction of shared systems.	There is no easy and accessible feedback mechanism in place for users to pass on their requirements to systems developers.

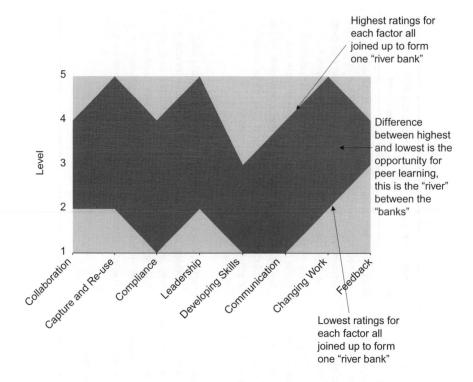

Figure 9.1: River diagram showing EDRMS maturity model factors

More details about how to use an extended version of this approach are available in the book *Learning to Fly*.[1] You may also choose to introduce a company or knowledge programme view at the end if you have other options to offer people who want to make improvements on particular factors.

Some hints and tips for getting the most from the peer learning process:

- Encourage people to start at the bottom (maturity level 1) and work up, rather than the top and work down when they are deciding how to rate their part of the organization.
- You may decide that three months is too short a timeframe for improvements in your organization. More than 18 months is unlikely to be helpful though in relation to EDRMS change programme.
- There will be a lot of discussion about what the eight factors mean for your organization. This is fine, as long as everyone understands and agrees with the final interpretation.
- The most value will be gained if you can repeat this process to track progress over time. This should be a productive learning process though, rather than a control and performance measurement process. A learning approach encourages collaborative conversations and peer learning, bringing all parts of the organization up to their highest desirable levels.

■ The discussion is the most useful part of this process – allow time for it and encourage it.

Real life stories

Implementing an EDRMS as a change management programme – DTI (Department of Trade and Industry)

The UK's DTI (since renamed Department for Business, Innovation and Skills) completed implementation of an EDRMS in March 2003 for about 5,000 staff in its HQ offices in London and 19 locations around the UK. The name given by the DTI to the project and EDRMS was "Matrix" and the project was completed on time and under budget. An excellent start, if regarded as just an IT project. However, the main challenge involved changing the culture (that is, working habits and attitudes towards managing information). Right from the initial planning stage this project was recognized as being more about the "management of change" than implementing an IT system and as a consequence, emphasis was placed on involving end-user staff, communication, and training. In addition a new "information manager" role was created in every work unit to support the new work processes.

On implementation, the DTI's policy on Information Management changed from "the official business record is paper stored in paper files", to "the official business record is electronic stored in electronic folders in Matrix".

The Government Department's remit was wide ranging and staff generally worked in small teams and mostly on policy matters. For many years staff had become used to saving emails in their own MS Outlook folders and draft documents in the personal drives of their PCs. Documents considered part of the business record would be printed and filed in paper folders, mainly by junior staff. Changing these working habits and long held attitudes to private stores of electronic information was the main challenge in ensuring full adoption of Matrix.

During the rollout of Matrix, the central team drove the project forward in partnership with local work units. However, once the system was implemented it was clear that ownership of the working practices and delivery of benefits should be taken up by the managers in local work units. To achieve this, a panel of senior staff, representing the main areas of DTI's remit, was formed. Known as the "Departmental Matrix Change Panel" (DMCP) and chaired by a DTI Board member (the Director General of Legal Services), its role was "Championing increasing and intelligent use of Matrix". To achieve this it had a four-pronged strategy.

1. Increasing Matrix usage by DTI HQ staff
2. Increasing skills and competency
3. Developing and sharing best practice
4. Developing new ways of working.

The DMCP used league tables, peer pressure, and awards to increase motivation, bite-size refresher training to improve skills, sharing good practice to illustrate actions required, and leadership to change the culture and working environment. Leadership proved to be the most significant factor. It is worth noting that the DMCP activities needed to integrate with other major initiatives during a period of significant business change, which included reducing staff numbers.

By March 2006, having achieved significant growth in usage (over 82% of staff using Matrix), DMCP decided to hold an event on 16 May 2006 to recognize and award people who, through their efforts and ideas, are helping to increase DTI's operational effectiveness and to publicize good practice. This event was called the "MOSCARS" an acronym of:

"Matrix – Opportunity (to) Share Celebrate And Review Successes"

Over 100 nominations were submitted with stories that illustrated good practice in using Matrix or in encouraging better practice that resulted in some benefit or added value for the Department. The winners were selected by a panel of internal and external judges.

Top tips

Some points to bear in mind in relation to the system are:

✓ Bring in a corporate governance perspective to drive good practice in helping others retrieve information.
✓ Aim for effective but balanced governance (for example, standardized tags on each document – including author's contact information – but avoid being too bureaucratic).
✓ Think about key system requirements: reducing document duplication, consistency of approach to using the system, effective search function, common look and feel, proper version control.
✓ Be clear about the access requirements of the system – who should be able to access the information and what will be their needs? Avoid blanket provisions.
✓ Think about how best to communicate with people about the system, accepting that everyone has different preferences about receiving information. Use Chapter 16 to help you tailor more effective messages.

Communication was identified as one of the key implementation factors, so we developed a "Highway Code" metaphor that you could adopt as part of your communications strategy shown in Box 1.

The research and the team involved

This project was carried out by a working group of knowledge managers from member organizations of the Henley KM Forum. Public and private sector organiza-

Box 1: The EDRMS "Highway Code"

For improved collaboration – "car share" and "stop, look, listen":

- Collaborate, don't duplicate.
- Use the system to prepare and review documents in parallel with others.
- Before creating a document, stop and see if it has been done before, look in the system, and listen to others.

For improved competitiveness and effectiveness – "keep the tank topped up", "see and be seen", and "become an advanced driver":

- Keep the information in the system current.
- Make it easy to find the information that you contribute.
- Having the right information always available makes it easier for people to cover for one another.

For improved compliance – "clunk, click every trip" and "one careful owner":

- Maintain the integrity of information you work with through regular reviews.
- Keep information organized and in one place.

Finally: "We know a man who can":

- Contact your expert users and the systems administrators if you need further help.

tions were included and academics also participated. It was carried out during 2005 and 2006 and was based on interviews with 16 users of EDRMS in four organizations, together with pre-implementation user surveys in three other organizations. The intention was to help knowledge managers engage in productive dialogues with colleagues about how the EDRMS can really add value by tapping into and enabling essential flows of knowledge across the organization. It is not intended to provide prescriptive advice for a particular business.

The Project was co-championed by Nick Silburn and Dr Christine van Winkelen of Henley Business School and Andrew Sinclair-Thomson of the Department of Trade and Industry. The working group included representatives from:

Davis Langdon
Department of Trade and Industry
GlaxoSmithKline
MWH
Nissan Technical Centre Europe
Unisys

Defence Procurement Agency
GCHQ
Metronet Rail
Nationwide Building Society
PRP Architects

Particular thanks are due to Mark Lawton who carried out the interviews as part of his MBA studies.

Final reflections from the research

Balancing integration and differentiation has been described as a dilemma all organizations must face.[2] This is the challenge of finding the optimum balance between drawing on different perspectives and knowledge bases to make sense of and adapt to a changing world, and being able to integrate these effectively in a coordinated and efficient way to enable a coherent pattern of effective decisions that achieve the purpose of the organization. We saw EDRMS being used to control activities (compliance), draw on different sources of knowledge from across the organization (collaboration), and reduce inefficiency in the coordination of the business (competitiveness); effectively all attempts to deal with the issue of organizational integration and differentiation in an efficient way. These very real tensions need to be considered by those implementing EDRMS.

- Collaboration is helped by just enough compliance in the form of sufficient standardization to allow efficient sharing of materials. Yet collaboration is also stifled by over-bureaucratic and highly regulated systems that achieve compliance through restricting access rights.
- Knowledge re-use (the competitiveness driver) requires sufficient compliance to standard formats and protocols, but also the minimum appropriate access restrictions to make the materials available as widely as possible.
- Collaboration supports the creation of new materials by bringing together different perspectives to allow new ways of looking at things, yet is also the vehicle for encouraging efficiencies from re-using existing distributed knowledge bases.

The most appropriate way of combining all three value drivers (the "3 Cs") needs to be identified for each organization. This will be a dynamic requirement as business objectives change and develop in different parts of the organization, suggesting that any technology system and associated working practices will need to be flexible to accommodate changes in priorities.

Notes

1. For more information about working with maturity models and using them for peer learning, see Collison, C. and Parcell, G. (2004) *Learning to Fly*, 2nd edn, Chichester: Capstone Publishing Ltd.
2. Lawrence, P.R. and Lorsch, J.W. (1967) *Organization and Environment: Managing Differentiation and Integration*, Boston: Harvard Business School Press.

Chapter 10

Snapshot

Communities of practice allow those interested in a particular area of knowledge to share knowledge and experiences with likeminded colleagues and to solve problems together. They are a way of ensuring that knowledge in a field is developed and maintained within the organization and that the overall level of competence is increased.

There are some principles and approaches that are generally useful in supporting communities of practice, but the way that these are interpreted needs to reflect the culture and business model of the organization. If the dominant approach is highly structured or process-oriented, then this probably needs to be reflected to some extent in the way communities of practice initiatives are undertaken. Conversely, if the organization values flexibility, then a "light touch" management approach will be more appropriate.

The most important aspect of an effective community of practice is the motivation of individuals to participate, which is directly related to the value that they anticipate gaining. Aligning this with the value delivered to the organization in return for supporting the community is the basis of an effective community. Alignment relies on the subject area being appropriate, the purpose of the community being clear, ensuring key roles are fulfilled, and providing relevant organizational support in the form of processes and technology.

It can be difficult to establish substantial communities of practice programmes, particularly in organizations in turbulent environments or subject to significant and ongoing internal change, because this requires a long-term perspective. In changing environments, it is important to ensure that organizational support is focused on communities that are most aligned with core and stable reference points in the organization, such as brand reputation, customer satisfaction, or operational effectiveness.

Why this matters

The flow of knowledge around an organization is at the heart of value generation in a knowledge-based organization (see Chapter 2 to analyse the key knowledge flows of your organization). However, often organization structures, hierarchies, and functions act as barriers to vital knowledge flows: knowledge may be shared very well within each, but then fail to flow across the boundary to those outside it. Professional associations manage and stimulate the flow of knowledge for some disciplines, which can mean that knowledge flows to and from the outside world more easily than across internal boundaries of an organization.

> "Instead of figuring out better ways of doing things after the event, communities of practice are a way of getting them right first time."
>
> *Louise Kennard, Marketing and Customer Services Knowledge Sharing Consultant, British Council*

In reality, in most organizations, those interested in a particular topic or subject area often find a way to talk to each other – particularly with the emergence of new collaborative technologies (see Chapter 13). Informal gatherings, both face-to-face around the "water cooler" and online in a variety of collaborative spaces, allow experts to connect and those interested in topics to find each other.

By helping those with an interest in a particular knowledge area to better communicate with each other, in effect amplifying these informal patterns of connections so that more people can share insights, experiences and knowledge, the organization benefits by having the widest possible expertise brought to bear on problems. At their best, these groups are essentially communities: groups who come together, either face-to-face or virtually, to share information and knowledge and to learn from one another. They are held together by a common interest in a given body of knowledge and want to share their problems, experiences, insights, templates, tools, and best practices. Their collective knowledge deepens over time.

These "communities of practice" are a useful structural mechanism to improve collaboration and knowledge sharing in organizations. They overlay rather than replace the existing formal structures, often being resilient to changes such as reorganizations as a consequence.[1]

The value that can be delivered by effective communities of practice comes from increasing the organization's intellectual capital in one form or another:

- *Human capital:* developing and retaining employees, improving competence levels and the quality of thinking.
- *Social capital:* aligning purpose and direction across the organization and building cross-organizational loyalty.
- *Structural capital:* pooling resources and sharing good practices to reduce costs and improve quality, stimulating innovation.
- *Relationship capital:* increasing sales/financial performance by improving reputation.

Although managers can amplify, enable, and support communities of practice, an essential characteristic is that active participation is largely a voluntary act by the individuals involved. Engaging with others in the community sufficiently for mean-ingful knowledge to be shared (rather than simply factual information) needs personal commitment and autonomous motivation.

To get the most from communities of practice, there are some principles and guidelines that can be helpful. These are relevant both to designing and managing individual communities of practice, and to thinking about how to sustain a more widespread programme involving multiple communities.

What this means for your organization

In looking at improving knowledge flows in Chapter 2, we used research that sug-gested that there are some basic factors that act as enablers. In the case of indi-viduals, the objective is that they can work without confusion, internal conflict, or unproductive stress.[2] They need to be motivated to achieve the purpose (they understand why it matters), have the skills to do the task (they know how to do it), be comfortable with and able to take the necessary actions (they know what to do), and do so in an environment that is conducive to such action (where it takes place is appropriate). If these four factors are in alignment, the process of achieving the outcome tends to run smoothly and efficiently because there is nothing blocking it. For individuals, motivation comes from their beliefs and values. Figure 10.1 illustrates this in a slightly different way to that used in Chapter 2, the nested layers emphasizing the way all the factors underpin each other. This representation also brings in the individual's sense of self, or identity, as an addi-tional aspect of alignment. It has proven to be a useful way of looking at what can support individuals in participating in communities of practice.

In effective communities, strong enough connections are made between people for them to feel that they belong at the "identity" level. Professional societies

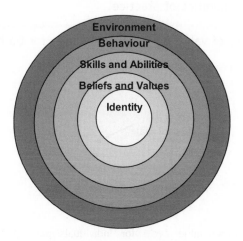

Figure 10.1: Alignment levels

have a similar effect, because an individual's sense of identity as a professional (for example lawyer, doctor, engineer, or teacher) may endure throughout a career and the behaviours, skills, and values endorsed by the profession may supersede organizational allegiances.

Individuals participate in organizational communities of practice for three general reasons: intellectual, emotional, and as a means to an end.

- *Intellectual reasons*: developing expertise, finding out about opportunities around the organization, understanding different perspectives, improving status, increasing influence, and sharing similar interests.
- *Emotional reasons*: satisfaction from helping others, peer recognition, increased confidence, building relationships, and a sense of belonging.
- *As a means to an end*: improving pay and benefits by improving performance.

There is a direct link between the success of the community and the motivation of individuals. If the community is successful, the individual will see value from participating, which will in turn increase motivation. For individuals, motivation always begins the process. Anticipation of value drives the initial motivation to participate and delivery of value sustains this as shown in Figure 10.2.

In contrast to this very clear sequence, the role of communities of practice in transforming an organizational need into delivered value is highly context-specific and there is not a single way of representing the relationship. This is shown on the right hand side of Figure 10.3 by dotted arrows that point in either direction. For example, there may be an existing emergent community that seems to address an organizational need and with some support can begin to deliver more value; alternatively, an organizational need may be identified and an intentional community designed and supported to address that need, eventually delivering the anticipated value.

The key message of this diagram is there are two broad principles involved in building effective communities of practice:

1. Sustain the delivery of value from the community for both individuals and the organization.

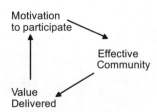

Figure 10.2: The motivation-value cycle for individuals participating in communities of practice

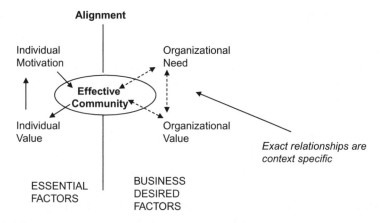

Figure 10.3: Aligning value delivery to build effective communities of practice

2. Align the "motivation-value" cycle that drives participation of individuals with the "need-value" process driving the organization.

"We run communities of practice (CoP) for local government to connect around issues, work together and solve problems. Involvement was initially spontaneous on an individual level. Now CoP are more mainstream and understood by senior people, organizations are putting together a more holistic strategy for getting involved, using a business initiation document and business case."

Lawrence Hall, Knowledge Manager with IDeA

Different types of organizations have different approaches to establishing and managing communities of practice according to their culture and business model. It is clear that what is desirable and acceptable in one organization can be undesirable and unacceptable in another. Observations of a number of communities in a variety of organizations suggest:

1. Organizations that operate in a structured or process-oriented environment tend to take a structured and interventionist approach to building communities and measuring the value that they deliver. Communities of practice are often designed intentionally with clear objectives that are directly related to business objectives. Measuring the value delivered can be a priority to maintain organizational support.
2. Organizations seeking to develop geographically distributed activities in fast-moving environments (particularly in high-technology sectors) tend to use technology to improve the effectiveness of existing emergent communities. The main intervention is to communicate community activities more widely so that more people can get involved and to coach facilitators about how to encourage knowledge-sharing behaviours. There may be little effort expended

in attempting to measure community value beyond the collection of anecdotal evidence.
3. Organizations that exist to be innovative, such as research and development firms, tend to value flexibility. Communities of practice are viewed as emergent and the main organizational support is to give time and space for participation in value-generating areas.

Establishing a formal programme involving multiple communities of practice takes time, certainly at least two or three years in a large organization. Many of the well-known success stories of substantial communities of practice programmes come from industries which are inherently more stable because the products require large capital investment and therefore long-term thinking, or they have a long product-development lifecycle. Examples include the car, oil, or pharmaceutical industries. These industries may have time to establish communities of practice programmes that measurably deliver benefits back to participants and the organization. However, there are many other examples of organizations that flounder after the first few apparently successful pilot communities of practice. More often than not, since the inception of the pilots some key element of the organization's strategy has shifted and the indicators of value being used to demonstrate the success of the communities are no longer recognized as important.

In these more turbulent or changeable environments, particular care over targeting investments to support a communities of practice programme is required. The benefits of developing a knowledge-sharing culture and improving efficiency and innovation are still important, it is just even more important to play to the characteristics of communities of practice. This means recognizing that they are self-organizing, they need to be in tune with the formal structures, and they need to evolve and change over time. Otherwise the value to individuals may be out of step with the value being delivered to the organization. An emergent community starts by delivering value to individuals informally through relationships. If the organization sees the potential for widespread value, then committing resources can make it more visible and effective. At some point, priorities change or objectives are met and the resources would be better allocated elsewhere. Individuals will probably continue the relationships they have established. Recognizing that communities have a lifecycle is important – for a while they rise into visibility in the organization and then they sink back into the shadows.

Creating an action plan

Enabling effective communities of practice

We have seen that individual motivation to participate and organizational value from investments in supporting the communities of practice (whether through "light touch" support for emergent communities or more substantial initiatives to design intentional communities) need to be aligned. The alignment levels model illustrated in Figure 10.1 is a useful way of summarizing actions that can be useful, as shown in Table 10.1. The way these are interpreted in practice should reflect the organizational context, culture, and business model as discussed in the previous section.

Sustaining a long-term communities of practice programme

Eight steps are helpful for setting up a large scale communities of practice programme that will be resilient to organizational change:[3]

1. Concentrate on a few areas that will make the most difference quickly and build from existing networks that are delivering value rather than expecting to create a top down all-encompassing programme.
2. Find the points of stability in the organization and stay close to these when investing time and other resources. Brand reputation, customer satisfaction, operational effectiveness, or the need to work together in a particular way could be examples of such stability points. The returns on investments in these areas are likely to be seen as most relevant for longest and success stories are therefore likely to be able to generate further commitment and interest and build momentum.
3. Stay as close to the external customer front line of the organization as possible. This is where the value is generated in the business. Keep the central function small and hand over ownership of both the individual communities of practice and the community of practice programme itself to local teams quickly and efficiently.
4. Design in sympathy with the predominant paradigm of the business (examples would be the need for process, structure, formality, informality, flexibility, or speed). This helps create resonance with other initiatives and builds reinforcing cycles of commitment and performance.
5. Make it easy for emergent communities to become visible when they can make a difference to the business objectives. This form of feedback tends to encourage greater adoption of these new ways of collaborative working and at the same time adds to the general learning of the organization. A single collaborative working technology platform that all communities can adopt easily is useful. It can allow everyone to see what is going on and to know how and when to participate. Encourage communities to be open rather than closed wherever possible – or at least to have part of their activities in the public arena.
6. Create the minimum process and toolkit for communities to adopt and use themselves. Invest time and effort sparingly in coaching key players in communities close to stability points or the customer front line and allow other communities to be self-sustaining.
7. Appreciate the importance of timing. When jobs are at risk, people aren't able to talk about the future. When they have recently been appointed to new roles, they are not yet ready to talk about how they fit into a bigger picture. Rolling

Table 10.1: Aligning value delivery to design effective communities

Alignment factor	What this involves	Examples
Environment	Provide appropriate organizational support: • Processes need to integrate communities into other organizational activities. • Technology needs to support communication and collaboration.	Social network analysis can be used to map the existing pattern of relationships and make sure that the right people are encouraged to participate in the community. Workshops can be used to build a shared understanding of what the purpose of the community is and to build relationships. These can be physical workshops or virtual workshops using conferencing technologies. Technology can be used to identify people with similar interests based on key-word analysis of their activities. Portal technology can be used to support messaging, document management, chat facilities, expert identifiers, and question and answer areas.
Behaviour	Encourage and reward trust and openness	Trust and openness are enablers of effective communities. Communities of practice do help create organizational cultures where these are valued. The knowledge-sharing behaviours that are needed can be encouraged through making visible success stories and positively reinforcing the role of the behaviours of participants.
Skills and Abilities	Ensure appropriate roles are fulfilled with properly trained people	A proactive and respected leader is the key role. This may not be the most senior person and the group may give them implicit authority. In emergent communities the term "leader" may not be appropriate. One organization preferred the term "catalyst". A high-level sponsor/champion is needed – particularly when intentional/deliberate communities are being created. This person supports the existence of the community. Other considerations in relation to roles are: • Subject matter experts add credibility and are needed by the community, but may be peripheral to the main activities. • A facilitator can encourage people to contribute and can also focus efforts to engage a wider audience. • Roles change over time depending on the way that the community evolves. • The number of formalized roles may depend on the size of the community. • Roles help create a sense of belonging for individuals and give the community an identity of its own.

continued on next page...

Table 10.1 - *Continued*

Alignment factor	What this involves	Examples
Beliefs and Values	Ensure there is a clear purpose and organizational support for the community.	This validates both participation in the community by individuals and the commitment of organizational support. A structured process may involve identifying potential members of a community around a specific topic, negotiating the outcomes desired by all stakeholders and synthesizing these into a set of community outcomes that define what the community will exist to do. This becomes the basis for deciding on the support the community will need and provides a clear basis for integrating it into the network of communities more broadly. Organizational support may be active or passive. There may be unqualified permission and support, toleration, or the requirement for business justification against hard financial measures. The minimum requirement is acquiescence: a willingness to tolerate working outside the formal structures and hierarchies, allowing individuals sufficient time and resources to participate. However, certain organizations may be better recognizing from the outset that to fit with the business paradigm, justifications against hard financial measures need to be created.
Identity	Encourage communities where there is an appropriate subject that relates to the identity of individuals as practitioners.	Subjects could include knowledge areas that are new to the organization, topical subjects, or those that are relevant to a particular business objective. In general, the knowledge domain should be important to the organization, something that people can get passionate about and sufficiently focused to attract new people and generate interest.[1]

out a community programme requires sensitivity to local conditions and an understanding of what is possible where and when.

8. More than anything else, become resilient to the unexpected. What you set out to do may not be what you end up being able to deliver. However, the insights that were gained along the way will make the contribution much more significant in the long run.

Real life stories

> "Be clear about what you want your communities of practice to achieve – and equally clear about how that is aligned with the interests of the people who will participate."
>
> Karen Fryatt, Business Improvement Manager, QinetiQ

> "Getting the enthusiastic endorsement of some key influencers has played a major part in establishing communities of practice within the organization."
>
> Tim Milner, Knowledge Project Manager, Improvement and Development Agency

At technical services firm QinetiQ, the emphasis is on focus. They argue that any organization wanting to build a community of practice needs to understand very clearly what its objectives are. The business context needs to be very clear, and the community's mission made very explicit.

At the Improvement and Development Agency, there is an emphasis on communicating that participation isn't an additional chore. Communities of practice aren't about adding to individuals' workloads, but instead are a tool to help people deal with their existing workload.

The British Council's community programme recognizes that if you don't provide an opportunity for people to meet occasionally, it can be difficult for a true sense of community to develop. They emphasize that face-to-face contact is very important, especially in the early stages of establishing communities of practice.

Top tips

✓ How can you make connections between people in the community in various ways? Do they understand each other's context, ways of behaving, skills, values, and sense of what it means to be a practitioner? If you are trying to build communities between people from different companies or national cultures, how can you "lower the fences" to make connections in each of these areas?

✓ What impact does the culture of your organization have on the community? Is the culture already one of trust and openness, or are you looking for the community to build these?

✓ Is the organization prepared to give the community "space" to exist and to operate? How much support is there for this way of people working together?

✓ How does your business operate? Is it process-oriented, structured, individualistic, or used to virtual working? Do you need to match the way you support communities to the way other things run within the business?

✓ Make it easy for emerging communities to become visible when they can make a difference to the organization's business objectives.

✓ Celebrate quick wins and publicize early success stories that highlight the contribution that communities of practice can make.

✓ Ensure communities of practice are integrated into other major organizational development and change initiatives. All the initiatives should reinforce each other, rather than appearing to be incompatible or to pull against each other.

The research and the team involved

This research was carried out in two phases. The first was undertaken during 2001 and 2002 by a working group of members of the Henley KM Forum.

Following a review of the literature, 18 communities in nine organizations were studied covering a wide range of industries and several UK public sector or recently privatized organizations. The knowledge manager of each organization collected information about the personal motivation and value derived by community participants, as well as the organizational need that the community addressed and the value derived from it. The research activities were intended to help managers identify useful practices for their organization in establishing effective communities of practice. They were not intended to provide prescriptive advice for a particular business.

Dr Christine van Winkelen from the KM Forum team and Visiting Fellow at Henley Business School was the academic co-champion for this research. The member co-champion was Philip Ramsell of Abbey National. Working group members included representatives from the following organizations:

Abbey National	Aegis
BT	Cadbury Schweppes
Defence Procurement Agency	EC Harris
Egon Zehnder	Ericsson
GCHQ	HECM
QinetiQ	SAP
Thames Water	Unisys

together with invited associate: John Burrows (formerly Buckman Laboratories).

The second phase of the work was undertaken during 2003 and 2004 and was a study involving three organizations (Thames Water, Orange, and RWE Innogy) led by Dr Edward Truch and Dr Christine van Winkelen, both Visiting Fellows at Henley Business School. The focus was on sustaining large scale programmes involving multiple communities of practice. Particular thanks are due to Dr Etienne Wenger and Professor Karl-Erik Sveiby who participated in aspects of this research.

Final reflections from the research

"One size does not fit all" in terms of communities of practice. An essential consideration is the culture of the organization, or "the way things are done around here". Although communities of practice bridge the formal structures and systems of an organization, the research suggested that they need to be initiated in a way that is in sympathy with the dominant paradigm, which includes the culture and business model. Following the vision of a leader who can see the value communities of practice will offer the organization may get the programme started. However, the programme will be very vulnerable to changes in leadership, restructuring, or new strategies to reflect a changing outside world if it is not aligned to what really matters to the organization and can't be evaluated in a way that is consistent with other programmes and initiatives. The "recipe" for alignment between individual motivation and organizational value which we argue is the basis for sustainable effective communities (an appropriate subject area, a clear purpose, the fulfilment of key roles, and appropriate support, enabled by a knowledge-sharing culture and sufficient organizational acquiescence) needs to be interpreted for each organization's context, culture, and business model.

Notes

1. Read more about communities of practice in the following: McDermott, R. (1999) Nurturing three dimensional communities of practice, *Knowledge Management Review*, 2(5); Wenger, E. (1998) *Communities of Practice: Learning, Meaning and Identity*, Cambridge: Cambridge University Press; Wenger, E., McDermott, R., and Snyder, W. (2002) *Cultivating Communities of Practice*, Harvard Business School Press; Wenger, E. and Snyder, W. (2000) Communities of practice: the organizational frontier, *Harvard Business Review*, 78(1), 139-145.
2. See for example Bateson, G. (1972) *Steps to an Ecology of the Mind*, New York: Ballantine Books and Dilts, R. (1990) *Changing Belief Systems with NLP*, Capitola CA: Meta Publications.
3. This list was first published in van Winkelen, C. and Truch, E. (2004) Embedding communities in turbulent times, *KM Review*, 7(2), 14-17.

Chapter 11

Snapshot

External collaborations offer organizations learning opportunities that are not available internally. Increasingly, everyone from government departments to isolated specialists within private organizations is trying to join up with others and collaborate across boundaries. These aren't formal, contractual arrangements, but looser, knowledge-based arrangements, designed to enable all the organizations involved to improve what they do. Many different forms of value can be achieved from these collaborations including individual capacity building, operational value, affirmation, reputation and relationship building, and learning about how to collaborate more effectively. The most difficult goal, and potentially the most valuable, is subject-specific organizational capability building but this needs visible long-term commitment by leaders to the collaboration.

Two main factors seemed to influence the extent of the value achieved from participating in external learning collaborations. Firstly, skilled, committed, and open-minded individuals need to represent the organization and be able to translate the implications of learning gained from the collaboration back into the organization. Secondly, the organization needs mechanisms and processes to transfer and amplify that learning, by joining up internal collaborative processes with the external collaboration activities.

Skilled, subject-knowledgeable facilitation in the learning collaboration helps ensure that inter-organizational dynamics are managed effectively. Particular attention needs to be paid to organizing systems and processes, social ties, power relations, trust, and risk. Practices that help achieve this are identified.

Why this matters

Increasingly organizations need access to a wider variety of learning opportunities than their own internal activities can generate. At a strategic level this is because:

- innovation needs the stimulus of new knowledge;
- new ways of looking at things help challenge existing mindsets and help the organization adapt and evolve;
- in the public sector, challenging social issues need cross-department and cross-sector thinking.

At a practical level, the reasons organizations give for participating in learning collaborations include:

- the need to think with others about difficult challenges;
- learning about and modelling partnership working for other purposes;
- building trust for other work with collaborative partners;
- the need for isolated specialists in organizations to find ways of sharing ideas and practices with like-minded people.

In general, there is a growing emphasis on alliances, partnerships, and collaborative networks between organizations (see Chapter 5 which discusses knowledge sharing under these more commercial conditions). A learning collaboration is one that involves representatives from two or more organizations set up with a deliberate expectation of learning from one another. This may be a precursor to some other more structured relationship involving a shared project or financial transactions.

Real collaborations are complex, often involving organizations from a variety of sectors and with the participants having a range of motivations and expectations. This can make it challenging to sustain the collaborations and to achieve the value that each participant expects. Clarity about the organizational intent in participating is an important starting point. Without this, it is not possible to determine clearly whether the value delivered is sufficient to warrant the resource commitment involved. Different kinds of value can be anticipated and achieved, the highest level being developing the organization's capability in a strategically useful field of knowledge. Leaders need to sustain commitment to the collaboration if this level of value is to be achieved.

What this means for your organization

Organizational learning happens at multiple interacting levels – between individuals, across groups and organizations, as well as inter-organizationally. The whole organizational learning system can be viewed as a series of nested levels, as shown in Figure 11.1. Managing and influencing the feedback loops across the levels is an essential part of effective learning, which means that inter-organizational learning cannot be viewed in isolation from the learning of the individuals who represent the organization, the groups they belong to, and the internal collaboration mecha-

Macro-environmental influences

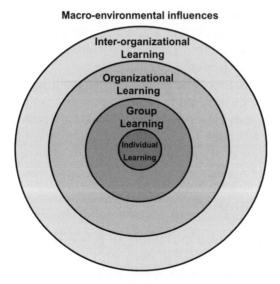

Figure 11.1: Viewing the organization as a learning system[1]

nisms that distribute externally-stimulated learning more widely within the organization.

There are three important organizational factors involved in being able to deliver value from involvement in external learning collaborations:[2]

- Knowing what is important and being able make sense of what it means for the organization (also called absorptive capacity[3]).
- Internal collaboration and knowledge transfer capacity to transfer the learning to where it is needed.
- Motivation to learn and teach.

In reality, few organizations achieve these fully. Informal approaches to knowledge transfer within the organization are common, so introducing new ways of working (including virtual teams and home working) makes knowledge transfer more difficult. Consequently achieving full value from participation in external learning collaborations often needs internal collaboration mechanisms to be improved too. In general, a strategic approach to collaboration is needed so that ways of joining up the internal and external collaboration can be identified.

The other important factor is the individuals who represent the organization in the learning collaborations. They generally do most of the work ensuring that learning is transferred from the collaboration back to the organization. Their subject-specific knowledge allows them to recognize the value of knowledge from the collaboration and acquire it on behalf of the organization. Individuals need to exert personal effort in thinking about the implications and then find ways of translating this back into the organization. Selecting the right people to represent the organization and then giving permission, emphasizing the remit, or giving responsibility to them to participate and act as channels for learning (whichever has the closest match with the organizational culture) is therefore an important aspect of achieving value from the collaboration.

Finally, if your organization is convening the collaboration, then someone skilled in facilitation needs to be involved to identify what mechanisms and processes will best ensure that outcomes valued by the participants are achieved. The facilitation approaches adopted will need to evolve as the relationships between the participants mature.

Creating an action plan

There are three steps involved in creating an action plan for effective organizational participation in a learning collaboration (with the third step having most relevance if your organization is convening the collaboration):

1. Be clear about the purpose of participating.
2. Pay attention to the individuals representing the organization in the collaboration.
3. Manage the dynamics of the collaboration.

These are discussed in turn in the following sections.

Identifying the purpose of the collaboration

Collaboration is used to achieve something difficult that an organization can't do on its own and it takes time, effort, and commitment to deliver ultimate value. Therefore successes en route need to be valued. Collaborations can generate a wide variety of different kinds of valued outcomes; some examples are shown in Table 11.1. Managers need to be clear about the outcomes that they are anticipating in order to commit appropriate resources. Taking the time to agree this at the outset both within the organization and then through consultation with potential partners in the collaboration means that it is much more likely that these outcomes will be achieved.

Learning relevant to operational activities, generating tangible deliverables together, and individual and organizational relationship building for other business purposes are all possible outcomes of many learning collaborations. However, subject-specific organizational capability building is much more difficult, though potentially more strategically valuable. Even when the subject-specific knowledge of individuals representing their organizations is improved, this may not translate to organizational capability building to any significant extent. Further learning transfer and amplification mechanisms are needed. These are largely based on adopting a strategic approach to "joining up" internal and external collaboration

Table 11.1: Forms of value that can be delivered from learning collaborations

Valued outcome	Examples of what this might mean in practice
Creating specific outputs together	Creating guidance for others around issues of shared concern. The guidance may be distributed in a variety of ways, for example an independently branded website for the collaboration can emphasize that a shared view and approach is being adopted.
Building the reputation of the organization	Demonstrating partnership working in action to other organizations. This can support inclusion in commercial or other collaborative arrangements.
Forming meaningful relationships	Trusting organizational and individual networking relationships established to support other activities outside the learning collaboration.
Helping solve operational problems	Discussing practical approaches to real problems with peers and learning from others facing similar challenges.
Affirmation of existing practices and ideas	Comparison of practices with those of other organizations. This is particularly valuable as a way for isolated professionals to compare practices with peers in other organizations.
Building the capacity of the individuals involved	Development of subject-specific knowledge and challenges to thinking through exposure to new ideas.
Organizational capability building	One form of capability building comes from being in the collaboration: building the capability to collaborate in partnerships effectively.
	The other is subject-specific organizational capability building derived from the topic around which the learning collaboration was established. This comes from developing trusting relationships to solve long-term difficult problems together.

and paying attention to the support given to the individuals representing the organization in the collaboration. If there are only opportunistic, unstructured, and ad hoc approaches to knowledge transfer and no further amplification mechanisms available, there is an inherent limit on the learning efficiency and longer term subject-related capability building.

The following section identifies some of the skills needed by individuals to be effective in representing the organization in learning collaborations, offering the opportunity for initial selection of the right people, as well as providing a basis for establishing development and performance assessment criteria. Other chapters in this book suggest approaches that will improve internal collaboration, with Chapter 2 offering a way of mapping valuable knowledge flows in a coherent way so that internal and external collaboration initiatives can be joined up.

Table 11.2: Knowledge sharing behaviours of individuals in learning collaborations

Knowledge sharing behaviour competency	What this means people do in practice
Networking	Networks, puts people together, values connections.
Trust and empowerment	Open, authentic, honest, trusting.
Consideration and recognition	Willing to listen and understand others, diplomatic.
Managing and sharing information	Subject knowledgeable. Find links from conversations to value for the organization and capture that value.
Gathering and developing knowledge	Curious to learn. Stimulated by intellectual input.
Communicating knowledge	Helpful, facilitative, enabling, self-confident.
Applying expertise	Energy, commitment, active. Credible and with influence back in the organization.

The individuals representing the organization

To the outside world, and in particular others involved in the learning collaboration, the individual is the organization. This means that individuals representing their organizations in the collaborations make a significant difference both to the relationships that form, the learning that takes place, and ultimately to the value delivered to the organization.

The knowledge-sharing behaviour competency framework (see Chapter 15) is a useful way of describing the kinds of behaviours individuals need if they are to be effective in these collaborations. How these behaviours are exhibited in learning collaborations is summarized in Table 11.2.

It is important to select organizational representatives who demonstrate effective knowledge-sharing behaviours. It is also important (and often forgotten) that it needs to be made clear that their remit in participating includes transferring learning back into the organization.

An additional consideration, which can be difficult for some organizations to achieve, is that when committed, skilled and open-minded individuals are identified to represent the organization, they need to stay involved as long as possible to establish effective trusting relationships within the collaboration so more meaningful knowledge can be developed and shared. In particular, if organizational capability building is the goal, then this can mean that leaders need to adopt a long-term perspective in committing resources to the collaboration.

Managing the dynamics of the collaboration

The way that the collaboration is organized and managed is important as this creates the collaborative "ambience" which encourages trusting relationships. This environment supports deeper learning and allows more complex issues to be addressed.

Managing the dynamics of the collaboration involves thinking about the systems and processes that are used to organize activities together, creating the opportunities for social ties to form and trust to be established, and ensuring that power and politics don't get in the way.[2] Practices that may be useful are outlined in Table 11.3.

To ensure success, those involved in the collaboration must avoid complacency and continue to emphasize the partnership role of all involved. The individual who acted as the convenor of one collaboration described himself as "an inquisitive member of the community" and "a member with a few more responsibilities" trying not to have "an overwhelming presence". This is perhaps a useful perspective to adopt in convening a learning-based collaboration.

Table 11.3: Practices that sustain the relationships between organizations in the collaborations

Aspect of managing inter-organizational dynamics	Illustrative practices
Systems and processes	Appointing a full or part-time collaboration manager.
	Ensuring that the facilitator has knowledge of the specific subject area and is skilled at selecting and using appropriate facilitation techniques.
	Capturing and distributing collaboration generated content by a skilled and informed person.
	Adopting a regular "rhythm" of activities and events to build a sense of community.
	Adopting a loose agenda at events to create space for people to raise issues and discuss emergent topics.
	Adopting collaborative technology (for example websites, wikis and other collaborative online tools).
Social ties	Allowing and valuing social time within the programme to allow participants to establish personal relationships.
	Considering whether appropriate qualifying criteria for participants need to be identified. This can ensure sufficient commonality and shared understanding for meaningful knowledge exchange.
	Ensuring continuity of individuals representing their organizations, particularly when difficult issues are being addressed.

continued on next page...

Table 11.3 - *Continued*

Aspect of managing inter-organizational dynamics	Illustrative practices
Trust and risk	Using a neutral venue can help separate people from day-to-day organizational pressures.
	Using skilled facilitation to generate a "safe" environment to discuss issues and share ideas and solutions openly.
	Working together on something specific leads to more active engagement – thinking something through together builds trust.
	Bringing real issues to the table for discussion shows that trust is forming.
Power relations	Limiting commercial/remit conflicts by screening participants.
	Ensuring that individuals representing their organizations are of a similar seniority.
	Allowing participants to design the content of collaboration activities, while the facilitator shapes the process followed.
	Reducing the visibility of differences in power between organizations or individuals to encourage peer learning.

Real life stories

Two learning collaborations are described here; the first one is a collaboration between four UK public sector agencies and the second Henley's KM Forum, a larger collaboration involving public, private, and not-for-profit organizations.[4]

Cross-government agencies

Participants: Four major UK government agencies.
Convener: One of the collaborators.
Valued outcomes from the collaboration: Shared independently branded website offering consistent guidance to the public sector, demonstration of partnership working in action, and trusting organizational relationships for other activities outside the collaboration.

The motivation for this collaboration is summarized in the following statement from one of the participants:

> Individual members of the public should expect to receive a seamless service from the public service. Everyone is looking at how everyone can work effectively together – citizen empowerment requires joined up information to be available.

This collaboration, which has been in existence for five years, is sponsored by four government agencies and strives to "build capacity for public sector managers and practitioners. It promotes its sponsors' collective knowledge and expertise on key improvement issues" . . . "helping to lay the foundations for successful partnership working in local areas". Information is disseminated by the collaboration to the public sector using a shared website. Additional improvement "tools and templates" are licensed by the partners and made available through the website. Collaboration between the four agencies is concerned with streamlining information and providing advice.

The collaborating partners are geographically dispersed. There are quarterly board meetings and the collaboration has a full-time convener. The convener develops the agenda, highlighting any important issues that have come up in the last quarter. Policy people from each of the four agencies are also involved in identifying trends and issues. Discussion is at a strategic level and key policy issues coming from central government that people need to be aware of are identified. The members then decide how to take this forward to its public presentation on the website.

A great benefit that was hoped for, but not entirely expected, is how inter-organizational relationships have developed between the sponsors. "At a strategic level we have been having conversations that we might not otherwise have had, and . . . our relationships are much closer personally and organizationally as a result."

However, there is a critical ongoing challenge in the role of the convener raising the collaboration profile. "I'm continually working with people doing their day jobs in the different organizations, and keeping it at the forefront of their minds."

Henley KM Forum

Participants: Knowledge managers from around 40 large multi-nationals and UK public sector bodies.

Convener: Henley Business School, UK.

Valued outcomes from the collaboration: Co-created practitioner guidance on specific KM issues, practical approaches for operational issues, challenges to thinking through exposure to new ideas, comparing practices with other organizations, professional networking.

Established in 2000, the KM Forum brings together business practitioners, industry thought-leaders, and experts in combination with academics. There is an ongoing programme of workshops, seminars, discussion groups, and highly focused research projects. Organizational representatives are usually senior executives with some responsibility for information and Knowledge Management. The member organizations each pay a fee and the vetting of members helps to ensure peer organizations participate and there is a minimum of competitive interaction.

The convener "provides a neutral venue where members can engage in relationship building, but usually with the aim of bringing learning back into their own organizations". The aim is to attract people who find it difficult to find like-minded people in their own organizations. Individuals participate "often because in their organizations they are outside the main functions. Here they fit in. They can share more easily with likeminded members in a collaborative, non-hierarchical way."

Individuals representing their organizations are keen to find value from solutions. "I have shamelessly stolen good information and applied it back at work. Templates from the research are very valuable ways of thinking about issues." However, there is also the opportunity to develop long-term relationships that may have value in the future.

One factor that enables this is the design of each event that seeks to minimize control and structure in order to provide the space for conversations to flow: ". . . at each event there are always deliberate gaps for networking . . . with long breaks". In addition the annual conference is a "great time for socializing".

The relationships that are formed at the face-to-face events are also supported by two activities, one is a members' wiki and the other is the series of projects that groups of members work on together each year. Since the same people regularly attend, trust has built up as they get to know each other. "There is lots of openness and lots of sharing . . ." and this enables better networking.

Individuals comment that they value the combination of being able to find immediate solutions for current issues in combination with developing relationships with knowledgeable and interesting peers. Longer term value comes from taking time out from the day job: "I have no time for creative thinking in job and hence [the KM Forum] provides an opportunity for more exploration of ideas."

Top tips

✓ Improve internal collaboration mechanisms and identify ways of joining these up with the learning from the external collaboration.

✓ Select organizational representatives who demonstrate effective knowledge-sharing behaviours and make clear that their remit in participating includes transferring learning back into the organization.

✓ When committed, skilled, and open-minded individuals have been identified to represent the organization, allow them to stay involved as long as possible to build relationships within the collaboration so more meaningful knowledge can be developed and shared.

✓ The collaborations evolve as the relationships between individuals and organizations mature. The facilitators need to be able to adjust the mechanisms and processes being used to support the collaborations as this happens. Continually seeking feedback and ensuring that valued outcomes are being achieved is essential for long-term success.

✓ Investing in creating a collaborative "ambience" within the collaboration helps build trusting relationships and shared identity which allows more complex issues to be addressed.

✓ There needs to be enough similarity between participants to encourage relationships to form, but also an appropriate mix and diversity of participants to generate a broad enough range of perspectives for the challenges being addressed.

✓ It is difficult to build organizational capability as this is a long-term process. It needs various things to be in place. Individuals involved in the collaborations need to be able to translate the implications of the learning back into the organization. The organization needs to have the systems and processes to transfer and amplify the learning that is brought back.

The research and the team involved

This research project took place during 2008 by a working group of members of the Henley KM Forum. The explicit intention was to study learning-based inter-organizational collaborations – not those for which there was a transactional exchange of goods or services involved. Data was mainly collected from inter-organizational collaborations within which working group members participated. Seven collaborations were studied in this research. Telephone interviews were used to collect the data (two participants and the convener (organizer) from each collaboration). An extensive review of the academic and practitioner literature was also undertaken.

The research activities were intended to help managers engage in productive dialogues with colleagues in various functions about how external learning-based collaborations could make a difference to the organization. They were not intended to provide prescriptive advice for a particular business.

Dr Christine van Winkelen from the KM Forum team and Visiting Fellow at Henley Business School was the academic co-champion for this research. The member co-champion was Graham O'Connell of the National School of Government. Keith Heron of Henley Business School was a researcher on the project. Working group members included representatives from the following organizations:

Audit Commission   *Government Office of the North West*
HM Treasury   *Improvement and Development Agency*
Ministry of Defence   *Nationwide Building Society*
National School of Government   *QinetiQ*
Unisys

together with invited associates: Andrew Sinclair-Thomson (Consensia Consulting Ltd) and Chris Collison (Knowledgeable Ltd).

Final reflections from the research

Subject-specific organizational capability building was rarely achieved in the collaborations we studied. This was because of two main factors: individuals not translating the implications of the learning back to their organization, and the organizations not having systems and processes to transfer and amplify the learning that was brought back. Potential and realized absorptive capacity describes these two factors conceptually.[3] Where capability building was achieved, there was visible long-term commitment to the collaboration by senior leaders in the collaborating organizations. In general, the leadership of the organization needs to positively acknowledge that collaboration is used to achieve something difficult that an organization cannot do on its own. It takes time, effort, and commitment to build capability. Success on the journey is likely to happen through other forms of value generation such as operational and affirmation value, reputation, and relationship building.

Notes

1. Based on Beesley, L. (2004) Multi-level complexity in the management of knowledge networks, *Journal of Knowledge Management*, 8(3), 71–88.
2. Easterby-Smith, M., Lyles, M.A., and Tsang, E.W.K. (2008) Inter-organizational knowledge transfer: current themes and future prospects, *Journal of Management Studies*, 45(4), 677–690.
3. Find out more about absorptive capacity from Zahra, S.A. and George, G. (2002) Absorptive capacity: A review, reconceptualization and extension, *Academy of Management Review*, 27(2), 185–203.
4. These cases were prepared during 2008 and represent the state of the collaborations at that time.

Section V

Become more agile

New technologies fuel the pace of change in a globalizing world and have driven business uncertainty and unpredictability to ever higher levels. Lack of interaction across time zones and spatial separation once acted as a buffer, insulating us from cascades of opinion and restricting access and awareness of knowledge opportunities. Web 2.0, the interactive world of social networks and collaborative technologies increases the connections and contradictions we have to manage in making decisions and undertaking organizational activities. It is a force for democratization that allows more people to have their say about what matters to them, to access knowledge and information at any time and in any place, to create their own influential material, and to stay connected and maintain relationships on the move. Potentially, it offers organizations access to varied sources of expertise faster and from farther afield. More participation amplifies opinion and insight and increases informal conversation both internally and externally. This can be a route to the sort of collective intelligence that improves business relevance through sensitization to customers' interests, increases informed planning and decision-making, reduces costly mistakes, and positively influences organizational reputation. Equally, if not well managed, it can be a shortcut to wasted time, biased decisions, damaged reputation, and reduced share price.

To thrive in this turbulence, organizations need to develop sufficient agility to respond to unpredictable and rapidly changing conditions. This means deliberately building flexibility and responsiveness into strategy and decision-making, organizational structures, and relationship networks. Learning has to be built into both the approach to strategy development and the strategies developed; feedback needs to be rapid and relevant to the many stakeholders affecting organizational performance today.

What do we mean by agility?

Organizational agility is a deeply embedded capability to initiate and sustain ongoing change in the structure and positioning of an organization so that it remains sufficiently well adapted to cope with, evolve and, where possible, proactively influence turbulent external demands.

Ultimately for all organizations, surviving and thriving depends on making sense of what matters to a broad community of influential stakeholders. This means identifying and accessing the knowledge required to meet their evolving needs, then reconfiguring the network of organizational relationships and processes to suit the revised goals. The challenge is that all this has to be achieved in dynamic circumstances where upheaval can occur faster than organizational structures can be reconfigured. An organization that cannot flex and adapt in a timely manner runs the risk of obsolescence.

How do you develop the key attributes of agility?

In this section, we consider three important and inter-related attributes affecting organizational agility. This is not a complete list. It does however reflect the priorities that have been troubling organizations in recent turbulent times. We start by considering how well knowledge is used to inform business decisions and the key factors that affect the process. Whether decisions are appropriate for the situation and encourage meaningful and worthwhile change depends on involving appropriate expertise, avoiding personal bias, using technology to access and integrate vital know-how into decisions, and using internal and external collaboration to ensure that the decision process is representative of the interests of many different stakeholders. The more managers can enhance these aspects of decision-making, as well as learning from and reflecting on the outcomes, the more responsive the organization will be.

The new social technologies have emerged quickly but not as part of business practice. They evolved as a way for individuals to build personal networks, have conversations, and share knowledge and opinion freely. Voluntary participation means that collaboration arises when people are excited by a common purpose. The social media have broken down some of the insulating barriers, power differentials, and personal inconveniences that prevent an individual having their say. In so doing, they have also increased the turbulence and pace of change facing many organizations.

Despite this, social media offer some viable opportunities to help organizations sense emerging priorities, to draw on a broader spectrum of expertise, and to improve the collaborative process, which are all vital for truly relevant decision-making. Many organizations are concerned about how to integrate social media into their existing structures and processes because they seem to work contrary to traditional organizing principles: control of the many by the few; a predetermined direction for the organization; competitive secrecy and commercial protection of intelligence; delineated boundaries between the inside and the outside of the organizations; decisions by a suitable hierarchical authority with responsibility for the outcome.

In this new economy, social media democratize influence, serendipity undermines planning, broadcasting and sharing can be more valued than secrecy and knowledge protection, and networks often circumvent the hierarchy and subvert bureaucracy. Some people resist the merging of work and social life that naturally evolves in this more interconnected life style. Others are particularly sensitive to the risks of the public sharing of imperfectly formed opinion. Some organizations may be nervous of publicly testing products before they are fully refined, or concerned about the impact of employees' public revelations on business reputation. But transparency, interaction, and frequent feedback have many benefits in terms of agility and responsiveness. They build trust, loyalty, and relevance. The more people use these virtual technologies, the more collaboration improves and the more confident people become in working and learning together, even when they are physically apart.

As people see the potential of social media for sharing ideas and opinion about things that matter to them and realize they can publicly influence issues they care about, the more they start to expect involvement in decisions affecting their working life. Employment contracts, rules, regulations, and bureaucratic procedures, all the conventional means of coordinating activity to deliver results, begin to feel more restrictive. Voluntary engagement rooted in personal pride, passion, and concern for something bigger, become a stronger incentive to participate and collaborate than money or bureaucratic coercion. This has been the path for many open innovation business models.[1]

As we move further from industrial economy production priorities and assumptions of decreasing returns from tangible resources, towards assumptions of economic value generated by knowledge work, we have to rethink the processes for leading and managing people as an organized collective. The organizational structures and processes developed in an industrial era may not suit the more democratic, participative world of today. Organizations are rethinking the future and trying to imagine what sort of processes, structures, and mechanisms would attract and engage mobile knowledge workers, and form the basis for what has been called Enterprise 2.0. Structures and relationships must simultaneously provide both stability and continuity, whilst allowing for agility and change. Organizations that are flatter, more fluid, and flexible will rely on reputation and trust to build relationships and engage talent.[2] This creates a virtuous circle of knowledge-sharing activity as in Figure V.1.

Generous knowledge sharing increases the opportunity to access valuable knowledge without the need to own it or lock it in forever. The evolutionary path to a future form of organizing which can really take advantage of what Shirky[1] has called the "cognitive surplus" in society could pass through one of three radically different generic scenarios. In Chapter 14 we look at what these scenarios might entail and how your organizational history may affect your progress towards these possible futures.

Imagining a potential future is a way to help your organization move forward constructively. The scenarios will not be exact descriptions of the future, but awareness of them increases sensitivity to trends and drivers of change. When knowledge becomes the main factor of production, the dynamics change to a situation where individuals, groups, and organizations negotiate common areas of interest before becoming involved together in something approaching a partnership. The risk of ignoring these dynamics is that organizations could become irrelevant and unattractive to new talent.

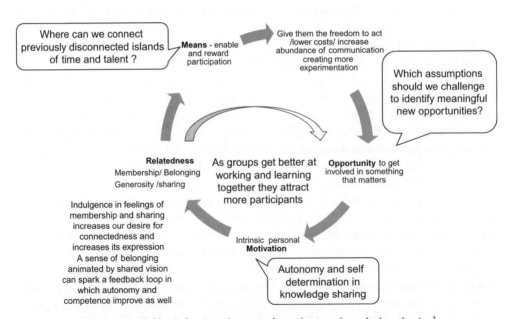

Figure V.1: Self reinforcing elements for voluntary knowledge sharing[3]

Key questions to ask yourself

As you start to use the ideas in the next three chapters ask:

- What is your organization doing to improve its capacity to make knowledgeable decisions by involving more people in the process of challenging out-of-date assumptions and principles of operation?
- How can you select and implement suitable social media to improve collaborative knowledge sharing inside the organization and across organizational boundaries so that the organizational activities evolve and remain relevant to external conditions?
- How can social media be used to both support structural reconfiguration that introduces more flexibility into the business operations and more diversity into the decision-making processes?
- What could your business look like if it employed all your knowledge-based resources? With a more flexible working structure and better knowledge sharing around a reliable and well engaged network could you bring more dynamic capability into the business?
- How could you change your people management practices to stimulate care and engagement?
- Given the pace and scale of change in your industry do you need to be looking at future scenarios and adjusting your decision-making processes and internal structures to encourage more people to be involved and engaged in shaping business direction?

Notes

1. For more information and real life examples take a look at Tapscott, D. and Williams, A. (2006) *Wikinomics. How Mass Collaboration Changes Everything*, New York: Portfolio, a member of Penguin USA; Chesbrough, H. (2006) *Open Business Models*, Harvard Business Press; Shirky, C. (2010) *Cognitive Surplus, Creativity and Generosity in a Connected Age*, Allen Lane, an imprint of Penguin Books; Leadbeater, C. (2009) *We-Think: Mass Innovation not Mass Production*, Profile Books.
2. Gagne, M. (2009) A Model of Knowledge-Sharing Motivation, *Human Resource Management*, 48, 571-589 suggests that the ways to influence knowledge-sharing motivation are to change job design, performance appraisal, and compensation schemes to offer more group-based and intrinsic rewards as well as positive feedback. Managerial style and training and development and selecting staff with comparable values are all important influences on the intention to share.
3. Based on Gagne, M. (2009) A Model of Knowledge-Sharing Motivation, *Human Resource Management*, 48, 571-589 and Shirky, C. (2010) *Cognitive Surplus Creativity and Generosity in a Connected Age*, Allen Lane, an imprint of Penguin Books. London.

Chapter 12

Snapshot

Good decision-making matters in all organizations. Today there are even more pressures on decision-makers to reflect the priorities of many different people and institutions, so "good" decision-making can be even harder to achieve. Decision-making is a knowledge-intensive activity. Consequently, initiatives may be needed to help decision-makers to access and use the best available knowledge. An integrated approach has been developed that draws on essential knowledge-related practices that affect decision-making. It is organized around five broad factors: using experts, using technology, using internal and external collaboration, organizational learning about decision-making, and developing individuals as decision-makers.

Evaluating how well your organization performs against these five factors is a useful starting point. You can do this by working with the maturity model that describes five levels of performance for each factor. It provides a systematic framework for examining your current position and planning how to improve. If one part of the organization is better than another at one of the factors, then managing a peer learning process can help build the capability of the whole organization.

Helping individuals to become more effective decision-makers requires particular attention. The research also offers a framework of five useful personal competencies: linking the big picture with the detail required for action, defining boundaries, influencing others, maintaining momentum, and weighing up the balance of influences. Individuals can work on developing these in conjunction with coaches, mentors, and their own personal reflection.

Why this matters

Good decision-making has always mattered. Today, people in organizations face even more pressures to make efficient and responsive decisions, whilst also complying with good governance and ethical approaches. Decision-making is a knowledge-intensive activity in which knowledge is, simultaneously, raw material, work-in-process, and deliverable. Many organizations, both private and public sector, are finding that they need to draw on a wider variety of knowledge to better serve the needs of increasingly demanding and sophisticated customers. Often access to knowledge comes through working within several interconnected networks of diverse individuals and organizations. Decision-making is often distributed across the organization to increase speed and flexibility, making it even more important for everyone to have a shared view of what the priorities are and what matters. It is a challenge for many organizations to ensure that decisions are based on the best available knowledge and do not work against one another. As decision-making is a very broad field, a useful definition to describe what we are looking at here is:

> A "decision" is a commitment to a course of action that is intended to yield results that are satisfying for specified individuals.[1]

This definition emphasizes that decisions need to result in purposeful action with the value of that action being determined by relevant organizational stakeholders. Improving conversations about what matters, as well as learning from the results of action to improve future decisions, are particular areas where managers can contribute to better organizational decision-making.

What this means for your organization

Good organizational decision-making is a capability that takes time and effort to develop. By understanding your organization's current strengths and weaknesses in this area, you can identify opportunities for improvement.

We found that five factors need to be considered together in an integrated and holistic way. The main actions needed to become good at each factor are listed below.

Using experts

- Recognizing decision-making situations which require expert input.
- The appropriate use of experts and expert panels to explore implications and provide advice.
- Ensuring the accessibility of experts to decision-makers.
- The development of experts in key areas which are particularly important to the organization.
- Ensuring that experts are proactive in passing on their knowledge to others.
- Learning from the contributions of external experts.

Using technology

- Widespread and disciplined use of appropriate information systems, decision support tools, and collaborative working systems by decision-makers.
- Provision of real-time information for operational decision-making.

- Understanding of the principles of evidence-based decision-making such that facts and information are sought to help make sense of a situation and establish an evidence base appropriate to the type of decision.
- Providing access to external resources and databases.
- Using technology to involve those who need to contribute to the decision, no matter what their location.
- Managing information repositories with good governance.

Using internal and external collaboration

- Recognizing situations when a range of knowledge and points of view are needed for good decisions to be made.
- Using communities and networks to build understanding and capability in key knowledge areas.
- Involving external parties where appropriate to contribute knowledge and different perspectives, with clear codes of conduct being used regarding the protection of valuable knowledge.
- "Joining up" internal and external collaboration activities through the use of technology and through joint involvement in networks and communities.
- A consultative approach to decision-making being the norm.

Organizational learning about decision-making

- Continuously appraising the ways decisions are being made, including whether experts, technology, and collaboration are being used appropriately and effectively.
- Understanding how to appraise risk in decisions and then reviewing the decision outcome to improve the appraisal process in the future.
- Sustaining an open culture in which debate and contributions to decisions are encouraged at appropriate points.
- Using a variety of processes to review and learn from decisions (including group and inter-group processes) and then being able to institutionalize changes when lessons have been learnt following a decision review. Also having a process to manage the future review of decisions to see if they need to be revised.
- Using people management processes (appraisal, reward etc.) that support consultative and team-based decision-making.

Developing individuals as decision-makers

The most effective way in which individuals can become better decision-makers is either through personal reflection or guided reflection in a coaching context. Both should raise awareness of their personal style, preferences, and mental and emotional biases. The organization can support and encourage individuals to do this through:

- Embracing and modelling reflective practice at all levels, including making time and space for reflection in the design of agendas, meetings, and events.

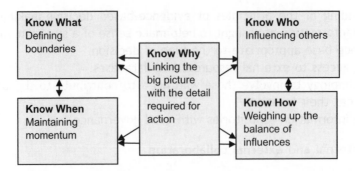

Figure 12.1: Knowledge-based competency framework for individual decision-makers

- Encouraging people to share personal learning from reflection, for example through blogs (with constructive ground rules) or collective learning situations.
- Encouraging people to look outside their usual environment (internal or external) to find new ways of understanding issues.
- Instituting coaching and mentoring programmes to support the development of decision-makers.
- Making available training in how to support participative decision-making, for example facilitation, negotiation, conflict resolution, leadership etc.
- Offering training to senior decision-makers in techniques such as framing insightful questions, strategic influence, and managing change in complex systems.

A competency framework was developed through the research that can be useful for individuals (or coaches working with individuals) as they plan how to tackle a big decision, work out what to do differently when things don't seem to be going to plan, or learn from experience once the decision has been implemented. This is outlined in Figure 12.1. The underpinning skills and abilities are summarized in Table 12.1.

Creating an action plan

You can use a maturity model that covers the five factors that enhance organizational decision-making capability to assess the strengths and weaknesses of different parts of your organization. Then you can facilitate knowledge sharing between them. This peer learning process is a very effective way to build organizational capability. The maturity model is shown in Table 12.2.

The steps you could follow to use this maturity model are:

1. Identify a group of people representing different parts of your organization (different teams, activities or functions). At least six is desirable – 10-12 is probably the maximum. Invite them to a 1.5–2-hour workshop.

Table 12.1: Developing decision-making competency

Personal skills and abilities required	
Understanding and awareness	Awareness of how the organizational context affects the decision
	Understanding of the organizational orientation to risk
	Ability to investigate the facts
Reflective practice	Modelling open and transparent behaviour
	Ability to challenge own thinking
	Ability to learn from experience
	Confidence to take risks and make mistakes
Communication	Effective communication skills
	Effective listening and questioning skills
Ways of relating to other people	Recognizing the value of other people's contributions
	Knowing who to involve
	Maintaining external relationships
	Networking
	Trusting
	Managing emotions
Awareness of time in relation to the effectiveness of decision-making	The timing of relevant external events
	The time pressures surrounding the decision and the time pressures on others
	The impact of timeliness on the acceptance of the decision
	The impact of time on risk
	Making time and space to think and reflect during and after the decision

2. At the start of the workshop give everyone a copy of the model and talk through what the five factor headings mean so everyone has a similar understanding.
3. For each factor ask them each to rate their team/group/activity (as appropriate) according to the five level definitions.
4. Then ask people to identify where they would want to get to on each factor within the next 12 months (identify the gap between the current and desirable rating).
5. Ask them to pick the two priority areas that they expect to make the most difference if they succeeded in moving them from where they are to where they want to be within 12 months.
6. Collect the information and use a flipchart to represent who has what rating (the River Diagram shown in Figure 12.2 can be a useful way of depicting the results for all groups and factors). Add in the desired ratings and what the priorities for improvement are (maybe in a different colour).
7. Look at who is strong at each factor and who wants to improve on it. Connect these people so they can discuss what the strong group is doing and how the weaker group can learn from this. These "peer assist" conversations should

Table 12.2: Knowledge enabled decision-making maturity model

	Using experts	Using technology	Using internal and external collaboration	Organizational learning about decision-making	Developing individuals as decision-makers
Ambient	Decision-makers are able to recognize situations which require internal and external expert input. Internal experts are accessible to decision-makers in terms of both time and their own ability to contribute. There are multiple ways for decision-makers to identify internal experts, and for experts to identify opportunities to contribute. Experts are active in passing on their knowledge to others, building the organizational knowledge base in their field.	There is pervasive use of information systems, decision support tools, and collaborative working systems by decision-makers. Decision-makers know when to adopt different tools and approaches for different situations. Systems provide real-time information for operational decision-making and can also be manipulated to generate new perspectives on situations. Collaborative technologies are widely used to widen participation in decision-making.	Decision-makers are able to recognize situations when a range of knowledge and points of view are needed for good decisions. An integrated approach to using internal and external knowledge sources is evident through the adoption of a wide range of collaborative methods and technologies, as well as communities and networks that include internal and external participants. Senior decision-makers adopt consultative approaches, demonstrating integrity in their behaviour and actions.	There is an organizational process to continuously appraise the approach to decision-making, including whether experts, technology, and collaboration are being used appropriately and effectively and how risk is being assessed. There is an open culture in which debate and challenge in relation to decisions is encouraged. Where lessons learnt following a decision review suggest an institutional change is needed, processes exist to embed it into structures or policies.	Reflective practice is embraced and modelled throughout the organization. Decision-makers are encouraged to look outside the usual boundaries (internal or external) to find new ways of understanding difficult issues. More sophisticated techniques such as framing insightful questions, achieving strategic influence, and achieving change in complex organizational systems are developed by senior decision-makers.

	Using experts	Using technology	Using internal and external collaboration	Organizational learning about decision-making	Developing individuals as decision-makers
Accepted	Senior decision-makers have been developed to know how to use internal and external expert advice effectively. Experts and expert panels are used to explore the implications and provide advice for significant decisions. The technical and professional development of internal experts is encouraged and supported. Experts know how to pass on their knowledge to others as they provide advice and through mentoring and coaching.	New technologies are adopted to support key business drivers and personalized access profiles can be created by decision-makers. Blogs support personal reflection on decisions and are encouraged within constructive ground rules. The principles of evidence-based decision-making (using data, information, and explicit knowledge) are understood and adopted in appropriate situations.	Different interpretations of a situation are regularly explored through various collaborative mechanisms as part of effective decision-making. External perspectives are actively sought, particularly by strategic decision-makers. Communities and interest groups are established around key business topics to build organizational understanding and capability for future decision-making. Codes of conduct regarding the protection of valuable knowledge are widely understood.	There is widespread use of a variety of decision review processes to learn from significant decisions, including inter-group reflection processes to support collective learning. Leadership teams are developed together to improve their decision-making. Risk appraisal methods incorporate learning from previous decisions, as well as considering the potential to learn from current decisions. The time at which a decision needs to be reviewed is recorded and a process maintained to action this.	There is an integrated approach to developing the capacity of individual decision-makers. Training, coaching, and mentoring support is widely available. Sharing personal learning from reflection is encouraged, for example through the use of blogs, within constructive ground rules. Organizational leaders share their own thinking and reflections in a constructive way, encouraging contributions whilst minimizing the potential for anxiety about change.

continued on next page…

Table 12.2 - *Continued*

Using experts	Using technology	Using internal and external collaboration	Organizational learning about decision-making	Developing individuals as decision-makers
Applied — Expert advice is sought as input to most significant decisions. An expertise directory is maintained to help identify in-house experts. These experts are also able to identify opportunities themselves where they can contribute. There is a coherent programme to develop and retain expertise within the organization. Efforts are made to retain learning gained from using external experts.	A range of decision support systems is available and decision-makers know how to use these in conjunction with in-house information systems, external resources, and databases to help make sense of a situation and establish an evidence base. Technological solutions are integrated and can provide a coherent picture across organizational boundaries. Information repositories are managed with good governance. Collaborative working technologies are generally used to bring together those who need to be involved, as well as to seek wider views as inputs to decisions.	Diverse views and contributions from within the organization are regularly sought by decision-makers. Effective training and communication means that decision-makers are confident in using technology to collaborate with colleagues from elsewhere in the organization. External intelligence is collected from various sources and is available to decision-makers. Internal and external collaboration initiatives are largely pursued independently. The organization actively supports employees' participation in various external professional and specialist networks.	Several parts of the organization have developed a "no blame" culture to support learning from decisions. Processes exist and are used to learn before, during, and after key decisions. Group reflection activities, such as facilitation, workshops, and standing agenda items, are used to collectively review and learn from decisions. People management practices (such as reward and appraisal) support team-based decision-making.	Several development initiatives encourage and support individual decision-makers to reflect on their practice (for example, coaching, mentoring, leadership development), though these do not consistently and coherently focus on improving decision-making. Clear efforts are made to provide time and space for reflection and this is modelled by more senior decision-makers. Corporate values are widely understood as a reference point for decision-making.

	Using experts	Using technology	Using internal and external collaboration	Organizational learning about decision-making	Developing individuals as decision-makers
Ad hoc	Decision-makers usually seek expert advice for key decisions, but there is no consistent basis for discerning the best opportunities for using expertise. External experts are often used and an ad hoc approach to involving internal and external experts means organizational learning is fragmented. Some training efforts address organizational knowledge gaps, but little coherent attention is given to building deep expertise.	There are some pockets of skill and confidence in using information, decision support, and collaborative working technologies to support better decision-making. Technology solutions are available, but their use is limited as there is not a clear strategy framing their purpose and application. Procedures, rather than training, are used to promote application.	The value of collaboration is not widely appreciated by decision-makers, though there are pockets of good practice. Initiatives to support better collaboration across the organization are in place, though without a coherent programme to ensure consistency. Groups and teams are formed to solve specific problems without a clear intention of improving the decisions made through a consistent approach to collaboration. Some people participate in external networks and this mainly improves their personal decision-making.	Some significant decisions and projects are subject to formal review after they are completed, but the mechanisms to take this learning forward to future decisions are not consistently available or applied. Processes to assess risk in relation to decisions are used, but rarely linked to evaluation of the consequences of the decision. Concerns about blame prevent open discussion of mistakes.	Senior decision-makers make visible to others the process they are using and the information that has informed their conclusion, though they rarely share their personal reflections and learning. Training is available in techniques that support participative approaches to decision-making, such as facilitation, negotiation, conflict resolution, leadership etc. Some development initiatives (such as leadership or mentoring programmes) do encourage individual reflection as the basis for learning.

continued on next page…

Table 12.2 - Continued

Using experts	Using technology	Using internal and external collaboration	Organizational learning about decision-making	Developing individuals as decision-makers
Decision-makers' personal preferences determine the use of experts. Experts are mainly identified through their role/job title or via personal networks. Some core areas of expertise are recognized and organizational efforts are made to develop knowledge in these areas, but most experts are responsible for their own development. Internal expertise shortages are mainly covered by buying in consulting services.	Some information systems are available to support decision-making, but they aren't "joined up" and may give an inconsistent picture, particularly across organizational boundaries. Governance is poor, which means information can be unreliable. The information systems and decision support tools available are not user-friendly, or decision-makers have not been trained in their use. Technology to support collaborative discussion around issues and to seek wider views is either not available, or not widely used.	Decision-makers tend to operate within organizational silos. Collaboration is mainly with local colleagues. Wider knowledge sharing to contribute to decision-making is limited due to "need to know" concerns, an organizational tendency towards protecting knowledge, or a "not invented here" culture. Some external knowledge sources are used, but an internal bias is evident in strategic discussions.	There are limited opportunities to learn from past decisions; this mainly happens when there have been significant mistakes. Databases do store some "lessons identified" from previous decisions and projects, but these are rarely re-used or referenced. Decision-makers leave the organization or change role frequently so that they do not have responsibility for their decisions and successors tend not to look at the records maintained by previous job holders. Judgements of risk in relation to decisions are often based on the perceptions of individuals with power in the organization.	Individual decision-makers tend to follow rules and procedures. An action orientation is encouraged through people management processes (such as recruitment, appraisal, and reward), with limited value being placed on taking time to think about difficult issues and reflect on learning. There are limited opportunities for individuals to share their reflections on decisions, where these have taken place.

Aware

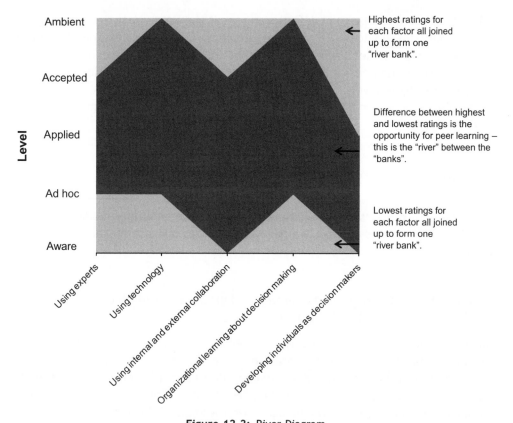

Figure 12.2: River Diagram

ideally be started at the workshop, then encouragement given for them to continue afterwards.

More details about how to use an extended version of this approach are available in the book *Learning to Fly*.[2] You may also choose to introduce a "company" or "KM programme" view at the end if you have other options to offer people who want to make improvements on particular factors.

Some hints and tips for getting the most from the peer learning process:

- Encourage people to start at the bottom (Aware level) and work up, rather than the top and work down, when they are deciding how to rate their part of the organization.
- You may decide that 12 months is too short a timeframe for improvements in your organization. More than three years is unlikely to be helpful though.
- There will be a lot of discussion about what the five factors mean for your organization. This is fine, as long as everyone understands and agrees with the final interpretation.

- The most value will be gained if you can repeat the assessment to track progress over time. This should be a productive learning process not an exercise in control and performance measurement. A learning approach encourages collaborative conversations and peer learning, bringing all parts of the organization up to their highest desirable levels.
- The discussion is the most useful part of this process – allow time for it and encourage it.

Real life stories

Different kinds of decisions need managers to apply the maturity model factors in different ways. In this section, we have stories from decision-makers about their approaches.

A simple decision that needed a strong evidence base: using technology and collaboration to collect and check facts

Simple decisions are not necessarily easy decisions, particularly when the issue is unpopular. This decision-maker needed to set priorities for the use of very limited shared resources. He worked with his team to carry out sufficient analysis of existing data to create an outline approach. He then explained the issue and the rationale for that approach to colleagues who would be affected, mainly in face-to-face meetings, following this up with the detail in emails with requests for answers to questions that would finalize the prioritization. The team created a "first cut" prioritization and put it out again for comments. This initial proposal was important because it allowed people to see the implications of the evidence that they had provided. Others saw how to improve their case for resource allocation. The final prioritization emerged from an iterative process in which everyone felt they had been given a fair hearing.

Using personal reflection and collaboration with others, including experts, to make sense of complex situations and develop options

When faced with a difficult aspect of a complex decision, this decision-maker said that he takes some time out. He would set aside a day, put everything out on a table, and apply some quality thinking to identify and understand the key concepts and establish a framework within which he needs to make the decision. By using this process in a recent complex decision he came up with two alternative models for a proposed way forward and shared them with a lot of people. These approaches evolved and didn't survive in their original form, but they were a useful foundation for moving things forward. His view was that if you offer people something tangible, it is easier to get to them engaged and they can quickly say what they like or dislike. In general, for difficult decisions he believes it is helpful to engage people with a potential solution, then listen hard to what is said about it. Some of the concerns will be due to lack of understanding, which can then be addressed. Others will represent added value as they bring in alternative perspectives. This approach also helps generate a more defensible decision; the debate and refinement means that you also won't be surprised by any questions at the end.

Using personal reflection, engaging people collaboratively, and using technology to collect evidence and communicate widely to achieve complex organizational change

This decision-maker considered how best to involve others in shaping the way forward in a complex decision about organizational change. He emphasized the need for a vision about what you want to get to, because it makes it easier to paint a clear enough picture about it for everyone to feel part of it. A decision-maker needs strong communication skills to be open, transparent, and clear with everyone. He commented that it never ceases to surprise him how much communication is actually needed. This decision-maker's organization tends to be very consultative and that can mean that the discussion continues until everyone agrees, which actually never happens. He said that in reality you need to find a balance between consultation and decision-making. The best approach is to identify where buy-in is needed. Project management tools can be used to provide opportunities for consultation and set the context for this. He commented that you need to know the difference between productive consultation and just creating opportunities for people to let off steam. This means being really clear about why you need consultation and what the outcome needs to be, and being ruthlessly honest about where people can contribute constructively. He added that honesty is important – there is a tendency to over-promise in terms of consultation but it is important that people feel they can contribute. People appreciate clarity about where and when the decision is being made. This means showing that there is a rational approach and evidence is being weighed.

Organizational learning about decision-making

This decision-maker commented that although his organization has a systematic process to evaluate decisions after the event, question the process, and identify lessons learnt, the lessons are largely carried with the people involved who share their stories and anecdotes. In general, he does not value knowledge repositories because all too often they don't get used. Where a review provides an institutional lesson that needs to be learnt, then it is important to change structures and policy so that the change becomes embedded in standard systems. Beyond this, in his view internal knowledge transfer happens best between individual people.

Top tips

One of the main benefits of using a maturity model approach for capability development is that it can stimulate higher quality conversations about issues that otherwise can be difficult to articulate. The framework creates a common language around the topic of organizational decision-making as well as a basis for objective assessment. Therefore, it is essential to make time for these conversations and to get a wide variety of people involved.

Other things to bear in mind in developing a knowledge-based approach to decision-making are:

- *Our own biases:* We use heuristics (rules of thumb) to speed up our decision-making all the time. However, these can create risks of bias if we use them inappropriately. Typical biases include preferring alternatives that keep things as they are and making choices that justify past decisions. All the recommendations to manage biases involve improving access to knowledge or increasing individual or organizational reflection. Encouraging people to use the competency framework will be helpful – encourage HR colleagues to consider incorporating it in the organization's competency framework.
- *Being aware of the types of decisions that we are making:* The consequences of a decision outcome may not always be clear ahead of time. It may not even be possible to make a full link between cause and effect in particularly complex situations. We need to develop an awareness of different types of decision and learn to draw on knowledge in different ways for each. A useful way of categorizing different types of decisions has been described by Dave Snowden and Mary Boone[3] and is summarized in Table 12.3. Practice using this to assess what kind of decision-making situation you are dealing with.

The research and the team involved

This project was carried out by a working group of knowledge managers from member organizations of the Henley KM Forum during 2009. Expert advisers and academics also participated. Nineteen telephone interviews with decision-makers in ten KM Forum member organizations (half public sector and half private sector) were used to collect the data and an extensive review of the academic and practitioner literature was also carried out.

The intention was to help knowledge managers engage in productive dialogues with colleagues in various functions about how Knowledge Management could build decision-making capability in the organization. It was not intended to provide prescriptive advice for a particular business.

The Project was co-championed by Professor Jane McKenzie of Henley Business School and Sindy Grewal of The Audit Commission. The researcher was Dr Christine van Winkelen of Henley Business School. Working group members included representatives from:

Table 12.3: Categorizing decision types

Type of decision	Characteristic	Decision-making approach needed
Simple	Clear cause and effect relationships are evident to all and right answers exist.	Reduce individual biases through a fact-based approach, good use of evidence, application of best practices and clear processes, and clear direct communication.
Complicated	Cause and effect relationships can be discovered, though they are not immediately apparent. Expert diagnosis is required and more than one right answer is possible.	Use high quality evidence with individual experts and expert panels to interpret it, challenging standard thinking through bringing in outside perspectives and encouraging creative thinking.
Complex	There are no right answers, but emergent and instructive patterns can be seen in retrospect. Efforts need to be made to probe the situation and sense what is happening to find the patterns of relationships.	Increase collaboration and communication to encourage discussion and surface issues and ideas, creating the conditions where patterns can emerge over time.
Chaotic	The relationships between cause and effect are impossible to determine because they shift constantly and no manageable patterns exist. Acting to establish order is needed through directive leadership.	Take action to find out what works through clear direct leadership, rather than seeking right answers. The aim is to move the decision situation away from chaotic to one of the above contexts (usually complex).

The Audit Commission
The British Council
DCSF

Balfour Beatty
Cranfield University
Ministry of Defence

Other member organizations of the KM Forum also identified interviewees to participate in the research:

Foreign and Commonwealth Office
Mills and Reeve
National College
Syngenta

HMRC
MWH
Permira

together with invited associates: Alex Goodall (previously Unisys) and Tim Andrews (Stretch Learning)

Table 12.4: Building decision-making capability as a series of intellectual capital investments

Intellectual Capital Component	IC investment area (maturity model factor)	Most significant contributions to decision-making
Human Capital	Identifying experts and developing expertise. Supporting reflective practice.	Sensemaking and identifying options. Managing individual decision-maker bias, increasing range and depth of experience, increasing debate, challenge and openness. Developing expertise. Reflection on practice and self-awareness to develop strategic decision-making skills.
Structural Capital	Using technology to structure, integrate, and provide access to explicit knowledge resources. Decision review process.	Access to current and well structured explicit knowledge to provide input for decision-making. Support experts in their decision-making. Recognizing different kinds of decision-making situations. Developing an appropriate repertoire of decision-making approaches.
Relational Capital	Adopting an integrated approach to internal and external collaboration.	Gathering intelligence. Accessing multiple perspectives to formulate the scope of the decision to be made in more complex situations. Making connections to create knowledge to generate new options.

Final reflections from the research

It may be helpful for managers to view developing organizational decision-making capability as a series of intellectual capital investments. The five factors that make up the maturity model can be mapped onto the core components of intellectual capital as shown in Table 12.4.

Notes

1. See p. 422 in Yates, J.F. and Tschirhart, M.D. (2006) "Decision-making expertise", in Ericsson, K.A. et al. (eds), *The Cambridge Handbook of Expertise and Expert Performance*, New York: Cambridge University Press, pp. 421–438.

2. For more information about working with maturity models and using them for peer learning, see Collison, C. and Parcell, G. (2004) *Learning to Fly* (2nd edn), Chichester: Capstone Publishing Ltd.

3. Snowden, D. J. and Boone, M.E. (2007) A leader's framework for decision making, *Harvard Business Review*, 85(11), 69-76.

Chapter 13

Snapshot

Here we explore how social media like wikis and blogs, and many other social networking technologies, can improve collaboration and knowledge sharing. Using social media such as wikis and blogs can enhance individuals' collaborative capability by reinforcing and building individuals' motivation to collaborate. Individuals do respond differently to the introduction of such technologies so five "user modes" offer a way to assess how to encourage and support people in the way that suits them. When there is a variety of technology options to choose from, groups will be quite effective in choosing the most appropriate tool for the job and finding out how to use it. Those who are used to working at a distance tend to become relatively more skilled at discussing and agreeing how to work together effectively and identifying social media that will help them.

People recognize the potential benefits of using social networking technologies for business knowledge sharing, but at present, they often feel that the benefits are outweighed by the perceived risks associated with mixing personal and professional networks. Clear policies supported by effective communication and training are needed to change these perceptions.

Why this matters

Web 2.0 technologies create a democratic environment that allows more people to have their say about what matters to them. They give people access to information and knowledge as they need it, but more importantly they help them stay connected with other people and manage their relationships on the move. They speed up access to relevant sources of expertise and increase the possibility of opportunistic connections.

The opportunity for more people to participate has implications for strategy, decision-making, reputation, and bottom line performance. Overall this challenges the way organizations communicate and collaborate, both internally and externally. There are two main reasons why finding new and better ways to collaborate matters for organizations.

> "The potential of social software is enormous. We're convinced that it's a superb way of allowing the lessons learned in one project to be made available to many other projects."
>
> *Peter Wilkinson, Knowledge Management Analyst, Taylor Woodrow*

Firstly, collaboration underpins knowledge sharing, and knowledge sharing stimulates new thinking and knowledge creation, which in turn leads to innovation. Innovation is an essential part of organizational agility.

Secondly, to make sense of rapidly changing technologies, customer requirements, and competitive conditions, organizations increasingly need to tap into knowledge from outside traditional organizational boundaries. They have to be sensitized to, and make sense of, the emerging signs of change. A wide network of external relationships, both at the level of individuals and with other organizations, is essential for accessing such knowledge. Externally generated ideas challenge the way managers and leaders think and can drive the ongoing strategic renewal and organizational development which all agile organizations need to achieve.

However, true collaboration does involve voluntary and engaged participation. Creating a culture of collaboration can be difficult in highly hierarchical organizations accustomed to top-down control because it requires more flexibility and trust than may be comfortable. Rather than trying to direct or manage collaboration, managers need to enable it, effectively creating the conditions where collaborative behaviours can flourish appropriately.

There are many ways to define collaboration, but a useful approach describes collaboration primarily in terms of relationships where trust, motivation, outlook, behaviour, and potential outcomes distinguish collaborative activities from other ways of working. Only truly collaborative relationships are likely to lead to breakthrough innovation as shown in Table 13.1.[1]

Table 13.1: The dimensions and dynamics of different working relationships

Relationship type	State of trust	Motivating force	Outlook	Behaviour	Potential outcomes
Collaborative	Highly invested	For the good of the whole	Synergy	Responsible	Breakthrough innovation
Co-operative	Transaction oriented	For successful project outcomes	Win-Win	Willing	Preconceived success
Competitive	Reluctant or cautious	To look good	Win within rules	Shrewd	Compromise
Adversarial	Distrust	Not to lose	Win at any cost	Cut-throat	Unpredictable

One aspect of creating the conditions for effective collaboration is the availability of appropriate technological tools. "Social media", alternatively known as "social technologies", "social software", "Web 2.0", "conversational technologies", "social computing", and "social networking," offer a range of interactive tools for different purposes. We will use social media as a generic term here, differentiating specific technologies as appropriate.

The social media called wikis and blogs became popular outside the business setting when applications like Wikipedia, Facebook, and MySpace created attractive customizable places for people to interact, creating a sense of belonging. The ability to co-create articles and develop shared understanding through wikis, or communicate daily thinking and reflections through blogs were in due course seen as useful business tools and are now moving into mainstream practice. Organizations have adopted wikis and blogs[2] for a range of different purposes and it must be said with different degrees of success. Nevertheless, in virtually every case their initial objectives are broadly the same: to be a route for employees to share documents and ideas, broadcast news and opinions, and author complex documents collaboratively.

The question that managers have been asking is whether social media are simply a set of tools that makes things easier for people who would collaborate anyway, or whether they represent such a radically different mode of interacting and working that they will transform organization structures making them inherently more democratic and collaborative. While many organizations have greeted that prospect with enthusiasm, others are struggling to identify the value of social media in their situation. Individual responses to the specific tools are also mixed.

Even when there is no official organizational support, research shows that it is not unknown for enthusiasts unwilling to take "no" for an answer to set up an unofficial wiki. Some people feel so strongly that social media facilitate their work that they go outside the firewall to use it when their organization does not encourage (or even allow) its use internally. This is why social media are sometimes referred to as subversive. If their use is happening outside the existing decision-making hierarchy, the organization could well be missing the potential benefits, even though it is trying to avoid some of the perceived risks. Many organizations that support social media – and relax their control over how employees use them – are learning to collaborate more effectively.

Social networking uses mobile and web-based technology to encourage large scale voluntary connections between interested people. This attracts more people to share their perspective on a topic and the emerging conversation can be used for sensing, organizing, and getting feedback about issues of mutual interest. It has been suggested that organizations can tap into the "Wisdom of Crowds", or "Collective Intelligence", though the risks of collective stupidity must be managed.[3]

Social networking is increasingly being used by organizations, politicians, and individuals to gain influence and support efficiency, improved performance, and enhanced accountability. Companies are using social networking technologies as a way to personalize their services and turn consumers into trusted brand advocates or advisors on product development. As more of the UK population begin to use social networking in their personal lives and the younger generation expect to have their say through these routes, people will also expect to access services online and to interact with the providers in these new ways.

What this means for your organization

There is a variety of fundamental questions that managers need to ask if they are thinking of implementing social media such as wikis and blogs for improved collaboration, or social networking technologies to interact with a wider audience. For example:

- Which tools should be used for which tasks?
- What blend of virtual and face-to-face working is appropriate in different contexts?
- Why do some organizations and individuals seem to embrace collaborative working, new technologies, and knowledge sharing whilst others find it difficult?

The technologies behind social media are still evolving and it is more helpful to think about the social phenomenon generated around them than the technical details of any particular application.

Wikis and blogs

The characteristics of wikis and blogs[2] are that they:

1. Enable content generation through conversations.
2. Provide a "history" or "trail".
3. Support asynchronous working (but not necessarily exclusively).

> "Less formal sorts of knowledge are often shared in face-to-face meetings. Wikis are a way of allowing people to share this type of knowledge without requiring them to be physically co-located – which is potentially very valuable in an organization like ours."
>
> Susan Frost, Knowledge Management Desk Officer, Ministry of Defence

In evaluating the benefits and risks of extending the use of these forms of social media, it was found that:

- Wikis and blogs improve access to other people for combining and exchanging knowledge. They can create worthwhile new connections that allow people to collaborate with peers and from the bottom up, whether this fits with the organizational hierarchy or not.

- Using these social media can build individuals' collaboration capability and can reinforce and increase individuals' motivation to collaborate because they realize unforeseen benefits and emotional support.
- The impact (and value) of these social media for an organization is influenced by the nature of the organization's hierarchy/bureaucracy and whether their introduction reflects or contradicts this. Coercive and enabling bureaucracies need different approaches, as discussed below.
- Individuals using these social media (officially or otherwise) can be catalysts for changing the social structure, particularly the nature of the hierarchy/ bureaucracy, in an organization.

However, organizations choosing not to use wikis and blogs give a number of reasons for this:

- Lack of knowledge and experience of the technology, sometimes exacerbated by lack of support or capacity in IT departments.
- Cultural barriers including resistance to change, not being ready, or not having a culture of using conversational tools.
- Not being clear what value wikis could add.
- Concerns over quality control and assurance.
- The perception that the organization isn't large enough to provide critical mass for a wiki.

Public sector organizations are also concerned about security and accountability.

Social networking technologies

In considering the use of social networking technologies, it is helpful to think in terms of the organization as many networks which connect both internally and externally.[4]

- Social networks consist of nodes (people) and ties (relationships) and are characterized by the patterns they form in terms of measures such as density, connectivity, and hierarchy. The strength of a tie is usually assessed with reference to factors such as frequency of contact, length of association, intimacy of the tie, and provision of reciprocal services.
- Some people seem more inclined than others to form strong or weak ties and to make bridging connections between groups and individuals. This propensity to connect with others is a useful way to understand individuals' networking styles and preferences.
- According to one theory, people presented with a technology event (such as the introduction of social networking websites to the workplace) choose different strategies based on whether they perceive the technology as an opportunity or

as a threat, and on the degree of control the users feel they have over the situation.

Through the social networks that are created, social capital develops, which is "the goodwill that is engendered by the fabric of social relations and that can be mobilised to facilitate action".[5] This creates opportunities for knowledge sharing and the stimulation of new thinking. There are risks in social networks though; if the ties become too strong between people in a particular group they can also act as barriers to new knowledge and ideas from elsewhere. A balance needs to be maintained across the network between bridging (links and relationships outside the group) and bonding (internal links and relationships) to sustain effective knowledge sharing and the stimulation of new thinking needed for organizational agility.

Social networking technologies have the potential to make it easier for people to create and maintain wide networks of relationships. Individual and collective responses to social networking websites will determine whether people choose to add them to their communication methods and change the pattern of their relationship building. These responses are likely to be shaped by many factors[6] including individuals' anticipation of value, individual networking style, social norms, the media capabilities of the websites, familiarity with the technology, the strength or weakness of existing network ties, and individuals' appraisal of how social networking websites will affect them.

Outside of the workplace, social networking sites such as Facebook, LinkedIn, and Twitter are making it easier for people to create and maintain very broad networks of relationships with high potential for serendipitous access to knowledge. However many factors influence the way people use (or don't use) social networking sites in the workplace. Norms around their use are still developing and concerns about privacy, reputation, governance, and interpretation lead to some reticence accepting them. Some people prefer to keep the social aspects of their daily interactions off record. Individuals and organizations have different expectations of value and different motivations for using them. As yet, there is no agreed best way for organizations to get value from encouraging more participation.

Creating an action plan

Getting started – deciding how to mix social media with other ways of collaborating

People accustomed to working together through a variety of technology tools, with or without face-to-face contact as part of this, seem to have a better understanding of how to work together effectively and efficiently than people who work only face-to-face. Discussing how to work together can lead to new, improved collaboration processes and people who have to work virtually (because of physical distance) find it necessary and hence ultimately easier to discuss ways of working than people who work mainly face-to-face who perhaps don't examine the process of collaboration or take it for granted.

- Mature teams experienced in technology make sensible choices when given access to a range of communication and collaboration technologies with different capabilities. The process of making choices builds team identity and spirit.

> "We have loads of collaboration tools, and part of my role is to show people all the options available. But it's up to teams to pick the tools that work for them and that suit the individuals and organizations they are collaborating with. Some have really taken to technology, whereas others are more traditional."
>
> *Michael Norton, Knowledge Management, IDeA*

- Mature teams inexperienced in technology use will find a way of collaborating effectively, but not necessarily efficiently.
- In contrast, teams at early stages of development and experienced with technology will use technology as an opportunity for structuring their interactions, which can accelerate team development, but this can be at the expense of team dynamics and team trust.

In extreme command-and-control environments where collaboration is particularly difficult, successful collaboration tends to happen when individuals are prepared to break the rules. In less extreme hierarchical environments, individuals in positions of authority can encourage collaboration and change by breaking the rules themselves and behaving in a non-hierarchical way when collaboration is needed.

These findings suggested the practical recommendations included in Table 13.2.

Table 13.2: Introducing social software technologies to improve collaboration

---

Practical ways to start introducing social software to the organization

---

Give people access to a range of face-to-face opportunities and technology tools for collaboration.

Let experienced people choose what tools they use and how they use them.

Let people customize their workspaces.

Encourage people to talk about how they work together.

If you're in a mainly face-to-face environment, give people access to technology tools and make sure they experience using them by encouraging them to resist face-to-face working for particular tasks.

If your organizational culture is strongly hierarchical, encourage people at the top of the hierarchy to "break the rules" and behave in a non-hierarchical way when collaboration is needed.

If collaboration just isn't in your organization's repertoire, find some colleagues to collaborate with and get on with it. Then if it's working well, show off about it!

Provide facilitation support for new teams to help people focus on processes as well as tasks.

Provide technical support and practice sessions for teams and individuals inexperienced in using technology.

Understanding the influence of the organizational context

The next important consideration is how the context of the organization influences the response when social media such as wikis or blogs are introduced. This depends on how the organization works in other ways.

The response to the use of social software seems to involve two inter-related dimensions.[7] The first describes the nature of the management hierarchy (this has been described as the prevailing bureaucracy) in the organization. The second describes individuals' motivation and capability.

- *The nature of the management hierarchy:* In terms of the prevailing bureaucracy, there are two useful descriptions: a coercive bureaucracy in which the environment for collaboration and knowledge creation/sharing doesn't exist, and an enabling bureaucracy in which it does.
- *The motivation of individuals:* The assumptions made by managers about individuals' motivation fall into three categories:

Rational-economic: people make rational decisions based on economic criteria and can therefore be controlled through rewards – emotions have no place at work.
Social: people are motivated by social needs – so need either to be supported at work as individuals, or placed in teams.
Self-actualizing man: people are self-motivated and don't need external incentives or controls.

At any point in time, if people's self-actualization needs are greater than their rational-economic needs, then their social needs will be focused on connecting and collaborating with peers rather than preserving (their position in) the organizational structure, and vice versa.

These two dimensions can be used to identify the likely effects of introducing social media such as wikis to an organization (Figure 13.1). To use this, you need to determine what kind of organization you have and how people's motivation is viewed, then select the appropriate intervention that can build the collaboration capability of individuals and organizations from Figure 13.2.

Understanding how individuals respond to social media

Some people contribute enthusiastically to tools such as wikis and blogs, while others are reluctant or even refuse to join in. Some wiki users report feeling "more in touch with other people and projects" – enthusing that wikis help to "create a sense of team" – others feel threatened, or hold back because they feel their contribution will be of little value.

Some links with personality were identified, for example, wikis level the playing field for introverts and extraverts. People who are not confident verbally can contribute to wikis without interrupting (as they might need to in a face-to-face

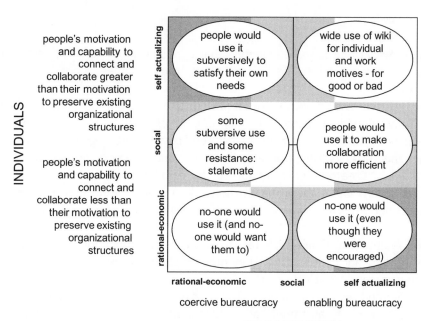

Figure 13.1: The likely effects of introducing a wiki in different contexts

	coercive bureaucracy	enabling bureaucracy
people's motivation and capability to connect and collaborate **greater than** motivation to preserve existing organizational structures	Give people permission to collaborate creatively within guidelines that deliver benefits to the organization as well as to the individuals. Ask people to identify uses for the wiki that will deliver organizational benefits and support these uses as pilots.	Build the organization's ability for ongoing positive transformation. Use the wiki to develop radical new ideas and directions that satisfy organizational and individual needs.
people's motivation and capability to connect and collaborate **equal to** motivation to preserve organizational structures	Demonstrate the benefits of bottom-up collaboration to the organization. Use the wiki for tasks that require collaboration between existing teams. Encourage motivated and capable individuals to support less motivated and capable individuals.	Make existing collaboration more efficient and increase the scope of collaborative decision-making. Configure the wiki to reflect existing organizational structures and use it for everything from writing agendas to setting strategy.
people's motivation and capability to connect and collaborate **less than** motivation to preserve existing organizational structures	Build people's motivation and capability for collaboration. Use the wiki for small, well-defined tasks that need to be done anyway. Choose tasks that are carried out by well-defined teams. Provide training and technical support.	Build people's motivation and capability for collaboration. Use the wiki for tasks that are important to individuals even if these tasks are not high priority for the organization. Provide training and technical support.

Figure 13.2: Using a wiki to build collaboration capability

meeting). Also, there is some evidence that people who make a lot of synthesizing contributions tend to be independent, tough-minded, conscientious, and unorthodox.

Five different user modes were identified. Users can operate in more than one mode. Some individuals behave as "consumers" of wikis and blogs, reading them but going no further. Others might be termed "respondents"; going beyond passive reading, they offer clarification and feedback, and make corrections to grammar and spelling. "Creators" go even further by contributing new material, offering drafts for review and elaborating on the work of others. Still other individuals are best described as "synthesizers" – authoring original contributions, organizing and restructuring others' contributions, and adding value through directing, encouraging, and facilitating. Finally, it's fair to say, a small proportion are "abstainers"; neither reading nor contributing, they may simply ignore wikis and blogs, or go so far as to comment negatively on them. Most synthesizers and creators also operate in consumer and respondent modes. The user modes are summarized in Table 13.3.

All modes except "abstainer" are valuable and can contribute to effective collaboration. There is no implied hierarchy in the different modes and no implied development path for individuals. Wiki communities benefit from a mix of modes and can become dysfunctional if some are missing. It was found that communities benefit from having at least one synthesizer. What's more, it was discovered that individuals can exhibit each of these tendencies at different times and under different circumstances. This is normal, to be expected and, indeed, encouraged because if the contribution made by social software to knowledge sharing is to be maximized, it is important for people to feel free to contribute at their own pace, in their own way.

Introducing social networking technologies

People value different kinds of networking methods to establish knowledge-sharing relationships in the workplace. We can compare and contrast participating in networks based on social networking technologies with more traditional approaches to networking. Again, the intention of doing this is to provide managers with insights into why some people will respond positively to the introduction of social networking technologies, whilst others will choose not to get involved.

Social networking websites are perceived as having a range of benefits: low cost; access to large numbers of people; access to people with relevant knowledge. However, for many individuals the perceived risks outweigh these benefits: people don't want to do their networking in public; social norms have yet to develop for the use of networking sites; many people don't like to mix their personal and professional lives. People are resisting the use of networking websites for professional purposes because they fear for their reputations.

This separation by most people between social and professional networking mimics the traditional ways in which professional and social lives are kept apart. Many people are using business networking sites such as LinkedIn to mimic tradi-

Table 13.3: User modes for social media such as wikis and blogs

User Mode	Behaviour	Outcome
Abstainer	Doesn't use the wiki at all. Might give many reasons for not using the wiki and might make negative comments about the wiki.	Missed knowledge-sharing and relationship building opportunities for the individual and the community. Abstainer can feel marginalized and other users can feel rejected.
Consumer	Visits wiki and reads contributions. Might subscribe to email alerts and RSS feeds.	Develops own knowledge base. Absorbs culture and norms of wiki. Builds understanding of how the community thinks and operates. Presence gives other users the sense of a wider audience. Can be perceived as secretive by other users.
Respondent	Posts content in response to other users' contributions. Includes asking questions, seeking clarification, offering feedback, and making corrections to grammar and spelling.	Increased confidence in own ability to contribute. Builds sense of community by providing feedback to other users. Correcting grammar and spelling can be irritating to other users.
Creator	Creates new pages, edits existing pages, and comments on others' contributions. Shares new ideas, offers drafts for review, and elaborates on others' contributions.	Own ideas and opinions are "published". Adds to the knowledge base. New ideas tested and refined. Elaborating on others' contributions affirms other users' thinking and builds sense of community. Adding new ideas that are not obviously connected to existing threads of content can be irritating to other users.
Synthesizer	Organizes and analyses others' contributions. Restructures pages, spaces, and sites. Makes comparisons, critically evaluates, draws conclusions, summarizes, directs, prompts, encourages, and facilitates.	Increased confidence in own ability to facilitate. Vibrant, self-sustaining community. Over-synthesizing can be frustrating for other users if they can't follow changed structures and can't find existing content.

tional face-to-face business networking methods, and Facebook for keeping in touch with friends and family. A few people are starting to mix personal and professional networking and are becoming adept at choosing methods that match the context.

If organizations as well as individuals are to maximize the potential benefits and minimize the risks of using social networking technologies, practical responses might be as follows:

- Use internal networking sites instead of public ones. This is likely to work only in very large organizations.
- Ban the use of public social networking websites – but this is difficult to enforce, particularly as people can increasingly access them from mobile devices. This doesn't maximize potential benefits, it just minimizes risks!
- Provide training and guidance. For example, organizations could train employees in the use of social networking technologies in the same way they train employees in how to deal with the press. This would benefit both employees and the organization. Training could include, for example, how to manage privacy settings on Facebook and how to behave online so that networking enhances reputation.

Ultimately the choice of whether to mix personal and professional networking is down to individuals, but if organizations don't find an appropriate way to support the use of social networking technologies they will not get any of the potential benefits.

Real life stories

This case has been selected because it illustrates the experience of an organization in the early stages of introducing a wiki.[8]

Care services improvement partnership (CSIP)

CSIP was formed in 2005 to support positive changes in services and in the well-being of vulnerable people with health and social care needs. It was part of the Care Services Directorate at the Department of Health and had over 400 staff in eight regional development centres.

CSIP worked with the statutory, voluntary, and private sectors to make the best use of the full range of resources and expertise available to improve services. Its knowledge-related aims included sharing positive practice and learning about what works and what doesn't, passing on research findings to organizations to help them improve services, and encouraging organizations to work in partnership across all sectors.

The organization used social media in two ways. It used a wiki as a real-time, collaborative authoring tool, and ran an online knowledge community (the KC) where people could hold conversations, set up specialist groups, and share content that already existed such as documents, videos, and images.

The wiki was designed specifically to support and encourage collaboration. CSIP believed in "collaborative advantage" – that working with others was more effective at producing innovation than working alone. Of the initial 600 wiki users, about half were CSIP staff. Because the organization was geographically dispersed, the wiki was also designed to create a "sense of team". One of the benefits of the wiki was that users could see who was online, and the virtual presence of colleagues gave people the feeling of being part of a team.

Examples of collaborative authoring using the wiki ranged from production of a 12-chapter e-book to the creation of meeting agendas. The impetus for the book came from its authors, who wanted something more flexible than a central editor coordinating Word inputs from 12 people. Using the wiki meant that 12 authors could work on 12 chapters simultaneously. Everyone could see what everyone else was doing so all the authors acted as reviewers and gave instant feedback. The result was rapid completion of the book, and chapters that complemented each other.

Based on experience gained from supporting the take-up and use of the KC, CSIP identified two kinds of user that would be needed to make the wiki succeed. The first was people who would be prepared to adopt and engage with wiki technology and help other people to use it. These people already existed in the KC, and they were given the explicit role of promoting and supporting use of the wiki. The second was people with a broad set of relationships – described by CSIP as "network leads". These people were trained to use the wiki so they could bring their networks and networking skills to the new environment. CSIP saw the wiki as a tool that needed a network of people or a piece of collaborative work to activate it. In the case of the e-book, both the people and the work existed before the wiki was used.

Although there were administrators for the wiki, there was no hierarchy of editing rights for its content. At first there was a fear that the content might be low quality, but this was not the case in practice: standards for content and behaviour emerged. These standards were not written down or policed by administrators – they were owned and applied by users. An example was the way different groups of people produce collaboratively authored documents. Some groups had an initiating author who wrote content, then other users commented and discussed changes before they were incorporated. In other groups users contributed and edited directly.

CSIP found that trust between users contributed to their motivation to use the wiki. CSIP worked hard to set user expectations and build a sense of shared commitment. Factors that contributed to the success of the wiki were the fact that it could be accessed over the Internet and its ease of use.

Differences in professional status can hinder wiki use. CSIP found it difficult to get senior care service professionals to contribute, and also found that some people don't contribute because they don't think they can add value. The technology itself can also be off-putting to users who are not comfortable with IT tools.

The wiki was used very heavily, but not across all user groups. About 15% of users contributed every day. A further 20% of users contributed at least once a week, and the remaining 65% made minimal contributions. Frequent contributors were usually the people who had been using the wiki the longest. Users new to the technology or the network tended to lurk before they contributed. Over the 18 months the wiki had existed, CSIP found that users became more active with experience – but believed there is value even to users who don't actively contribute because the wiki is an effective way of transferring dynamic knowledge to passive consumers.

Although the wiki was designed for use by existing networks of people or to complete existing tasks that need collaboration, the way it was set up has created new connections because users can see what others are doing. The most active and dynamic groups seem to hold a magnetic attraction for others and pull in new users.

Future plans included enhancing users' online presence and creating forms of interaction – particularly verbal interaction – taking the wiki beyond the collaborative authoring of content.

Top tips

Develop a social networking technologies strategy to maximize the benefits and minimize the pitfalls of using social networking websites in the workplace. The Improvement and Development Agency draft social media and social networking strategy could be an example. This suggests:

- Exploring the use of social networking websites at a corporate level.
- Developing and adopting a social networking/media code of conduct and usage policy for staff.
- Supporting and developing training programmes for staff in using social networking/media tools and techniques.
- Opening up vital knowledge-sharing, Knowledge Management, and professional social networking websites through clearly defined web access policies.
- Recognizing and supporting the development and use of internal social networking sites (such as Yammer).
- Adopting a Creative Commons licence as the default intellectual property policy.
- Rewarding appropriate behaviour.

The research and the team involved

The study of social media in relation to collaboration within organizations and the adoption of social networking technologies was an ongoing area of investigation within the Henley KM Forum between 2007 and 2009. Three phases of research were carried out, all led by Dr Judy Payne of the Henley KM Forum. The research was intended to generate a better understanding of issues and possible practices. It was not intended to provide prescriptive recommendations for any organization.

The first phase looked specifically at the adoption of wikis and blogs in organizations and the behaviour patterns of individuals in response to this. Following a survey to identify suitable case study organizations, interviews were conducted in five organizations that had adopted wikis and blogs for different purposes.

In the second phase, the emphasis moved to the role social media played within a broad internal collaboration strategy, and in particular how and when to adopt certain technologies and approaches. Five cases were selected as examples of successful collaborative working and interviews carried out with those involved.

In the final phase, the contribution of social networking technologies to knowledge sharing in the workplace was studied through focus groups in three very different organizations. Individuals actively using social networking technology and those not using it were deliberately paired in constructing the focus groups. The most valuable methods for building knowledge-sharing relationships were identified and ranked.

The member co-champion of the first phase was Fred Child from Nationwide, of the second phase Susan Frost from the MOD and Adrian Malone from Faithful+Gould, and in the final phase, the co-champion was Michael Norton from the Improvement and Development Agency.

The working groups for the three phases of this research included representatives from the following KM Forum member organizations:

Audit Commission	AWE
Balfour Beatty	BERR
BG Group	The British Council
Cancer Research UK	CSIP
DFID	Faithful+Gould
GCHQ	Highways Agency
HMRC	HM Treasury
Hyder Consulting	IDeA
Information Centre for Health and Social Care	Lendlease
Mills & Reeve	MOD
MOD DGS & EDBS	MWH
Nationwide	NHS West Midlands RDC
Office of the Parliamentary and Health Services Ombudsman	PRP Architects
QinetiQ	RBS
Syngenta	Taylor Woodrow
Unisys	United Utilities
Vodafone	

together with invited associates: Geoff Parcell of Practical KM and Livio Hughes of Headshift.

Final reflections from the research

The way in which people use technology is influenced by existing social and organizational structures and by structures built into the technology. Through the use of the technology (which is a social interaction), new sources of structure emerge over time. Users' adoption of technology depends on many factors, including anxiety levels, personal innovativeness, and prior experience with technology. Their adaptation strategies can be viewed as choices based on a combination of personality and social structures in work and life environments. The widespread adoption of social software for personal use can be viewed as a series of structuring events in which people are challenging existing society structures on a global scale. Technologies present particular opportunities for structuring and therefore particular opportunities for change.[9]

Notes

1. See for example Hattori, R.A. and Lapidus, T. (2004) Collaboration, trust and innovative change, *Journal of Change Management*, 4(2), 97-104 and Huxham, C. (2003) Theorizing collaboration practice, *Public Management Review*, 5(3), 401-423.

2. The following definitions for "wiki" and "blog'" were copied from Wikipedia on 20 April 2007:

   A wiki is a website that allows visitors to add, remove, edit and change content, typically without the need for registration. It also allows for linking among any number of pages. This ease of interaction and operation makes a wiki an effective tool for mass collaborative authoring. The term wiki can also refer to the collaborative software itself (wiki engine) that facilitates the operation of such a site, or to specific wiki sites, including the computer science site WikiWikiWeb (the original wiki) and online encyclopedias such as Wikipedia.

   A blog (short for web log) is a user-generated website where entries are made in journal style and displayed in a reverse chronological order.

   Blogs provide commentary or news on a particular subject, such as food, politics, or local news; some function as more personal online diaries. A typical blog combines text, images, and links to other blogs, web pages, and other media related to its topic. The ability for readers to leave comments in an interactive format is an important part of most early blogs. Most blogs are primarily textual although some focus on photographs (photoblog), sketchblog, videos (vlog), or audio (podcasting), and are part of a wider network of social media.

   The term "blog" is a portmanteau, or, in other words, a blend of the words web and log (Web log). "Blog" can also be used as a verb, meaning to maintain or add content to a blog.

3. See for example Surowiecki, J. (2004) *The Wisdom of Crowds*, Random House. Thomas Malone, Rober Laubacher and Chrysanthos Dellarocas, wrote an excellent article called the "Collective intelligence genome" in *Sloan Management Review* (Spring 2010) that indicates when and how to use the potential of collective intelligence with respect to any proposed decision or project.

4. See for example: Granovetter, M. (1973) The strength of weak ties, *American Journal of Sociology*, 78(6), 1360-1380; Haythornthwaite, C. (2002) Strong, weak and latent ties and the impact of new media, *The Information Society*, 18, 385-401.

5. See for example: Adler, P. and Kwon, S.-W. (2002) Social capital: prospects for a new concept, *Academy of Management Review*, 27(1), 17-40; Nahapiet, J. and Ghoshal, S. (1998) Social capital, intellectual capital, and the organizational advantage, *Academy of Management Review*, 23(2), 242-266; Edelman, L.F., Bresnen, M., Newell, S., Scarborough, H., and Swan, J. (2004) The benefits and pitfalls of social capital: empirical evidence from two organizations in the United Kingdom, *British Journal of Management*, 15, S59-S69.

6. The individuals' anticipation of value is explored in the following papers:
   Nahapiet, J. and Ghoshal, S. (1998) Social capital, intellectual capital, and the organizational advantage, *Academy of Management Review*, 23(2), 242-266; Cross, R. and Prusak, L. (2002) The people who make organizations go – or stop, *Harvard Business Review*, 80(6), 104-111; Totterdell, P., Holman, D., and Hukin, A. (2008) Social networkers: measuring and examining individual differences in propensity to connect to others, *Social Networks*, 30, 283-296; Dennis, A.R., Fuller, R.M., and Valacich, J.S. (2008) Media, tasks, and communication processes: a theory of media synchronicity, *MIS Quarterly*, 32(3), 575-600; Yates, J., Orlikowski, W.J., and Jackson, A. (2008) The six key dimensions of understanding media, *MIT Sloan Management Review*, 49(2), 63-69; Barry, B. and Fulmer, I.S. (2004) The medium and the message: the adaptive use of communication media in dyadic influence, *Academy of Management Review*, 29(2), 272-292; Beaudry, A. and Pinsonneault, A. (2005) Understanding user responses to information technology: a coping model of user adaptation, *MIS Quarterly*, 29(3), 493-524.

7. The framework is based on ideas from the following two sources: Adler, P. and Borys, B. (1996) Two types of bureaucracy: enabling and coercive, *Administrative Science Quarterly*, 41(1), 61-89; Schein, E. (1965) *Organizational Psychology*, New York: Prentice Hall.

8. The case was prepared in 2007. Reproduced with permission.

9. You can explore these ideas further in the following two articles: Dennis, A.R., Wixom, B.H., and Vandenberg, R.J. (2001) Understanding fit and appropriation effects in group support systems via meta-analysis, *MIS Quarterly*, 25(2), 167-193; DeSanctis, G. and Poole, M.S. (1994) Capturing the complexity in advanced technology use: Adaptive Structuration Theory, *Organization Science*, 5(2), 121-147.

Chapter 14

Snapshot

How should your organization be structured and what kinds of relationships does it need to invest in to be effective in the global knowledge economy? The starting point is acknowledging and challenging the fundamental assumptions of the industrial era that govern the practices of most organizations today because these may limit an agile response to changing conditions. A set of tools and techniques are provided that managers can use to engage in different conversations about the future with other strategic thinkers in their organizations. This can stimulate new ideas about how to organize and manage more effectively.

A set of scenarios created using these techniques is included here to stimulate discussion. Through developing these scenarios, it became clear that new relationships and organizational structures would help respond to some of the drivers creating important shifts within the knowledge economy: shifts involving power, time, contradictory values, and new spaces and places where connections happen. Some of the understanding that was developed about key dimensions of these drivers is included here. However, the main objective is not to provide a comprehensive guide, but to encourage you to actively engage with the ongoing development of thinking and practice in areas that are crucial to success in the knowledge economy.

Why this matters

The organizations involved in this research coined the term "Transformational Knowledge Management" (TKM) to describe what is involved in re-thinking and re-framing an organization to be better adapted to the knowledge economy. TKM is about questioning the fundamental assumptions of the industrial era. This means examining the critical changes influencing business and organizational performance. The fundamental premise of TKM is that:

> To adapt successfully to the changing world, organizations, individuals and societies must transform the way they use knowledge.

One example of this new kind of thinking is re-evaluating how organizations relate to those who work for them. The majority of knowledge workers are still managed and rewarded in traditional ways, which bear little relation to the potential returns from their expertise or the contribution this makes to society. Employee engagement has become a hot topic in management journals, which is a clear acknowledgement of the need for new kinds of relationships in the workplace. Some thought provoking observations about employee engagement are:[1]

- 74% of organizations began formally focusing on employee engagement between 2000 and 2004.
- A 2003 Gallup survey in the US and Canada found that only 25% were actively engaged in their work, 56-60% were not engaged, and 17% were actively disengaged. The actively disengaged workers were estimated to cost US business between $270 and $343 billion per year due to low productivity.

It is difficult for organizations to keep up with the exponential growth of new knowledge. Talented individuals working anywhere in the world are gaining more democratic power through the internet and social technologies. Attracting and engaging their interest and passion is increasingly important to deliver the required levels of performance in a global economy. Additionally, although there are definite changes to the way work is organized, for example, flatter hierarchies, project-based working, virtual teams, communities, distributed leadership, tele-working, outsourcing, in-sourcing, partnering, clustering, corporate social responsibility, the sustainability agenda, and the life-long learning agenda to name but a few, only a minority of firms have mastered all of these in the integrated and holistic way which will contribute to real agility in a changing world.

What this means for your organization

Thinking about the future

It isn't possible to predict the future, but scenarios can help managers imagine possibilities and can act as the focus for discussion and new thinking to improve decision-making. Three scenarios were developed to describe possible futures in the knowledge economy. These scenarios were defined by two key dimensions:

1. The business assumptions on which the organization transacts with society: moving from the familiar industrial view in which largely tangible products are created and the primary focus is generating profit for shareholders, to one founded more on the application of knowledge for added value and to solve client and societal problems, and a recognition and acknowledgement of

the multiple stakeholders' expectations and their effect on organizational decisions.

2. The way individuals transact with organizations: here the move is from an "employment" model in which the basis for pay is largely related to time spent and the assumption is that financial reward is a prime motivator, to one in which the individual engages with work activity as a more self-driven, creative learning process and the assumption is that achievement and fulfilment are also primary motivators.

The interaction of these two dimensions defines the three potential future scenarios we envisaged for the continuing evolution of the knowledge economy. These are intended to challenge managers to think about their business models and how they want to relate to people within the organization, as well as to external stakeholders. Reflecting on the ideas captured within these scenarios is a useful starting point for transformational thinking about how to organize and manage. The scenarios are mapped against these dimensions in Figure 14.1.

Key characteristics of the three scenarios (called The Trust Conundrum; Suburbia – A Great Place to Be; and The State of Mine respectively) are also summarized in Table 14.1 and compared to the present day.

Through analysis, appreciative inquiry, and creativity processes, the three scenarios were visualized as maps (see Figure 14.2) and described through imagined motivational speeches of leaders of organizations within each scenario (Table 14.2).

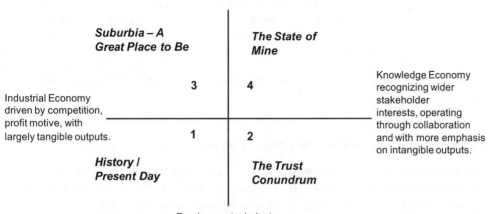

Figure 14.1: Boundaries for the scenarios

Table 14.1: Characteristics of the scenarios

Scenarios:	History/Present Day	The Trust Conundrum	Suburbia – A Great Place to Be	The State of Mine
Predominant model (Underpinning assumptions about value creation)	Industrial economy (Profit through competitive output of goods)	Knowledge economy (Satisfaction of stakeholder groups through differentiated output of beneficial services)	Industrial economy (Profit through collaborative stakeholder involvement so that knowledge enhances goods and services)	Knowledge economy (Differentiated value for individual societal stakeholders)
Approach to the relationship between the organization and individuals	Employment	Employment	Engagement	Engagement
Primary factor of production	Tangible goods and capital	Intangibles	Tangible goods and capital	Intangibles
Knowledge purpose	The efficient coordination of goods and activities to maximize return on investment. Knowledge not considered a major contributor to performance.	The coordination and integration of knowledge to satisfy broad stakeholder interests steadily and responsibly through organizational control.	Product innovation – to amplify the value delivered by tangible products through the addition of knowledge in order to grow the wealth of society.	Process innovation – to use knowledge to improve the quality of life fulfilment/ happiness for everyone involved.

Changing structures and relationships to be more agile

At the heart of these scenarios is a need to rethink who owns knowledge and how to reward knowledge sharing. There is also a need for new spaces and places to connect individuals and groups having specialist knowledge with organizational needs. Examples of this are already being created through the internet. Websites have been created to allow individuals and organizations to share problems in search of solutions, and to act as a market in which either party can sell solutions to unrecognized problems that they do not have the knowledge or capability to commercialize.

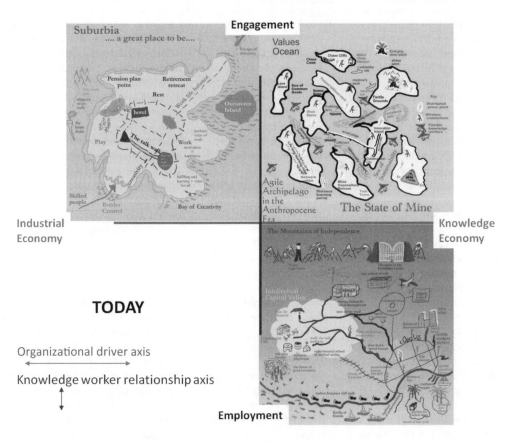

Figure 14.2: Visualizing the scenarios as maps

Various forms of networked organizational structures are increasingly evident. Often there is a kind of federalized infrastructure around which individuals and groups come together because they identify with some shared purpose. Usually the core is small and the network is distributed. Most are designed to encourage more agility, flexibility, and responsiveness. They all revolve around three basic criteria.

1. How centralized or distributed the power derived from critical knowledge is.
2. How they create a sufficiently strong identity to attract interested people to engage with their activities.
3. How permeable the boundary of the collective is and hence how open it is to external influence and change.

Each organization needs to consider how best to manage these dynamics depending on where the critical knowledge is based. For example:

Table 14.2: "Quest" stories: leaders' motivational speeches to employees within each scenario

Suburbia – A Great Place to Be	Trust Conundrum	The State of Mine
We know one size doesn't fit all! We are individuals with unique lives, interests, passions and ambitions that make us special and different. We respect and value your decision to work with this organization and trust you to efficiently and productively collaborate with us to keep this business at the front of the field. Continuing to deliver profitable growth is at the heart of our purpose. We will continue to be in the top 3 profitable businesses in each sector that we operate in. We know that achieving this relies on your passion and commitment. There are many ways for you to be part of our organization – whatever route you have chosen, you can tap into this passion and share it with us through our communities and the many technologies we have invested in to allow us to collaborate with each other across the world to deliver our purpose. We have learnt how to welcome good people to work with our organization in many ways. We have learnt how to truly collaborate in an open and honest way. We know that these both underpin our performance because the old adage "people are our greatest strength" really is true today. Delivering a high performing organization is why we have come together; what keeps us together is the respect we have for each other. This organization is a great place to be: to be yourself today, and to become what you want to be tomorrow.	We make a difference! What we are doing together is good for everyone because while we do good business, we know it also matters that we are good partners, employers, customers, and citizens of the world. We will continue to grow at the rate that allows us to do all these things well. We will learn how to be better at everything we do. We value thinking, reward effort, and because we care about doing the right thing and doing things right, Information and Knowledge Management are at the heart of our business as they provide the markers to keep us on track. We have learnt how to measure what we are doing to ensure that we are doing it well. We also know how to reward those who work hard for us. The old adage "what gets measures gets managed" has never been more true. We introduced the triple bottom line (financial, social, environmental) to show ourselves and the rest of the world that we are living up to our standards. As we go forward into our next challenge together, we hold to these ideals.	Here's what we stand for: we don't seek the easy way out and we do what is right to the best of our ability, through consultation, collaboration, and open-mindedness. Through your commitment to work with us in this way, we have become a lithe, innovative, and flexible organization that continues to perform well, whilst meeting our social and environmental responsibilities. We will continue to evolve this organization as opportunities present themselves, driven by our passions and our commitment to innovation and thinking in new ways. Learning is at the heart of how we will achieve this and we will continue to learn from each other and our partners – challenging ourselves to improve what we do and how we do it. We seek opportunities to share what we have learnt about how to be good corporate citizens, as well as to learn from others. Your passion and commitment continues to give us the energy to achieve this. We have learnt how to learn together: we know the importance of dialogue, reflection, and being open to different perspectives. We have also learnt that our shared values are what keep us together, helping us work through the complex challenges of today's world with confidence and integrity. We know how to use technology to keep us connected with each other – communication is at the heart of effective collaboration – and we are continuing to learn how to build and sustain effective relationships – with each other, with our partners, customers, and all those who care about the things we care about. We don't know what the future holds for us, but we are looking forward to the opportunities it will present to us. We hope you will choose to continue on the journey with us.

- If customers hold knowledge that adds value to a business offering and the customer base is widely distributed, then the organization needs to provide spaces and places, both physical and virtual, to interact with them. This allows the organization to understand and integrate what matters and is valued by these critical stakeholders.
- If the core knowledge that makes a difference sits with suppliers, or a network of knowledgeable individuals who can influence the success or failure of business intentions, then ways to negotiate within this network need to be developed.
- If the core knowledge and expertise is that of individuals employed by the organization, such as in consultancies or education institutions, then the focus must be on retaining access to critical talent.

It isn't difficult to imagine that eventually the definition of an organization and its boundary could become simply the knowledge/expertise assembled to achieve a specific purpose. But ultimately this is at the heart of agility. The most appropriate structure will be strongly dependent on the organization's purpose. For example, a hierarchical organization may still be best where security, stability, and repeatability remain of paramount importance. Even then, other values such as environmental concerns, ethics, community, and cultural values will still play a part in the process of attracting and holding people together. As ever, there will be trade-offs to balance conflicting needs and priorities.

In the public sector, accountability is highly valued and existing structures have been developed for that purpose. This means that distributing decision-making and harnessing the network effect can only be used to advantage in certain areas. External drivers have the most power to change public sector organizations. Typical drivers for change will often be legislation or new government agendas based on international or national economic issues. For example, the Freedom of Information Act in the UK (or equivalent elsewhere) has exerted pressure in many areas; the recent global financial crisis is another example.

One possible conclusion from all this is that it is inappropriate to look for one good or indeed one stable way of organizing. Instead, managers should adopt a contingent approach to structure based on how access to knowledge throughout the organization's whole internal and external network adds value (see Chapter 2). In a more open ecology, any organization must decide what knowledge it retains and protects internally and what it sells or shares externally, either to attract more interested parties to its knowledge activities, or to allow knowledge to be used more efficiently by others in combination with their expertise.

Creating an action plan

Starting a dialogue about the future

As we have emphasized, it isn't possible to predict the future, but it is possible to prepare for it by thinking more systematically about what might happen. By monitoring current trends and signals, internally consistent scenarios can be devised. These aren't predictions, but are a view of possible paths to the future. Their main benefit is that they challenge mindsets and create more alertness and responsiveness to changes in the environment, potentially improving decision-making.

A variety of approaches can be used together to stimulate and challenge thinking by the group of people involved in creating the scenarios. We used all of the techniques outlined in Table 14.3 in creating the scenarios described above. We recommend using these or similar techniques to create your own collective views of possible futures.

Table 14.3: Techniques to create conversations about the future

Technique	Brief description
Appreciative Planning and Action	This is an alternative to conventional problem solving, which tends to assume something is broken. In contrast, Appreciative Planning and Action involves a structured process of finding the best of what is currently happening, envisioning what could be, designing what should be, then planning what will be done to achieve that.[2] Within the envisioning stage (the "Dream" stage of the process), creative visualization can usefully involve workshop participants in creating an image of the desirable state of the organization. Collective exploration of the knowledge flows that would be happening in and around the organization in the future can then take place.
Ice breakers and creativity techniques	At the start of each workshop these can be helpful to encourage people to get to know each other, build trust between them, and help people get into the right frame of mind. Within a workshop process, exploring ideas through the use of metaphors, challenging perspectives on a topic, and using poetry to encourage different ways of thinking can stimulate people to shift their mindsets.[3]
Macro-environmental analysis	The wider environment (or macro-environment) includes factors that affect everyone trying to do business in the same place at the same time – such as laws, trading rules, social norms and patterns, new technology opportunities, and so on. Exactly what is included does depend to some extent on the industry or sector – it would be an unmanageably large task to include everything – however, it is important not to be too narrow in the way that you define the brief for this kind of analysis. Useful factors include sociological factors (demographics, life styles, social values etc.), political factors (the political trends and regulatory environment), economic factors, and technological factors.

continued on next page...

Table 14.3 - *Continued*

Technique	Brief description
Scenario analysis	Following the macro-environmental analysis and creative thinking about the future, the next step is to identify key dimensions that represent issues that seem to be crucial in determining how the future plays out. Typically 2–4 scenarios are created. Each is internally consistent and not a variation on the same theme. Best and worst scenarios or extreme worlds (where positives reinforce each other, as do the negatives) can be ways of shaping alternatives. Name the scenarios. Carry out further research to better understand the uncertainties and trends associated with each. Develop and evaluate strategic options for the business that would be appropriate within each scenario.[4]
Creative visualization through mapping	Change is commonly described as being "like a journey". This is a helpful metaphor and can be exploited to create a common language around the issues involved in moving towards each scenario. Journeys need maps, and maps are rich in potential imagery of the change process: rivers, roads, and mountain passes might be enablers of progress; cliffs, mountain ranges, deserts, and so on are barriers or difficulties to be overcome. Participants represent their change process, or target end-state, as a map of the imaginary and metaphorical terrain. In this technique, imagery is used creatively and imaginatively to produce a picture that represents change as if it were an actual journey – in the form of a map.[5]
Storytelling	Many approaches can be used to craft stories. A useful one involves crafting a Quest story – here a central character challenges the status quo, has setbacks, but ultimately succeeds. It is a plot of progress and adventure. The story is structured to include an emotionally charged story line, a view of how this is going to end up, and a narrative structure with a beginning, middle, and end.[6]

New ways of organizing and new types of relationships

The main action here is to start to follow current thinking about key topics and then to work with colleagues to develop innovative policies and practices which distinguish the organization to attract individuals, groups, and other organizations with valuable knowledge.

Employee engagement

Employee engagement initiatives in many organizations involve giving increased attention to creating effective dialogue, using storytelling to build deep under-standing and establish shared meaning around issues, and building an internal brand that people can identify with. These are very much in line with the kind of knowledge-based engagement that is potentially transformative.[1] Transformative engagement is about finding ways to positively engage people in learning and knowledge sharing so that there is deep attention to knowledge in the organization. This means that people care enough to find what they need to do their jobs well (a "pull" approach, rather than the organization "pushing" knowledge to them), and they care enough to make available what they have learnt so that other people can do their jobs well (a collaborative and knowledge-sharing mindset prevails). Whatever the organizing structure, there need to be effective channels for knowledge to flow. When this kind of structure and culture exist, the organization becomes a place where people collectively know what is known, and can talk to customers based on this knowledge. New opportunities are sought based on the knowledge, playing to the strengths of the organization rather than trying to fit people to what comes along. Individuals interested in developing their careers in these knowledge areas are attracted towards the organization so the knowledge is refined and developed.

Talent management

The changing nature of work emphasizes jobs involving complex interactions that require a high level of judgement. Generating value from the knowledge available to the organization means placing learning and knowledge creation at the heart of designing a sustainable organization. Getting the best from individuals associated with the organization means giving them opportunities to access the knowledge they need to do their jobs well, as well as to share what they know and have learnt. Retaining and developing knowledge, and more specifically expertise, is now high on the agenda of many organizations.[7]

Organizing for collaboration

The best way to describe the kind of organization that is needed is an "ecology": an evolving, dynamic, interactive, mutually dependent mix of individuals, small groups, large organizations, and partnerships.

Knowledge flows (rather than stocks) generate value in organizations. Collaboration between those involved with the organization is the mechanism by which knowledge flows and is combined in productive or creative ways. In virtual interactions and/or short-lived teams, collaboration can be effective only if the parties are willing to open up to one another and cooperate to achieve a goal, carry out a task, and solve problems. Developing an ecology in which there is a culture that enables trusting relationships to be established virtually and with collaborative partners is essential in a knowledge economy.

In the public sector, long-term information often needs to be maintained. This means that a strong and stable infrastructure is needed to support this, limiting the flexibility in structures that can be adopted. Good Information Management always underpins good Knowledge Management, and this is even more the case in the public sector, organizations owning long-life capital assets, or those whose activities potentially lead to long-term liabilities.

The social context for knowledge work

Knowledge-intensive work requires highly educated workers. Countries that can attract such workers have an advantage. Factors that attract such people include the quality of living, cultural environment, and services. Maintaining high standards of education requires political will and investment. This is an emerging field. There are various definitions of a knowledge city including: "a city that is purposefully designed to encourage the nurturing of knowledge". A paradox of the knowledge economy is that firms have to become more flexible with the virtual abolition of frontiers and the internationalization of the economy, yet "they are ever more tied to a location because of dependence on highly educated staff and the integration into local networks".[8]

Real life stories

New organizational forms – the leaderful organization

Karl-Erik Sveiby, Professor of Knowledge Management at Hanken Business School in Helsinki, has studied the decision-making processes in the most sustainable society on Earth. By working with an Aboriginal cultural custodian from the Nhunghaburra people, he has crafted the concept of "leaderful" organizations.[9] The tribe has a non-hierarchical view of leadership in which knowledgeable individuals work within a self-sustaining ecology. Wisdom is developed through mentoring and a commitment to continuous questioning and re-learning – all rooted in a deep understanding of the web of connections between knowledge, appropriate action, and the knock-on impact on an entire ecology. Consequently, each person takes on a leadership role when their knowledge and expertise is needed, not because they have a higher status or more power.

Although the idea of a leaderful organization might seem impractical, there are successful examples in today's commercial world. The Dutch finance consultancy company Finext has chosen to use a unique organizational structure that allows adaptation and improvisation without direct decision-maker control. The firm itself says: "Our distinctive organizational structure offers more than 150 professionals all possibilities to make the most of themselves. This leads to involvement, creativity and entrepreneurship which we quickly relay to the heart of the matter." The firm operates as a set of self-managed teams which self-organize around products or markets according to their interest. Finext has been in existence for more than a decade. There are no senior managers to direct and coordinate resources; instead a rotating leadership approach is used: a facilitator function responsible for paying special attention to group dynamics. Knowledge-sharing meetings are an essential component of how the organization functions. Decisions are taken with care at every level, and the result is an organization that has prospered without a central decision-making body despite an economic recession.

Networked organizations – Collaborative Innovation Networks

To kick start successful and relevant innovation, some organizations have turned to COINs – COllaborative Innovation Networks which tap into what has been called swarm creativity.[10] Swarm creativity draws on lessons from ant and bee colonies, which can adapt and thrive by acting together without everyone always deliberately working in harmony, and without any particular individual having a disproportionate influence on the way the collective responds.

In essence, COINs are a swarm of highly motivated and passionate people who care about a cause, and coalesce to act independently, without a predetermined end game. In a high trust environment, governed by few rules, they collaborate to uncover and realize new ways of doing business. They bring massive creativity because their divergent views and expertise constantly confront existing assumptions. Yet, they maintain coherence by adhering strictly to a simple set of rules about respect, courtesy, mutual help, and concern for others' time and energy.

COINs have gained momentum in recent years as the internet began to break down barriers to participation and to increase access to different perspectives. This has produced some extraordinary and unexpected outcomes. For example, they have been a source of real discontinuity in certain industries. Linux is a familiar example of a COIN that has undermined monopolies in the software industry. The Daimler Chrysler Global Procurement and Supply COIN, which set out simply to leverage e-business technologies in the automotive supply chain, ultimately created an online marketplace – a worldwide automotive exchange that has competitors like Ford, General Motors, Renault, and Nissan contributing as major partners.

New forms of relationships giving access to new sources of knowledge

In the extreme, the permeability of organizational boundaries to knowledge flows is completely changed to allow the free-flow of knowledge. IBM did this when they made a conscious decision to change their business model and become part of the Open Source movement.[11] McKenzie (2007) writes:

> For the price of sacrificing bureaucracy, and internal sign offs, IBM were able to ratchet up $100 million development costs into $1 billion of technical advances, just by belonging [to the Open Source Movement]. By releasing code they were also able to change the focus of their competitive orientation from operating systems to added value applications, integration and services. This gave IBM a viable platform uniquely tailored to their needs, infinitely flexible and constantly developing for 20% of the cost of a proprietary operating system. They gained agility, cost savings and innovation. Linux benefited too

- from the reflected reputation of Big Blue's reliability, access to more expert minds and momentum for the move to open source acceptance. Increasing returns for both.

In contrast, where firms have both tangible and intangible elements to their products then there is likely always to be a need for some degree of control over the permeability of the boundary of the organization to knowledge flows to be retained.

Examples of organizations who have adopted a hybrid approach to knowledge-sharing relationships in different industries are:[12]

- Toyota and in particular the partnership between GM and Toyota formulated as NUMMI. As a result of the Toyota quality success and a challenge from GM to incorporate their way of working into a more individualistic culture in an under-performing plant of GM, the internal systems and processes were redesigned to harness the distributed knowledge of all company workers to focus more on learning than compliance.
- eBay and Amazon have opened up their boundaries through the web. They actively encourage customer preferences and opinions to define what is offered to them as a priority based on prior searches and purchases, as well as influencing what or where others buy based on reviews and collective valuation of the best experience. However, they centralize things such as payment mechanisms, where the value of security overrides the value of openness and choice.

Top tips

Developing the kind of organization that can match available knowledge with potential need means learning how to use:

- Large scale facilitation techniques that allow many different stakeholders to participate constructively and to collaborate effectively.
- Open business models that engage consumers of knowledge with the producers of knowledge.
- Techniques that identify and motivate key individuals and groups that act as knowledge catalysts, driving the organization forward and creating a momentum behind ideas.

Engaging the passion of knowledgeable individuals is essential to attract talented people to contribute to the organization. Communities of practice are known to be most successful when they emerge from passion and real interest. But most of all, engagement is about knowing what matters to individuals and why it matters to them. This involves integrating widespread dialogue and a different kind of facilitation that challenges assumptions and collectively explores values into much more sophisticated communications programmes.

The research and the team involved

This research was carried out in two phases between September 2006 and December 2007.

In the first phase, an expert panel of 18 experienced KM practitioners and academics from a range of organizations (UK public sector, not-for-profit, and large private sector with significant operations in the UK) was assembled from members of the Henley KM Forum. In a series of facilitated workshops over six months, these experts collaborated in an interactive research process. The aim was to develop three scenarios that would help explain the routes organizations might take in response to the challenges of the knowledge economy. The workshops used a combination of creative thinking techniques and structured methods of inquiry to combine literature and experience into credible pictures of the future.

In the second phase, the group developed their understanding of drivers of value and the coordination mechanisms needed to organize in the knowledge economy. The starting point was issues that had been identified as influential within the development of the scenarios. Expert speakers were invited to share current thinking with the group, in addition to further literature-based research.

The two phases of the project were led by Professor Jane McKenzie and Dr Christine van Winkelen of Henley Business School, together with Robert Taylor from Unisys, the member co-champion. The research was intended to stimulate thinking and develop understanding. It was not intended to generate prescriptive recommendations for any particular organization.

The working group consisted of representatives from the following organizations:

Cancer Research UK   *Defence Procurement Agency*
Energy Saving Trust   *LexisNexis Butterworths*
MOD   *MWH*
National School of Government *Nationwide*
QinetiQ   *Taylor Woodrow*
Unisys

together with invited associates: Richard Potter (previously from QinetiQ), Peter Hall (previously from Orange), David Gurteen (Gurteen Knowledge), and Andrew Sinclair-Thomson (previously from DTI).

Final reflections from the research

Being a manager or leader who can lead the kind of transformational change that is needed to truly be effective in the knowledge economy means developing new ways of thinking. In particular it means getting better at handling uncertainty, ambiguity, and change. This involves not establishing the decision parameters of problems too quickly just to avoid the psychological discomfort that comes from uncertainty, but adopting more fluid sense-making processes that lead to alternative ways of looking at the issue. It also means accepting and working with contradiction as a mechanism for creativity. Overall it means not feeling threatened by making choices that satisfy more stakeholders.

Notes

1. Useful sources to explore in relation to employee engagement are:
   Employee Engagement: How to build a high-performance workforce, Executive summary available from the research reports area of http://www.melcrum.com; Robinson D., Perryman S., and Hayday S., *The Drivers of Employee Engagement,* IES Report 408, April 2004, http://www.employment-studies.co.uk/summary/summary.php?id=408
   Reflections on Employee Engagement, UK's Chartered Institute of Personnel and Development, CIPD Report, 2006 http://www.cipd.co.uk/subjects/empreltns/general/_rflempngmt.htm
   Working Life: Employee Attitudes and Engagement 2006, Katie Truss, CIPD, http://www.cipd.co.uk.
2. Find out more about Appreciative Planning and Action from http://appreciativeinquiry.case.edu.
3. Explore new creativity techniques, for example Using Ice Breakers in Meetings, http://nonprofitmanagement.suite101.com/article.cfm/using_meeting_ice_breakers and Poetry in the Workplace: "What poetry brings to business" by Clare Morgan, University of Michigan, 2010.
4. More information about scenario planning can be found at: Schoemaker, P.J.H., When and how to use scenario planning (1991) *Journal of Forecasting,* 10, 549-564; Schoemaker, P.J.H., Scenario planning: a tool for strategic thinking (1995) *Sloan Management Review,* 36(2), 25-40; http://www.ncvo-vol.org.uk/uploadedFiles/NCVO/Publications/Publications_Catalogue/Sector_Research/Picture_This.pdf.
5. For examples of the use of maps to describe business issues see, http://www.companymap.com and Crainer & Dearlove (2005) *The Business World Atlas,* Meteor Press, which use a technique called "Associative Cartography".
6. To find out more about this approach to crafting stories see Downing, S.J. (1997) Learning the plot: emotional momentum in search of dramatic logic, *Management Learning,* 28(1), 27-44 and Downing, S.J. (2006) Managing a merger? Don't lose the plot, *Health Service Journal,* 2nd November, 21-22.
7. Find out more about talent management from Cheese, P., Thomas, R.J. and Craig, E. (2007) *The Talent Powered Organization: Strategies for Globalization, Talent Management and High Performance,* Kogan Page Ltd; Ready D. and Conger J. (2007) Make your company a talent factory, *Harvard Business Review,* June, 69-77; "The battle for brainpower: a survey of talent," *The Economist,* Survey, 7 October 2006; and track further developments at The Work Foundation: http://www.theworkfoundation.com.

8. Find out more about the social context for knowledge work: Bounfour, A. and Edvinsson, L. (2006) *Intellectual Capital for Communities: Nations, Regions and Cities*, Elsevier; Carrillo, F.J. (2006) *Knowledge Cities: Approaches, Experiences and Perspectives*, Butterworth Heinemann; van den Berg, L., Pol, P.M.J., van Winden, W., and Woets, P. (2005) *European Cities in the Knowledge Economy*, Ashgate. Various ideapolis reports from the Work Foundation, including Williams, L., Lee, N., Jones, A. and Coats, D. (2006) "Creating an ideapolis: the case study of Manchester", http://www.theworkfoundation.com/products/publications/azpublications/creatinganideopolis.aspx.

9. Read more about this in Sveiby, K.-E. (2006) *Treading Lightly: The Hidden Wisdom of the World's Oldest People*, Australia: Allen & Unwin.

10. Gloor, P. (2006) *Swarm Creativity: Competitive Advantage through Collaborative Innovation Networks*, Oxford University Press.

11. See for example Tapscott, D. and Williams, A.D. (2006) *Wikinomics. How Mass Collaboration Changes Everything*, New York: Portfolio, A member of Penguin USA; also McKenzie, J. (2007) *Making Connections and Embracing Contradictions: A Key to the Management Enigma?* Inaugural Lecture, Henley on Thames, Henley Management College.

12. Toyota and GM: see for example Adler, P.S. and Cole, R.E. (1993) Designed for Learning – A Tale of Two Auto Plants, *Sloan Management Review*, 34, 85-94; also Chesborough, H. (2006) *Open Business Models. How to Thrive in the New Innovation Landscapes*, Boston MA: Harvard Business School Press.

    eBay and Amazon: see for example Brafman, O. and Beckstrom, R.A. (2006) *The Starfish and the Spider: The Unstoppable Power of Leaderless Organizations*, London: Portfolio, Penguin.

Section VI

Make change stick

What makes change so difficult?

Evolution and change is a natural part of any ecology, but it always involves loss and learning. As human beings, our identity and mental view of the world is wrapped up in our past experience. In a work context, when what we have known has brought us success, it may seem hard to give up a track record of reward for the uncertainty of something new.

Simply telling people what to do is not enough for them to change. People may have to re-evaluate many deep seated personal assumptions, beliefs, values, as well as relinquish hard-won knowledge, expertise, and familiar behaviours to adapt to a new environment. Convincing people that the journey will be worthwhile and beneficial needs careful thought about how to approach them in terms that are meaningful for them. Managers need to communicate why and how change might happen in a way that people can easily absorb and which resonates with what matters to them. Conversations about change are either places where people can make the necessary mental adjustments, or where the fear of loss and learning are reinforced to the point of generating resistance. Language is the medium of conversation, and generally language is imprecise and open to interpretation. This is due to past experience, and mental and cultural filters.

Spreading change across organizations involves rethinking long-held assumptions about priorities and the way to manage assets. It is even harder to shift the collective mind of the organization away from the dominant logic that has developed over time than it is to shift individual beliefs. As we saw in Chapter 14, moving from a tangible industrial economy to a more intangible knowledge-based business needs changes in organizational behaviour, as well as the ability to flex and adapt the core knowledge that makes the firm distinctive. This often means significant collective re-learning. Managers have tools that they can use to shift collective behaviours, such as performance management systems, training and development, or even selection and reward, but fundamental beliefs and assumptions may drag the change back into well-trodden patterns of behaviour unless there is sustained effort.

How can you make it easier for people to accept change?

In helping people to accept change, a good first step is to win some allies. Engage the enthusiasts: help them understand the sort of skills and behaviours associated with effective knowledge-related initiatives. They can then become advocates to support the spread of good practice by modelling good behaviour, coaching others, encouraging implementation of knowledge initiatives, and generally infecting others with their enthusiasm and abilities. For knowledge sharing to become a good habit, it is helpful to embed the principles in different human resource development and management processes too, so that there are other triggers to spread the change in behaviour.

However, we also know that processes and procedures, even if ostensibly followed to the letter, may not be followed in spirit. They are open to interpretation and can become a nominal tick box exercise if people do not really understand or buy into the purpose and benefits of compliance. This limits the potential for creating the kind of engagement needed to exchange more complex and difficult to articulate knowledge. Understanding what motivates and drives people's behaviours, (whether in terms of the impact of personality on willingness to share knowledge, the cultural predispositions that shape instinctive responses to change initiatives, or the mental filters, biases, and interpretations we unconsciously apply to communications) allows you to have greater influence as you try to embed better practices into the daily pattern of operations.

In this section, there are several checklists and frameworks to help you influence others more effectively. These include ways to prepare for and reflect on conversations and communications as you try to implement knowledge related initiatives. By becoming more aware of the often unspoken inhibitors to change that are rooted in the inner workings of our minds, it is possible to become more convincing in your communications, more effective in conversations, and more influential in achieving the desired outcomes for knowledge initiatives.

If you work internationally, this also requires a heightened sensitivity to different preferences that are imbued into nationalities as a result of formative experiences and what is considered accepted behaviour within their societies.

The best way to raise your awareness and sensitivity to the impact of changes that you are instigating is through honest and disciplined reflection. This can be done alone or in a structured conversation with a coach or mentor. Such reflection can take place before an event: reflect forward on what might happen, how you might respond, what you might do instinctively, and whether that is right for a situation. Alternatively you can reflect after the event: look back on what happened and review how you actually reacted, what you might do differently next time. Over time, with the help of the sort of structured frameworks offered in this section, the discipline of reflecting will become more instinctive; it will require less conscious effort and you will begin to reflect in the midst of action and adjust your behaviour, so that continuous learning becomes a natural part of the process of connecting with others.

Key questions to ask yourself

As you start to use the ideas in the next four chapters ask:

- When you start a project, plan an initiative, or need to make a decision, where should you build in time for structured reflection to improve the process of engaging others with your ideas, expectations, and requirements?
- Who will be your natural allies, who will spread enthusiasm and active engagement with knowledge-sharing initiatives? How can you help them to develop their ability to lead local and international conversations and create effective communications and convincing arguments?
- When trying to roll out knowledge-related activities across cultures what do you need to know about local cultural preferences in order to achieve global consistency and local acceptance?

Chapter 15

Snapshot

A deep understanding of what "knowledge-sharing behaviour" really involves allows managers to select people for important roles and to design initiatives to encourage positive behaviours. The Henley Knowledge Sharing Behaviours model has been translated into a competency framework that provides a useful reference point for many development initiatives. Awareness of the elements of the model can support processes such as performance management and leadership development within the organization, ideally through integration into existing competency frameworks. When individuals are aware of these competencies, it can also help them focus self-development activities. Understanding the link to personality is also useful because in general it is easier for people to change their behaviour in a way that is in tune with their preferred style. It is also important to recognize that behaviours that may "come naturally" to some people may be difficult for others to sustain.

In addition to encouraging widespread knowledge-sharing behaviours, in most organizations the team dedicated to planning and implementing knowledge-related initiatives is very small. Those responsible for improving the use of knowledge in the organization need to engage allies and encourage local knowledge activists. There are nine characteristics of an effective knowledge activist, which are essentially a refined application of the broader knowledge-sharing behaviours competency model. The characteristics have been used to prepare a framework to help managers understand what to look for in their knowledge activists and how to develop these people.

Why this matters

Knowledge-sharing behaviours affect business capability

From collaborative product development through to factory floor process improvement, the ability to share knowledge effectively – with supply chain partners and customers, or among employees – is of critical importance. Increasingly, it is businesses' ability to unlock the information held in people's heads that makes the difference between success and failure, with failure, in some cases, impacting on corporate survival itself. But even as growing numbers of managers within organizations come to understand this, they face an awkward dilemma: knowing that knowledge sharing is important is one thing, and knowing how best to actually share that knowledge quite another.

The bottom line is that by understanding what influences knowledge-sharing behaviour, managers can improve the way knowledge is shared within their business. The three fundamentals of effective knowledge-sharing behaviour are: Building Relationships, Building a Knowledge Base, and Building Knowledge Value. These are underpinned by seven knowledge-sharing "competencies": personal behavioural characteristics that impact on how well (or not) knowledge is shared. Understanding, recognizing, and developing these competencies is vital for improving the way that knowledge sharing takes place within organizations.

Knowledge activists encourage knowledge sharing

Knowledge Management is not something that can be "done" to an organization by a knowledge manager – all managers and employees have a role to play in managing the organization's knowledge effectively. Knowledge sharing is a key aspect of that role. Most organizations only have a very small team or even a single manager dedicated to thinking about knowledge issues. Other people in the organization must be engaged as allies and local knowledge activists in order to get things done.

> "Knowledge activism should be a characteristic of all good managers. Stressing the need to be active, rather than simply using the label 'activist' helps to achieve this."
>
> *Chris Collison, Director, Knowledgeable Ltd*

In any business where a focus on knowledge can contribute to improved effectiveness, you'll find people playing the role of "knowledge activists". They are people who see the value of knowledge to the organization and who support the implementation of knowledge-related initiatives. As such, they play a vital role: encouraging knowledge activities, participating in projects to create and share new knowledge, and connecting seekers of knowledge with reliable sources. This raises the question: "what characteristics and skills make knowledge activists effective?"

What this means for your organization

Competencies underlying knowledge-sharing behaviour

The Henley Knowledge Sharing Behaviours model has three key components: Building Relationships, Building a Knowledge Base, and Building Knowledge Value.

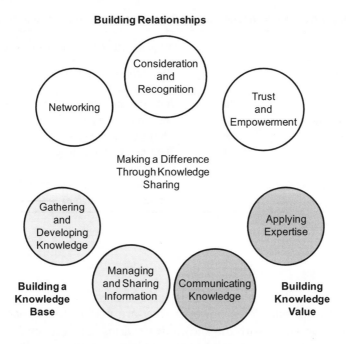

Figure 15.1: Knowledge-Sharing Behaviour competency framework

"In building a knowledge base, less is often more: I see a lot of effort wasted in archiving information – often of poor quality – that will never be used."

Robert Taylor, Business Excellence Director, Unisys

The logic is that first, better relationships contribute towards greater sharing; second, the more in-depth and detailed a body of knowledge is, the more likely it is to be of business value; third, that its value will be enhanced by more effectively organizing its capture, storage, and sharing. Each component has more than one competency. Figure 15.1 shows how the competencies link to the components.

Characteristics and skills of effective knowledge activists

Knowledge activists are allies who promote the implementation of knowledge-related initiatives. They have some local responsibility for knowledge activities, but may have other responsibilities as well. They engage in relationships, participate in projects, and create new knowledge. They also connect seekers with sources of knowledge and develop these relationships. Some knowledge activists are experts in a particular field, others have a broader understanding of the business. The three broad categories of effective knowledge-sharing behaviour (Building Relationships, Building a Knowledge Base, and Building Knowledge Value) describe

Table 15.1: Applying the Knowledge-Sharing Behaviours framework to knowledge activists

		Characteristics and skills of knowledge activists
Building Relationships	✻	Developing relationships
	✻	Internal belief
	✻	Cultural alignment with organization
Building a Knowledge Base	✳	Action-oriented
	✻	Project management
	✳	Information brokering
	✳	Creativity
Building Knowledge Value	✻	Dialogue and communication
	✻	Credibility through experience

✻ = Strong, ✳ = Moderate.

their characteristics and skills, however they are manifested in particular ways. These aren't inconsistent with the knowledge-sharing competency framework, just a specific interpretation for these key individuals.

There are nine typical characteristics and skills of effective knowledge activists. Some of the characteristics and skills are more pervasive than others. Each is therefore described as *strong* or *moderate* in Table 15.1.

In addition to these characteristics and "soft" skills of activists, there is also a whole raft of harder, "technical" skills that these people might need: content architecture, database management, IT application skills and so on – depending on your organization's knowledge strategy.

Creating an action plan

Using the Knowledge-Sharing Behaviours competency framework

> "Building high-quality relationships is critical, because it's through relationships that knowledge flows, and value is created."
>
> *Debbie Lawley, Director, Willow Transformations (formerly at Orange)*

The development of the Henley Knowledge-Sharing Behaviours model into a detailed competency framework is provided in Tables 15.2-15.8. These include what each of the seven components involves, how certain personality traits may influence it, and what someone can do to develop it. You can integrate this into your own organization's competency framework, or use it as a standalone element within other initiatives that would benefit from better knowledge sharing.

Table 15.2: Building relationships - networking

What the competency is	What it is not	The influence of personality
Seeking contacts and building relationships with others. Knowing who has specific skills, experience, and knowledge and how to contact them. Involving people with relevant expertise in projects and activities.	Wasting time "re-inventing the wheel" by not involving the right people. Focusing solely on your own area of the business and treating your own department as an island to be defended. Limiting the knowledge base that you draw on to make decisions. Working separately from others and/or competing with them.	People who are ambitious and concerned about things going well and about how others see them, place more importance on networking as a matter of course. Those who set themselves less ambitious work targets or don't worry about the views of others may need to pay more attention to developing this competency.

Developing the competency

Identify key people and key teams across the business who you need to cooperate with. Arrange meetings and discuss how you can work together more effectively.

Maintain a list of people who can provide you with assistance. Record their areas of expertise and contact details. Alternatively, use your organization's skills database if it exists – and keep your own record updated in the system.

Participate in appropriate forums and professional bodies.

Contact people in your network regularly to foster mutually beneficial relationships. Don't just contact them when you need something.

Selecting for the characteristics and skills of knowledge activists

To help you identify knowledge activists who can help drive change initiatives, use Table 15.9 to decide what to look out for, or what to design into recruitment criteria.

Real life stories

Using the Knowledge-Sharing Behaviours competency framework

In this section, two organizations explain how they intended to use the framework[1] following a survey of knowledge-sharing behaviour competency levels (including the perceived value of that competency) across several teams.

Table 15.3: Building relationships – consideration and recognition

What the competency is	What it is not	The influence of personality
Listening attentively to the contributions of others. Reacting to others with consideration and tolerance. Building rapport and motivating others through recognition, encouragement, and reward.	Forcing your own opinions onto other people. Ignoring input from others. Making assumptions about what others are thinking. Claiming the glory for yourself and not acknowledging the wider contribution.	People who are keen to achieve high standards, are outgoing and comfortable in social situations, and are keen to present a positive image of themselves may find it easier to build rapport with others and recognize the contribution that other people can make. A pragmatic and common sense approach to life can also make it more likely that someone will be tolerant and considerate to others. In contrast, people who set less ambitious targets, are reserved, self-critical, and/or have a particularly conceptual view of the world, may need to pay more attention to developing this competency.

Developing this competency

When a colleague is communicating an idea, listen and ensure that you understand what he or she has said before you respond. Check understanding by asking questions or by reflecting back what has been said by paraphrasing the key points of what you have heard.

Try to understand another's point of view based on who they are, the likely pressures they are under, and their goals.

Be objective and non-judgemental when interacting with others. Confront the issues, not the person.

Use people's names when you speak to them.

Mobile Phone Operator

Employees of this Mobile Phone Operator scored higher than the average in the competency areas of *Communicating knowledge* and *Applying expertise*. The internal culture had tended to foster and respect clear communication. This was very much in line with the company's brand approach which aimed to clearly and simply convey products and service offerings to customers. It spilled over into the way

Table 15.4: Building relationships – trust and empowerment

What the competency is	What it is not	The influence of personality
Providing others with the knowledge, tools, and other resources to complete a task successfully. Considering knowledge as a resource to be used for the "common good". Openly sharing knowledge that others may find useful or relevant. Treating others in a fair and consistent manner.	Preventing others from making significant contributions. Keeping key pieces of information to oneself. Using information as power. Ignoring opportunities to coach or provide feedback to others.	People who are keen to meet high standards, are confident with others and are supportive and tolerant of the needs of others are more likely to act fairly and give people the authority and resources they need to succeed. In contrast, those who set less ambitious targets, don't necessarily worry about how things will turn out, and prefer their own company may be less interested in the needs of others and may need to focus on developing this competency.

Developing this competency
Actively seek to receive feedback about your behaviour with regard to knowledge sharing.
Improve the level of genuine and honest feedback you provide to others.
Find ways to coach others in real time. Offer to act as a coach for a particularly stressful event by giving the opportunity to rehearse before and debrief afterwards.
Identify tasks that would be challenging to others and delegate to them where appropriate.
Set the terms of reference for work and not the detailed plan.

the company worked internally, emphasizing the use of simple, friendly language that makes the point. Being practical, having valuable competence in applying and achieving results has been very important to them.

Increasingly, *Managing and sharing information* had become more important in the organization. This was expressed in the comparatively higher than average rating given to the importance of this competency. As a large company with operations in many different countries, understanding what is known within the organization had becoming a strategic issue. Many senior level messages highlighted the need to share and learn from each other.

The Mobile Phone Operator intended to use the competency framework in three ways:

Table 15.5: Building a knowledge base - gathering and developing knowledge

What the competency is	What it is not	The influence of personality
Continual regard to personal and professional development. Working to build on previous experience. Seeking out ideas and opinions from other people. Aiming to keep your own knowledge up-to-date.	Failing to take advantage of knowledge and skills across your organization. Ignoring coaching or feedback opportunities. Disregarding own development needs. Alienating yourself from others at work.	People who are ambitious, keen to achieve high standards, and are outgoing and interested in other people may find it easier to develop and keep their knowledge up-to-date. In contrast, people who set themselves lower targets and are relatively less comfortable with and interested in other people, may need to focus on developing this competency.

Developing this competency

Always be willing to learn. Encourage your colleagues to express ideas to you openly.

Find a mentor with whom you can regularly review progress and who will provide constructive feedback and give coaching where necessary.

Find every opportunity to discuss your work with others (other teams, senior managers, etc.) and to find out about their projects.

Organize lunch meetings where individuals can share best practice on key work issues.

Visit leading edge firms and transfer ideas back to your team.

Organizational competency development: The internal culture programme includes leadership development. The focus would be on understanding the important implications of this work for self-development in leaders.

Aid to selecting facilitators and community leaders: The full set of personality traits that have been linked to knowledge-sharing behaviours include imagination, achieving, and gregariousness. Understanding these relationships is very helpful for those who have the responsibility for selecting knowledge leaders in the company.

Trouble shooting in collaborative situations: The set of seven knowledge-sharing behaviours, together with the definitions of what competency means and does not mean, would be used within communities and other collaborative contexts when it was felt that improvement is needed. It would act as a coaching aid, helping groups to understand what good knowledge sharing looks like and to pinpoint areas for development.

Table 15.6: Building a knowledge base – managing and sharing information

What the competency is	What it is not	The influence of personality
Creating and supporting systems and procedures that individuals can use to file, catalogue, and share knowledge.	Waiting to be asked for information rather than offering it to others.	People who are ambitious and keen to meet high standards may tend to use and
Making effective use of available media to share knowledge across the organization.	Adopting a silo mentality within teams and departments.	encourage others to use Knowledge Management and Information Management systems in the organization.
Encouraging others to use knowledge-sharing systems.	Taking a back seat in discussions rather than offering relevant knowledge or the benefit of your experience.	In contrast, people who are less ambitious and set lower targets and/or place their priorities outside of work may need to pay more
Encouraging communication and collaboration.	Failing to keep everyone up-to-date with progress.	attention to developing this competency.

Developing the competency

Remember that sharing your information might save someone "re-inventing the wheel".

Ensure that you have access to, and are able to use the systems available for sharing knowledge in the organization.

When receiving new information, ask who else would be interested or who needs it.

Volunteer knowledge, views, and opinions before being asked.

Share what you have learnt from your experiences – successes and failures.

Participate actively in communities relating to your work practices.

Thames Water

> "It's important to recognize that knowledge matters: until you do that, you haven't left the starting block. Some organizations recognize this – but many don't."
>
> *Peter Hemmings, Principal Consultant, KN Associates*
> *(formerly at Thames Water)*

Thames Water is part of one of the world's largest water enterprises operating actively around the globe. The KM Programme had been running for two years at the time this survey was completed and had developed a Balanced Scorecard approach to monitoring and measuring progress in key areas, linked to the KM Strategy goals based around four strategic building blocks:

- Making Knowledge Visible
- Building Knowledge Intensity

Table 15.7: Building knowledge value - communicating knowledge

What the competency is	What it is not	The influence of personality
Explaining and expressing ideas, concepts, and opinions in a clear and fluent manner both in writing and via presentations.	Providing knowledge that recipients do not need.	People who find that they enjoy explaining their ideas to others may be particularly creative and enjoy thinking about new ideas in general. If they are also relatively outgoing, even though they may be tense before important events, then they are likely to find it easier to adapt the style of a presentation or document to the needs of the audience. In contrast, people who are particularly pragmatic, tend to be nonchalant, and/or are reserved with strangers, may need to pay attention to developing this competency.
	Not allowing the opportunity for people to check that they have understood your message.	
Adapting your presentation style according to the communication channel/ audience.	Failing to adapt your approach to the audience.	
	Communicating the "nice to know" rather than the "need to know".	
Being aware of the needs of the audience.		

Developing the competency

Research the needs and points of view of those attending your presentations and reading your documents.

Be clear about the purpose of the communication.

Ask others to give a summary of what you have said to check how well you have communicated.

Ask a colleague to evaluate your work critically and give you some tips on areas of improvement.

Make an effort to mix with a variety of people, inside and outside your organization, and try consciously to identify the different styles that they adopt. Practice adapting your style to fit with theirs.

- Developing Knowledge Culture
- Building Knowledge Infrastructure

The respondents to the Knowledge-Sharing Behaviours and Personality survey were from all areas and levels within the organization. Most had some involvement with Knowledge Management, including community participation. The pattern of results reflected the emphasis that the organization placed on networking and applying expertise: performance against both these competencies was rated comparatively highly.

Table 15.8: Building knowledge value – applying expertise

What the competency is	What it is not	The influence of personality
Understanding the technical aspects of your job. Ensuring that you apply your knowledge and previous experience effectively. Making the most of available technologies to ensure that work is completed effectively and efficiently.	"Re-inventing the wheel" by failing to look at the work others have already carried out. Withholding information that you know will be useful to others. Failing to take action that you know is appropriate.	People who are intellectually curious and keen to meet high standards (including worrying about how things will turn out) are likely to pay particular attention to applying technical expertise and job knowledge. In contrast, those who adopt a more down to earth approach, place their priorities outside of work and are easy-going and even nonchalant, may need to work harder to develop this competency.

Developing the competency

Review your current level of knowledge in your job and identify any key gaps. Seek out training and development opportunities to fill each of the identified gaps.

Seek opportunities for involvement in a technically challenging project where you will have to update your skills and knowledge.

Identify areas of future technical or commercial knowledge or skill that are likely to become critical to success in your job and focus on developing these.

Organize discussions at work with other specialists in your field. Meet regularly to review and discuss relevant and topical issues. Participate in relevant communities of practice and professional associations.

Table 15.9: Identifying knowledge activists

	Characteristics and skills of knowledge activists	Typical descriptor	Able to:
Building Relationships	Developing relationships	Strong networker, particularly through informal routes. Good facilitator. "Building up contacts and making connections."	Create mutual trust and build strong relationships. Link other people together. Establish through dialogue what receivers of knowledge already know to make knowledge sharing more effective.

continued on next page...

Table 15.9 - *Continued*

	Characteristics and skills of knowledge activists	Typical descriptor	Able to:
	Internal belief	Highly committed to knowledge sharing and collaboration. "Passion and confidence."	Convince others to participate in knowledge-related initiatives. Demonstrate their own commitment by sharing their own personal knowledge.
	Cultural alignment with organization	Aligned with the culture or a particular subculture in the organization.	Get things done by working with the existing culture.
Building a Knowledge Base	Action-oriented	"Persistent juggler." "Completer finisher."	Implement tools, processes, systems structures, and cultures.
	Project management	"Take away the ambiguity of the idea and make it real."	Break the knowledge vision down into practical activities. Plan and organize. Demonstrate good attention to detail.
	Information brokering	"A connector of information and content." "A facilitator of information."	Create links across the organization and keep subgroups joined together. Maintain networks and knowledge flows. Create new connections outside the organization.
	Creativity	"Creative influencing."	Seek out new knowledge. Enquire creatively when seeking knowledge from others. Invent novel ways of communicating the benefits of knowledge activities.

continued on next page...

Table 15.9 - *Continued*

	Characteristics and skills of knowledge activists	Typical descriptor	Able to:
Building Knowledge Value	Dialogue and communication	"Communicate with simplicity." "Provide a common language."	Convey mental models with a rich vocabulary, drawings, and body language. Tell effective stories. Speak in terms that knowledge receivers understand.
	Credibility through experience	Well regarded in own area, usually with a long track record.	Interact with practitioners across the organization. Demonstrate depth of knowledge in own area. Engage in detailed technical discussion in own area.

The importance of knowledge sharing and behavioural attributes was recognized. The company sought to embed them across the organization through the performance development process based on the Thames Water Competency Dictionary. Future plans included using key attributes from the Competency Dictionary as part of the organization's recruitment process and building them into leadership development across the business. These areas linked directly with "Developing a Knowledge Culture", one of the four building blocks of the Knowledge Management Strategy.

Top tips

✓ Integrate the Knowledge-Sharing Behaviours competency framework into your own competency system. This embeds knowledge sharing into people management practices.

✓ Tailor development of Knowledge-Sharing Behaviours to personal areas of strength by taking into account personality and style preferences. Try to avoid a "one size fits all" approach.

✓ Use the Knowledge-Sharing Behaviours model to audit communities of practice, virtual teams, and other groups where effective knowledge sharing is essential for performance.

✓ When looking for knowledge activists, it is useful to focus on knowledge-sharing behaviours. Technical skills can be easier to develop than underlying behaviours.

✓ Effective knowledge activists are far more likely to come from inside the organization than outside.

✓ Knowledge managers and activists learn a lot from external networking. This gives them access to other people in similar roles at different stages of development.

The research and the teams involved

The research that produced the Henley Knowledge-Sharing Behaviours model, its associated competency framework, and investigated the links to personality was conducted between 2002 and 2003. A literature review was carried out to explore the research that had previously been done in the area of both personality and knowledge sharing. The study of personality in relation to work behaviours and performance in the workplace is a well-established area, which offered the opportunity to use an existing tool for measuring personality traits. The personality attributes were from the SHL IMAGES™ questionnaire, which provided a broad high-level view of personality, consistent with what is known as the "five factor model". As there was no existing tool to measure knowledge-sharing behaviours, focus groups, supported by the literature review, were used to create a model and inventory using competency components and item content from the SHL Competency Framework. A preliminary round of data collection was used to derive a short form of the inventory with 42 items (six items per scale). This Inventory and the IMAGES™ questionnaire were emailed to participants who were asked to complete both, and also to rate the importance of each of the seven competencies for their own jobs. Where possible, questionnaires were emailed to peers, who were asked to rate the participants on the seven competencies. The total sample consisted of 241 participants from 28 organizations. Peer ratings were received for 54 people. Factor analysis of the data provided support for the Knowledge-Sharing Behaviour competency model and suggested that the seven competencies are distinct and stable. Correlations were used to examine the relationship between the six personality scales and the competency scales.

The research was co-championed by Anna Truch of Henley Business School and Dr David Bartram of SHL Ltd. Dr Christine van Winkelen of Henley Business School provided project support. Companies involved in the working group included:

DTI	*EC Harris*
Ericsson	*EZI*
Getronics	*Orange*
QinetiQ	*Thames Water*
Unisys	

Professor Malcolm Higgs and Dr Judy Payne, both of Henley Business School, also supported this research.

The research into the characteristics of knowledge activists was carried out during 2004 and 2005. Following a review of the literature to generate an expected profile of characteristics and skills, the extent to which they were reflected in practice was explored through interviews with knowledge managers, knowledge activists, and the customers of KM initiatives in three companies. The Project was co-championed by Dr Judy Payne of Henley Business School and Debbie Lawley of Orange. Keith Farquharson of EDF Energy provided research support. Companies involved in the working group included:

Aegis	*AWE*
Buckman Laboratories	*Defence Procurement Agency*
DLO Andover	*GSK*
Highways Agency	*Metronet Rail*
Nissan	*Orange*
QinetiQ	*Unisys*

Both phases of the research were intended to provide insights into knowledge-sharing behaviours that could support practical initiatives in organizations. They were not intended to provide prescriptive advice for any particular organization.

Final reflections from the research

It is important to realize that there is no "good" or "bad" personality profile, it is just that we each have different preferences. By being aware that there are differences, managers can tailor development initiatives so that people can play to their strengths, as well as learning ways of coping in situations that don't come so naturally to them. Our personalities remain relatively static as adults (there can be some changes, but for many people these are relatively minor). As knowledge sharing becomes increasingly important in distributed, virtual, ever-changing organizational teams, giving people some clarity around what is expected, what effective behaviour looks like and what support is available for development in line with their personal style is the basis for improved performance.

Note

1. The cases were prepared in 2003. Reproduced by permission.

Chapter 16

Snapshot

"Selling solutions" to improve knowledge flows in organizations does not always work; focusing on what motivates people to engage with the initiatives themselves can be more effective. To get this kind of buy-in requires clarity about the outcomes of the initiative and what those mean for the target audience. It also involves recognizing the barriers to people's engagement and identifying resources to address those which realistically can be overcome. Finally, it involves understanding the filtering patterns that affect how people receive information and tailoring communications in the most effective way to suit the predominant patterns of the audience.

A four-part, eight-step process is offered to help you systematically design your proposition so that knowledge-related initiatives will become "compelling buys" for their target audiences.

Why this matters

Knowledge sharing challenges well-established assumptions about the value of power and authority, responsibility, leadership, hierarchy, competition, and cooperation.[1] Also, assumptions about how to manage tangible resources have been so deeply ingrained that people don't necessarily accept that new ways are needed to manage knowledge. Despite the evident worth of initiatives to those who create them and those who intuitively "get" what it means to be a knowledge-based organization, all too often, for a variety of reasons, knowledge-related initiatives fail to deliver their anticipated value. This reduces motivation to pursue future initiatives and ultimately undermines the organizational potential for sustained success in the knowledge economy.

The way to handle this is to adopt a more systematic and carefully considered approach to designing initiatives that:

- start with a sharp and positive definition of the expected business outcome;
- objectively review the resources that enable and the barriers that obstruct the desired outcome;
- create lasting change by tapping into the triggers that motivate and engage the people involved. This means taking account of their ingrained predispositions and instinctive preferences.

These steps allow managers to construct more acceptable or even compelling arguments for initiatives and to refine and target communication accordingly.

What this means for your organization

The main implication of this approach is that it requires considerable thought about how to engage with the target audience for an initiative. Two frameworks are suggested to help with this: alignment levels and filtering patterns.

Alignment levels

As we saw in Chapter 2, there is research to suggest that there are some basic factors that affect an individual's responses to a situation, which need to be aligned if they are to work without confusion, internal conflict, or unproductive stress.[2] They need to be motivated to achieve the purpose (they understand why it matters), have the skills to do the task (they know how to do it), be comfortable with and able to take the necessary actions (they know what to do), and do so in an environment that is conducive to such action (where it takes place is appropriate). If these four factors are in alignment, the process of achieving the outcome tends to run smoothly and efficiently because there is nothing blocking it. For individuals, motivation comes from their beliefs and values. When we looked at engaging people in communities of practice (Chapter 10), we represented these factors as a series of nested levels (as shown in Figure 16.1), adding in the individual's sense of self, or identity, as the deepest aspect of alignment. Engagement can be shaped by interventions at any of the levels.

Filtering patterns

Words are the mechanism by which we mentally codify our own assumptions, as well as the way we coordinate the behaviour of others. The way we frame our words can change their impact. Each individual through their experiences develops a set of filters through which they make sense of the world.[3] These filters delete, distort, and generalize and so shape their model of the world. Different people use different filters, but there are certain repetitive patterns that can be identified through analysis of a person's behaviour and/or speech patterns. These subconscious filter patterns mean that individuals pay selective attention to the informa-

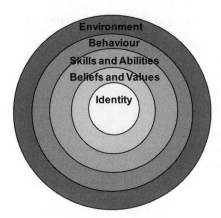

Figure 16.1: Alignment levels

tion presented. Once recognized, it has been argued that you can more easily attract a person's attention by couching the message in the words and communication structures that naturally resonate with their preferred orientation. The proposition here is that if you are aware of the predominant filter patterns of your target audience and shape your communication with them accordingly, you will be able to engage their attention and interest more effectively.

Many common filter patterns have been identified and these can provide insight into individual orientations. Tables 16.1 to 16.8 summarize recognized filters, together with ways you can identify them through conversation and questions. The final column of each includes suggested responses that are relevant to engaging someone in a knowledge-related project. All of the patterns have been described in relation to a business context and are based on the work of psychologists who identified the filtering patterns.[3]

Creating an action plan

These principles can be used as part of a process for planning a knowledge-related initiative, or evaluating how well previous projects have been designed. Insights about what could have been better can make implementation easier in future. The four parts of the process are Definition, Diagnosis, Design, and Determine feasibility.

Definition aims to move the project definition from a "solution focused" specification to an "outcomes focused" one. It is important that the specification spells out who is affected, what needs to happen, where and when it will occur, and why it is worth doing.

Diagnosis focuses on how to achieve the outcome. To do this it is important to review separately the influences on the way individuals within the target audience create meaning. You can do this by assessing the predominant filter patterns and the key orientations on the multi-layer alignment level model.

Table 16.1: Filter patterns relating to operational preferences

Focus of the filter	How the filter will shape the orientations of individuals and groups	Ways to identify the filter in general conversation	Suggested response to help turn a knowledge-related project into a compelling buy
Drive to act	Tends to *initiate* and jump into the fray.	People with this filter will talk about action, and explain things in short crisp sentences.	Tap into these people early. They are likely to be KM activists – people who, once convinced, like to get things done. Talk to these people in terms of starting, initiating, major leaps forward, innovations.
	Tends to be *passive/reactive*.	People with this filter will use words that suggest thinking about things: trying, waiting, they could if . . .	Such people are followers, and are more likely to wait for the dust to settle before they engage. Strong messages from people they respect may help. Talk to these people in terms of patience, all in good time, responding to signals.
The potential outcome of an activity	Focuses strongly on moving *towards* goals and objectives. Pays most attention to future possibilities.	Listen for words like gain, achieve, get, include – and for positive statements of what someone wants.	For people with this preference, explain the project goals and benefits. Wherever possible suggest how they align with the individual's/group's own objectives. Relate plans for change to delivery of future benefits and rewards. Talk about outcomes in terms of positive benefits: "increase re-use of good ideas" rather than "avoid re-inventing the wheel".

continued on next page...

Table 16.1 - *Continued*

Focus of the filter	How the filter will shape the orientations of individuals and groups	Ways to identify the filter in general conversation	Suggested response to help turn a knowledge-related project into a compelling buy
	Motivated by moving *away from* risks. Good at finding and correcting problems through analysis.	Listen for words like avoid and exclude. Recognize problems and negative statements about what someone dislikes, is concerned or uneasy about.	Explain the benefits of a project in terms of how it can help people avoid problems and errors; stop them encountering things they dislike, fear, or do not enjoy; or prevent them making mistakes.
Evaluating decisions	Prefers to make decisions based on their *own internal criteria* of what is right and wrong in a particular situation. People with this preference gather information for their own use and tend to make decisions intuitively.	If asked the question *"how do you know you have done a good job?"* this sort of person will say they just know, they can tell for themselves, or it feels right to them.	Tell these people that they need to decide for themselves, it is up to them to do what they believe is right. Having solicited information about what these people believe is really important, shape explanations to positively align with their beliefs and values, so that the criteria they use for evaluating their decisions are automatically aligned.
	Tends to *rely on external sources* of advice and information from others to help them decide. May be overly concerned about what others think of their actions and choices.	If asked the question *"how do you know you have done a good job?"* this sort of person will say they know when others tell them, or there is external evidence of their success.	Build into a project plenty of opportunities for feedback, guidance, group discussion, peer assists, reviews during the process. Multiple messages through different routes will reinforce confidence in their decisions.

continued on next page...

Table 16.1 - *Continued*

Focus of the filter	How the filter will shape the orientations of individuals and groups	Ways to identify the filter in general conversation	Suggested response to help turn a knowledge-related project into a compelling buy
Task preference	Always looking for a better way to do things. Actively seeks to *expand options*. Enjoys learning and innovation.	When asked why they chose their job, this sort of person will say that it gave them more possibilities, choices, variety, alternatives, routes to improvement etc.	Explain how the project will open doors and enable them to do new things and give the business new options. Emphasize the learning opportunities and the new openings that will ensue.
	Highly efficient when *following clearly defined procedures*. Adhering to standards and rules appeals to them.	When asked why they chose their job, this sort of person will go into lengthy explanations about how they got the job, the steps they took, the interview process, and the way the recruitment process was structured. They will not give you active reasons for choosing it.	Interest these people by outlining the steps that need to be taken to achieve the outcome. Explain how the project will help them do things the right way. Emphasize benefits such as standardization, orderliness. Show how their role could become more structured and methodical.
Information preference	Works with and thinks in *large "chunks" of information*. Needs to understand the big picture to accept new information.	Listen to the way this person tells a story. A big chunk person will give you an overview of a situation with little detail, and events may be explained in a random order.	In any communication, written or verbal, start by presenting a short overview, a summary of features (positive benefits and ways to avoid problems). This is the elevator pitch, which draws in big chunk people.

continued on next page...

Table 16.1 - *Continued*

Focus of the filter	How the filter will shape the orientations of individuals and groups	Ways to identify the filter in general conversation	Suggested response to help turn a knowledge-related project into a compelling buy
	Likes to receive information in *small "chunks"*. Detail conscious and needs to be comfortable that all the "I"s are dotted and "T"s crossed.	Listen to the way this person tells a story. A small chunk person will give you lots of detail, and build the story cumulatively and often linearly.	Immediately support general arguments that appeal to the big chunk people with factual evidence and detailed arguments that support the overview, so that "small chunk" people have some meaty information to get their teeth into.
Communication and interaction	Gives greatest emphasis to *non-verbal communication*. Sensitive to subtle signals and undercurrents in communications.		In any communication programme, consciously include a mix of visual images, hands-on trials, and nods of agreement to ensure that those who value this sort of input can engage with the content. The communicator must be "authentic" (without doubts about the message) or these people will sense mixed messages.
	Pays most attention to the *content of the message* itself.		Straightforward simple content, avoiding jargon and technical language and building on a shared language makes it easier for the receiver to understand the content of the message.

continued on next page...

Table 16.1 - *Continued*

Focus of the filter	How the filter will shape the orientations of individuals and groups	Ways to identify the filter in general conversation	Suggested response to help turn a knowledge-related project into a compelling buy
Work environment	Wants to work with people around. Wants to work alone.		Emphasize the communal nature of the project. Emphasize how the project will facilitate independence and self sufficiency for the user.
Responsibility	Wants *sole responsibility* for the work they perform.	Ask this person what they like about their work and they will talk about independence. They will use the word "I" predominantly in their descriptions.	Involve these people in pre-project data collection, or in research activities with precisely delineated outcomes that they can take singular responsibility for achieving. Show how a project could enhance their individual performance.
	Want to *share responsibility* with others and prefers team projects.	Ask this person what they like about their work and they will talk about teams. They will use the word "we" predominantly in their descriptions. Some people may fit in between these two categories and talk about being in control with others around.	Emphasize the collaborative nature of knowledge projects and how the combined contributions will make a significant impact on the end results.

Table 16.2: Filter patterns relating to adherence to norms

Focus of the filter	How the filter will shape the orientations of individuals and groups	Ways to identify the filter in general conversation	Suggested response to help turn a knowledge-related project into a compelling buy
Assertion	Knows the policies and rules. Willing and able to tell others what to do (*). Believes it is inappropriate to tell others what to do.	Useful questions to ask here are: *What is a good way to increase your success at work?* and *How could someone else improve their success?* It will be clear from the answers where a person's preferences lie in terms of rules and whether they care about the way others work.	For those with filter patterns marked (*), explain how the initiative fits with the current strategy and organizational policy. Engage these people in activities that allow them to explain to others what is involved. Those with filter patterns *not* marked (*) do not care for involvement or interaction with others. Even if they are persuaded themselves, they will never be your best champions so it is better to focus on those who will promote the project or get involved.
Involvement	Have rules for their own lives and don't involve themselves in others' work habits. Care about others and are concerned about other people's actions at work (*).		
Complacency	Are willing to follow the rules and policies of the organization (*). Do not feel the need to conform to the organization's rules.		
Tolerance	Know the rules and policies for themselves, but do not feel it is appropriate to impose them on others. Is intolerant of the actions of others.		

Table 16.3: Filter patterns relating to what convinces someone

Focus of the filter	How the filter will shape the orientations of individuals and groups	Ways to identify the filter in general conversation	Suggested response to help turn a knowledge-related project into a compelling buy
See	Must be able to see something "with their own eyes" to be convinced.	Ask how do you know someone else in a similar position to you is good at their work? You will hear responses that contain visual words like see, show, and notice.	Include visuals, diagrams in project reports and documentation. Do demonstrations which "show". Show videos of other users.
Hear	Must hear how, or hear about something in order to be convinced.	Ask how do you know someone else in a similar position to you is good at their work? You will hear responses that contain auditory words like hear good reviews, sounds like they know what they are doing etc.	Gather testimonials. Listen to customer experiences and market signals. Tell stories about the project. Engage people in discussions about lessons that have been learnt.
Read	Must read information or instructions to be convinced.	Ask how do you know someone else in a similar position to you is good at their work? You will hear responses that contain words about information, reading, text, and numerical evidence.	Provide detailed documentation on how to use the project output. Tables, statistical data, manuals give these people the confidence that it is worth them engaging with a project.
Do	Must actually do or experience something themselves in order to be convinced.	Ask how do you know someone else in a similar position to you is good at their work? You will hear responses that contain the words about doing, action, performing.	Involve these people in testing prototypes. Encourage these people to trial new products and give feedback.

continued on next page...

Table 16.3 - *Continued*

Focus of the filter	How the filter will shape the orientations of individuals and groups	Ways to identify the filter in general conversation	Suggested response to help turn a knowledge-related project into a compelling buy
Number of examples	Must have data or an experience a particular number of times for them to be convinced.	When asked the same question this person will quantify how many times they need to see, hear, do, or read to be convinced.	Repeat communications several times presenting various different types of information and exemplars to demonstrate the utility of a project.
Automatic	Only need a small amount or even partial information, and then quickly project the rest of the information. Then, they decide based on their projections.	When asked the same question this person will tend to say "pretty quickly", or "I give people the benefit of the doubt".	Engage these people early in a project, by targeting them with an early briefing that appeals to their main filters. Once they are on board, they can help you build momentum for acceptance.
Consistent	Never quite convinced. Need to get information every single time to remain somewhat convinced.	This person will go into long explanations of many things that are required to convince them.	Don't waste time trying to persuade these people, focus your efforts where you will get more rewards.
Period of time	Need to have data remain consistent for a period of time for them to be convinced.	When asked the same question this person will generally give you a period of time as part of the answer.	Keep repeating the same messages from many different angles and through many different routes.

Table 16.4: Filter patterns relating to approaches to work

Focus of the filter	How the filter will shape the orientations of individuals and groups	Suggested response to help turn a knowledge-related project into a compelling buy
Practice	This person simply begins the task; they work best when they can get the first step out of the way immediately.	Break down project into small steps. Give these people some early wins.
Concept	This person completely develops an idea or theory; needs time to think things through before they take action.	Explain the rationale and logic behind the project and help them understand how it fits conceptually with other aspects of the business.
Structure	This person organizes the resources; establishes lists and identifies the relationships that will be important before they take action.	Project plans, resource and network maps will make this person feel more comfortable that it is worth their while engaging in this project.

Table 16.5: Filter patterns relating to temporal focus

Focus of the filter	How the filter will shape the orientations of individuals and groups	Ways to identify the filter in general conversation	Suggested response to help turn a knowledge-related project into a compelling buy
Past	Concentrates on the past and relies on experience to help make decisions.	This person will refer to previous events or experiences frequently in conversation.	Focuses on past successes. Show how this project can build on experience and existing expertise.
Present	Concentrates on the present, the "now" and tends to be practical. May not learn the lessons from the past.	This person may show frustration if you talk about the past or the future. They will prefer to talk about now and may make statements such as "it is what we do now which matters".	Explain the immediate benefits, and pitfalls. Outline requirements for first steps. If this is a decision-maker, ensure you are the last person to communicate with them before a decision is made as this person may change their mind with the next conversation they have.
Future	Concentrates on the future and tends to be a dreamer. Finds it hard to enjoy the fruits of earlier planning.	This person will talk about future plans, about what can be done tomorrow or further ahead in time.	Visionaries and innovators need support from others in a team if a project is going to run to plan. Engage these people with a compelling future vision or story.

Table 16.6: Filter patterns relating to motivational criteria

Focus of the filter	How the filter will shape the orientations of individuals and groups	Ways to identify the filter in general conversation	Suggested response to help turn a knowledge-related project into a compelling buy
Power	Motivated by situations where they have power, authority, and control over people and things.	Listen for an emphasis on words like authority, influence, prestige, control, and direct impact.	Show where in the project the user can exert their influence and make a difference.
Popularity	Motivated by situations where people like them, they can participate in taking care of people, and they can be part of a group.	Listen for words about friendship, belonging, participating.	Show how the project helps others, and encourages inter-personal relationships.
Performance (achievement)	Motivated by situations where they can achieve. They want to be noticed for what they have achieved.	Listen for words about achievements, challenge, competition, success.	Show how the project can improve performance.

Design involves developing a process that is focused on removing the barriers and accessing the necessary resources to achieve the required ends. At this point filtering patterns can be used in a different way, to plan a compelling and convincing communication process.

Determine feasibility. The final step in the process is to review the completed analysis to check that it makes sense. Is what is being proposed feasible and coherent? It can be easy to analyse a situation too much and break it down into so many constituent parts that one loses a sense of the whole picture. It is important to ask *will it achieve the outcomes, and is it sufficiently focused and well defined that success will be evident? Is it realistic and achievable?*

These four parts translate into an eight-step process as shown in Table 16.9.

Real life stories

At first sight, this can appear to be a complicated process to follow so a substantial example is included here. The knowledge manager of a construction firm (Construct) used the eight-step process to plan an initiative to improve the engagement of

Table 16.7: Filter patterns relating to relationship sorting

Focus of the filter	How the filter will shape the orientations of individuals and groups	Ways to identify the filter in general conversation	Suggested response to help turn a knowledge-related project into a compelling buy
Sameness	Notices similarities and prefers things to remain the same.	When asked what is the relationship between their job this year and what they were doing last year, this sort of person will explain the similarities between the two, and suggest that little has changed.	Explanations that show how the project deliverables are similar to something the "user" already knows or is comfortable with will make it easier to win over people in this category.
Progress	Wants things to evolve over time, adapts to steady change, but resists radical change.	When asked what is the relationship between their job this year and what they were doing last year, this sort of person will talk about more or less, better or worse, as a comparison between this year and last.	Explanations and justifications that show how the potential "user" can transition from where they are now to where they could be, and the stages in between, will win the hearts and minds of this sort of person.
Difference	Notices differences, stagnates in stable environments, and thrives on frequent change.	When asked what is the relationship between their job this year and what they were doing last year, this sort of person will talk about what has changed, what is new and what is unique.	Explanations and justifications that highlight novelty, major improvements, and what needs to be done differently are important for engaging this category of people. Creativity and innovation processes that enable the transfer of knowledge between different people will be appealing.

Table 16.8: Filter patterns relating to primary interests in terms of the content of work

Focus of the filter	How the filter will shape the orientations of individuals and groups	Ways to identify the filter in general conversation	Suggested response to help turn a knowledge-related project into a compelling buy
People	Works best with people and their feelings.	If you ask someone to say what they enjoy about their work they will talk a lot about feelings, responses, and about their reactions to others.	To feel successful this sort of person wants to have involvement with aspects of the project that are people-related. Talk to them about the impact of the project on people.
Tools	Works best with tangible tools and instruments.	If you ask someone to say what they enjoy about their work they will focus on the application of tools and techniques, the joy of technology, and the satisfaction of using a tool well.	To feel successful this sort of person wants to have involvement with aspects of the project that involve the application of tools. Demonstrate the process through active application of a tool or framework.
Systems	Works best with the process of things.	Ask this person to say what they enjoy about their work and you will hear a lot about procedures, following rules, and about smoothly running mechanisms.	To feel successful this sort of person wants to have involvement with aspects of the project that involve things like flow charts, decision trees, and procedures manuals. All of these process-oriented descriptors will help this person engage more fully with a KM project.
Information	Works best with facts and knowledge.	Ask this person to say what they enjoy about their work and you will hear a lot about concepts, ideas, information theories, ways of understanding, and about the knowledge that they contribute.	Provide plenty of supporting factual information, access to databases, and knowledge resources to refer to for this type of person.

continued on next page...

Table 16.8 - *Continued*

Focus of the filter	How the filter will shape the orientations of individuals and groups	Ways to identify the filter in general conversation	Suggested response to help turn a knowledge-related project into a compelling buy
Money	Is concerned about money and keeping score.	Ask this person about what they enjoy in their job and you will hear about measurement, recording of figures, financial rewards, bottom lines etc.	Show how this project will impact the bottom line and how the financial impact of the project will be measured.
Place	Concerned about the geographic or social/ political position.	Ask this person about what they enjoy in their job and they may tell you about travel, status and position, and experiencing international cultures.	Show how the KM project relates to the individual's current social group or to their place in the organization's hierarchy of power or influence. Talk about any regional focus for larger projects.
Time	Is concerned about allotting time and keeping to schedule.	Ask this person about the satisfaction they get from their job and you will hear about meeting deadlines, about planning and scheduling projects.	Present timelines and project resource commitment plans. Explain any contingencies that may be required.
Activity	Focuses on activity and needs to manipulate activities.	A person like this will explain their enjoyment of the job in terms of doing things, organizing events, and getting things started.	Talk about how the person can get involved, what they personally can contribute, and how to do this.

technical people in business development activities; effectively they were being asked to share their knowledge to help develop new business for the organization. In Table 16.10 the application of each step is followed by reflections on the value of that step in terms of the knowledge manager's own thinking processes, and finally his recommendations for others wishing to work with the model.

Table 16.9: Eight steps to create more convincing initiatives

Step 1 – Define the business issue	Describe the business issue you want to address. State it in the negative (as a problem). If you can, include a cause and effect: because of x, we can't y. You may want to return and redefine the issue having completed the steps which follow.
Step 1a – How is this issue created or sustained?	Describe the "people" factors that you think have created or are sustaining the problem. Identify relevant filter patterns using the earlier tables.
Step 2 – Define the desired business outcome	Describe the business outcome you want to achieve. State it in the positive. Make it as specific as possible – consider who, what, why, when, where, and for whom. You might also consider how you might achieve the outcome – but not in any detail at this stage. Describe how you will know when the outcome has been achieved – what evidence will there be? Make sure that what you are aiming for is within your (or the organization's) control. Check that if the outcome is achieved it will really lead to business value. You may want to loop back to step 1 here.
Step 2a – What might help or hinder achievement of this outcome?	Describe the "people" factors that might support or hinder the achievement of your desired outcome. Identify relevant filter patterns using the earlier tables.
Step 3 – Who is the target audience in the business?	From the steps so far, identify the target audience for the intervention you are about to plan. Be as specific as you can.
Step 4 – Identify barriers and resources	Pick the alignment levels where you feel you have permission to intervene, and where you can be most effective. Identify what is stopping the outcome happening (barriers) and what would be needed for the outcome to be achieved (resources).
Step 5 – Identify the filter patterns relevant to barriers and resources	Identify which barriers and resources are most significant in blocking or enabling the outcome and where you have permission to act. For these barriers and resources, identify which people factors or filter patterns are most likely to influence the target audience.
Step 6 – Use the insights from steps 4 and 5 to design an intervention	Use insights from steps 5 and 6 to design knowledge-related interventions which might help achieve the outcome identified in step 2. The interventions should remove barriers or provide resources identified in step 4.
Step 7 – Which filter patterns should be explored?	Focus at this stage at the alignment level (or levels) which you selected at step 4. The people factors or filter patterns identified at this stage are likely to be a refinement of those identified at step 5.
Step 8 – Assessing the feasibility	Check that the intervention designed is within your control to implement, and that it will achieve the outcome producing measurable evidence that the outcome has been achieved.

Table 16.10: Application of the eight-step process by a knowledge manager at Construct

Process Step	Application of the step by Construct	Reflections by Construct on what was learnt by applying the step.	Recommendations for other users as a consequence of working with the model.
Step 1 - Define the business issue	People not having an awareness of their individual business development contribution means that they do not contribute to the new marketing initiative.	We knew what the problem was already. By stating the issue as a cause and effect problem, it forced us to think more deeply about what the underlying cause of the issue was – this is far more useful as it then becomes something that we can design interventions to resolve. This ensured that we are working on the underlying cause of the issue, rather than the symptom.	You need to loop through a number of times. Also it is likely that there will be more than one issue. You need to consider whether one is more significant than others (are issues hierarchical with one creating the others?) or are the issues inter-related in a more complex way? If this is the case, where should you start and how can issues be chunked or sub-divided into manageable initiatives?
Step 1a - How is this issue created or sustained?	Individual's initiation patterns may be important for how and when they will engage with the plan. Those with a tendency to be passive may be waiting for the initiative to take off before "getting on board". Convincer patterns may also be important, individuals who are convinced by a number of examples will not yet have these available because this is a new initiative. Those who are convinced by seeing/doing/hearing about might need experiences which match their individual filters before they shift from an awareness of the marketing plan into an engagement.	It provided insights that we had as a management team developed our thinking in terms of what we wanted to do; we now had to go back to basics in order to communicate this to the rest of the team.	

Process Step	Application of the step by Construct	Reflections by Construct on what was learnt by applying the step.	Recommendations for other users as a consequence of working with the model.
Step 2 - Define the desired business outcome	To support individuals at the Technology Centre in engaging with the marketing plan through providing them with opportunities and information which allows them to generate their own personal engagement with the marketing plan in a way which is aligned with the business objective.	Ensure that we have defined something that we can do to fix the issue. By sticking to the rules of defining a well formed outcome, we were forced to think about an outcome defined as something we wanted to do, rather than something we wanted to have happen.	There may be a loop back to the issue. Need to check that the outcome does fix the issue.
Step 2a - What might help or hinder achievement of this outcome?	*Evaluating decisions*: some individuals will decide for themselves, some will want to receive advice from others - how can we provide an opportunity for both approaches?	Helped us to think about the process of change we wanted, rather than just the end product of that change. This means that we have to think about the type of intervention we want and what and what will work in terms of the context of our organization (as well as what the indirect consequences will be).	Care should be taken not to list every filter pattern as ultimately every pattern will have some influence, but only the most important ones should be prioritized.
	Information preference: chunk size - how do we present the plan as both an overview and with detail so that the audience can pick out the messages that are right for them?	Providing prompts to think through the project. Each filter pattern was a prompt to ask "is this relevant, if so how?" which helped ensure that we thought about the project from more than one perspective.	Care should also be taken to understand the definitions of the filter patterns correctly. It is very easy to relate the name of the filter pattern back to personal assumptions and misuse the label.
	Adherence to norms: can we ask those who will tell others the rules to help spread the message? (i.e. the knowledge activists see Chapter 15)	The most useful prompt here is the reminder that the way I am thinking about a project is influenced by my own thinking styles and patterns. This helped to break down the issue/outcome into sub-projects which require different types of people to achieve - the differences between people in the target audience become opportunities rather than barriers.	
	Approach to work: some people will want to get started straight away, others may prefer to develop relationships or understand the concepts first. How do we support/allow this to happen?		
	Temporal: need to provide examples from past, present, and future.	The quality of our thinking was higher due to greater depth of thinking about the individuals and groups of people who need to be influenced or considered to make the project work.	
	Relationship sorting: show how this is both new and evolving from previous initiatives.		

continued on next page...

Table 16.10 - Continued

Process Step	Application of the step by Construct	Reflections by Construct on what was learnt by applying the step.	Recommendations for other users as a consequence of working with the model.
Step 3 - Who is the target audience in the business?	All individuals within the organization's Technology Centre.	Helped us identify where we needed to focus our efforts in order to achieve success. Gave the insight that we needed to transfer our focus of activity outside of the management team (which was appropriate for the first stage of developing the strategy) out into the wider team who will be asked to implement the strategy. Making this shift a conscious action helps to define the two stages of development.	Make sure the target audience is the right audience to resolve the issue.
Step 4 - Identify barriers and resources	*Environment* *Barriers:* time is a barrier - targets set to recover time on fee earning work versus business development activity. *Resource:* need to create suitable time and space within which individuals can develop understanding. *Behaviour* *Barriers:* individuals focused on "doing" need also to develop skill of planning forward and thinking strategically. *Resource:* individuals who have this skill set can share it with colleagues. Formal training where appropriate/necessary.	The "level" categories were useful to provide different perspectives on the same problem. It became clear that the problem existed on a number of levels and that some of these were either more relevant or easier to influence than others through an intervention. We identified some barriers that we might not otherwise have thought about. Looking at the resources required was useful in identifying some aspects of the project that were not fully thought through (for example provision of training - which training and for whom?).	Be clear about the difference between the levels. They are distinct and each adds their own value.

Process Step	Application of the step by Construct	Reflections by Construct on what was learnt by applying the step.	Recommendations for other users as a consequence of working with the model.
	Skills and abilities *Barriers*: linked to behaviour as not all individuals have/believe they have the full spectrum of skills required. *Resource*: provision of training/mentoring. Link to skills mapping project to set up peer learning opportunities. *Values and beliefs* *Barriers*: some individuals may not recognize that this is part of their role, especially as we have a dedicated resource. *Resource*: understanding of the new strategy and what this means at all levels needs an effective communications plan. *Identity* *Barriers*: we do not have clear statements of who we are to reflect recent changes in the business. *Resource*: need to define our purpose clearly in terms of both internal and external elements of the business and translate these for individual team members and groups.	Breaking down the problem into these levels forced a change of pace in the project planning process. It forced a quality of thinking at an important stage. We identified that some barriers were more important than others, modifying the issue slightly having completed this stage.	

continued on next page....

Table 16.10 - *Continued*

Process Step	Application of the step by Construct	Reflections by Construct on what was learnt by applying the step.	Recommendations for other users as a consequence of working with the model.
Step 5 - Identify the filter patterns relevant to barriers and resources	*Drive to act*: tendency to be active/passive - focus on "active" group initially as these people will take the initiative forward in the first stages. Follow up then with those who are more comfortable following advice and guidance. *Responsibility*: some individuals may wish to work on the initiative on their own, others as a collective effort. Need to provide opportunities for all, but also make sure that those who prefer solo responsibility are not isolated or unsupported. Are we ensuring that those who are "active" have sufficient opportunity to lead? If not, we are missing an opportunity, but will also frustrate (and therefore disengage) these people. Are we ensuring that those who prefer to "follow" can receive the support/guidance they need to be able to contribute?	Helped to focus on the people we have in the team and how to engage them with the project. This helped to design a project which focuses on the individuals and how we can get the most out of them. A traditional approach would be to work out what needs to be done, then to pull together the people from the team who collectively will provide the skills and experience needed to do it. This approach was different, the focus instead was a combination of what needs to be done, with who we have in the team and what their individual strengths and weaknesses might be as a result of their filtering patterns. This resulted in a project design that potentially will engage more of the team as we are looking at how to fit the project around the individuals, rather than fitting the individuals around the project.	Care must be taken not to assume too much - for example "tendency to be passive" does not mean that these people will not initiate anything. Care must be taken not to engineer too much theory about how people will behave from these patterns.

Process Step	Application of the step by Construct	Reflections by Construct on what was learnt by applying the step.	Recommendations for other users as a consequence of working with the model.
	Convincer patterns: are we providing messages in the right channel? Do we need to review the way in which we are trying to get people to engage and ensure that we are supporting the range of different communication preferences?		
Step 6 - Use the insights from steps 4 and 5 to design an intervention	*Intervention to remove barriers*: need frequent team briefings and communication to the team which is delivered at different levels, e.g. a high-level message followed by detailed examples. Provide communication that is good for people who prefer to see, hear, do. Provide training and mentoring opportunities and select/ allow self-selection of appropriate methods for/by individuals.	This step translated thinking back into tangible knowledge-related interventions. These interventions might have been arrived at without going through the process, but the way in which they will be implemented and the reason for doing so are both much better defined as a result of using this process.	A knowledge-specialist will probably have interventions in mind throughout the process. It is important to at least challenge whether these were the right assumptions. This requires self-awareness of these assumptions throughout the process.
	Intervention to provide resources: use recently completed skills mapping project to provide opportunities for peer to peer sharing of knowledge.		

continued on next page....

Table 16.10 – *Continued*

Process Step	Application of the step by Construct	Reflections by Construct on what was learnt by applying the step.	Recommendations for other users as a consequence of working with the model.
Step 7 - Which filter patterns should be explored?	*Information preference*: communication material and methods need to match individuals' preferences. *Convincer patterns*: group learning and individual learning opportunities need to be created. *Work environment*: need to provide opportunities within the communication and setting up of the initiative to ensure that individuals can get started/work out the relationships/understand the concepts to match their preferences. Can work structure be engineered to match the right person to the requirements of the task? *Temporal*: provide examples from the past, examples of what can be done now, and also examples of what we want to achieve in the future.	This ensures that the difference between individuals is incorporated into the solution design, therefore ensuring that the implementation plan contains the quality of thinking that has preceded this stage.	
Step 8 - Assessing the feasibility	Carried out with the team.		

Top tips

✓ Define a compelling vision: to build, sustain, and extend the engagement of others, a well-defined, compelling, positively phrased vision is an essential pre-requisite for any project.

✓ Know your audience well: it is worth investing the time to systematically assess how their thinking style will impact on their willingness to engage with your intentions. This does mean that you need to define precisely the audience, possibly segmenting it.

✓ Vary your message to suit your audience: design the communications to fit their filters.

✓ Know yourself and your own preferences: significant reflection is needed on the impact of one's own preferences on the way a project is designed and communicated.

✓ Careful reflection and repeated sanity checking are essential: the process is easy to do superficially and badly. To get value from it requires careful thought about some quite subtle facets of human responses. Frequently you will need to go around the questions several times to refine your answers to ensure that they are internally consistent and therefore coherent as a whole. Often at the outset you may define the audience too broadly to make the project feasible.

✓ Looking backward or planning forward? Whilst it is primarily designed to be a planning tool, the process can equally well be used to guide an after action review. It provides a structured mechanism for assessing where a project may not have been designed to be sufficiently attractive to the audience. This may trigger ideas for future activities and communication programmes that will better engage users with established opportunities.

The research and the team involved

This research was carried out during 2005 and 2006 by a working group of members of the Henley KM Forum. Following a review of the literature, the four-part eight-step process was developed then refined and tested by members of the working group through an action learning process. The research activities were intended to help managers shape and communicate effective knowledge-related initiatives in their own context by better understanding how to engage the attention and interest of individuals. They were not intended to provide prescriptive advice for a particular business.

Professor Jane McKenzie was the academic co-champion for this research. The member co-champion was Adrian Malone of Taylor Woodrow Consulting. Working group members included representatives from the following organizations:

Cadbury Schweppes   *Defence Procurement Agency*
Energy Saving Trust   *GSK*
Hyder Consulting   *Mills and Reeve*
Ministry of Defence   *Nationwide Building Society*
Orange   *PRP Architects*
Unisys

Together with invited associates: Geoff Parcell (Practical KM Ltd)

Final reflections from the research

Designing an effective knowledge-related intervention is much less about providing solutions and much more about understanding what motivates people to engage with knowledge sharing and communicating intentions in a way that the user can easily absorb. Such a conclusion is not really surprising, but up until now we have not had a straightforward process to help managers to thoroughly think through their approach. This process provides a way to do that, without training necessarily being needed in the subtleties of human psychology, or investments in organization-wide surveys to understand the orientations of the audience.

Notes

1. Toffler, A. (1990) *Powershift; Knowledge Wealth and Violence at the Edge of the 21st Century*, Bantam.
2. See for example Bateson, G. (1972) *Steps to an Ecology of the Mind*, New York: Ballantine Books and Dilts, R. (1990) *Changing Belief Systems with NLP*, Capitola CA: Meta Publications.
3. You can read more about this in Chomsky, N. (1976) *Reflections on Language*, New York: Pantheon and in Charvet, S.R. (1997) *Words that Change Minds*, Iowa: Kendal Hunt Publishing. James, T. and Woodsmall, W. (1988) *Time Line Therapy and the Basis of Personality*, California: Meta Publications contains some personal examples of how these filtering patterns affect human behaviour. The initial set of filtering patterns was then identified and described by Leslie Cameron-Bandler in collaboration with David Gordon, Robert Dilts, and Maribeth Meyers-Anderson.

Chapter 17

Snapshot

Although on average managers spend around 80% of their time in conversation, not all of these are as productive as they could be. Conversation encompasses many forms of interaction, including what could be called dialogue, debate, or simply communication. It can be a one-off process between two individuals, or a series of longer term interactions involving several people.

High quality conversation is the basis for effective knowledge sharing so it is important that individuals and organizations work at improving it. We take conversational skills for granted, so it needs deliberate planning ahead and then reflection after a conversation to identify the lessons for improvement. A framework based on effective knowledge-sharing and dialogue principles is offered as a way of structuring these processes. It includes a step-by-step way to think through the conversation in relation to key factors.

Good conversations include a healthy balance between listening and telling, between reflection and action orientation, and between play and analysis. Consciously assessing the balance of these factors, as well as the power structure, emotional ambience, and mindsets of those involved, all contributes to productive conversations.

Making time to work with the framework can seem difficult in organizations where conversation is not viewed as a productive use of time. However, recognizing the knowledge implications and the potential for improved decision-making makes it worth investing effort. Feedback suggests that with practice its use becomes a mental habit that improves outcomes for the users. The motivation, engagement, and commitment of all those involved are also likely to improve when there are good conversations, as opposed to unproductive, negative, or frustrating ones.

Why this matters

Conversation is a generic term which encompasses many different interactive processes over a variety of timeframes. Some conversations take place at the same

"We run after-action reviews, and have trained facilitators to create the dynamics and conditions for constructive conversations within them. People say they don't have time for conversations, but it's essential if we are to learn as an organization. You have to fight for it, or you will lose the battle over conversations in organizations that are focused on the bottom line."

Ditte Kolbaek, Knowledge Manager EMEA, Oracle

time and in the same place, others are facilitated through various types of technology, either at the same time but in different places, or even at different times in different places. A conversation about a specific topic may require several discussions with a range of individuals, or there may be a series of one-to-one interactions that are spread out over time. All of these situations are included as conversations here.

Conversation is the most natural and intuitive form of information exchange: we learn to converse in our formative years and therefore assume that we know how to do it well. The knowledge that has the most potential value in an organization is the knowledge that is most difficult to write down (tacit knowledge). It is only through conversation in which experiences and ideas are shared in a productive way that there is the potential for people to exchange tacit knowledge.

It has been suggested that managers spend around 80% of their time in conversation. This may be in formal situations such as meetings, but may also be in spontaneous, relaxed, and less formal settings where people may be more comfortable sharing knowledge. Even so, many conversations fail to generate action, are ignored by participants, or become contentious and unproductive. This reinforces the belief that conversation is a waste of time. Even worse, misunderstandings, misdirections, and mistakes arise all too frequently from conversations with even the most receptive and sympathetic colleagues.

Conversation as an important form of work is not always valued or legitimized in organizations. There may be contradictory messages, signals, and performance measures that emphasize "doing" rather than discussion and considered reflection.

All this suggests that there is considerable room for improvement in the way that we anticipate, carry out, and learn from workplace conversations. Time and effort spent improving conversations as a vehicle for exchanging valuable knowledge is a worthwhile investment.

By building in a process of disciplined planning and reflection for strategically important conversations, organizations can improve collective understanding of the issues that are detracting from organizational effectiveness. The improved knowledge sharing resulting from higher quality conversations has a direct and positive impact on decision-making and performance. Encouraging reflection on the components of decision-making (including conversations) is one aspect of building an organization's decision-making capability (see Chapter 12).

What this means for your organization

In considering how to improve conversations, it is helpful to consider a conversation as having four phases:

1. *Initiating – to explore possibilities.* This requires people to share knowledge that can be difficult to articulate (tacit knowledge), so needs people to feel at ease. The surroundings and risk involved for participants need to be considered too.
2. *Understanding – to get buy-in.* Here, deeper understanding of meaning and purpose needs to be established, which will take time. If people are resistant, this can need particular attention.
3. *Performance – initiating action.* A commitment to action is the outcome of a productive conversation. An active emotional ambience is needed to achieve this, as well as the management of risk.
4. *Closure – learning.* Here learning and conclusions are embedded and any loose ends tidied up so they don't affect future conversations.

Key aspects of a conversational process have been brought together into a framework for managing knowledge-intensive conversations as shown in Figure 17.1.

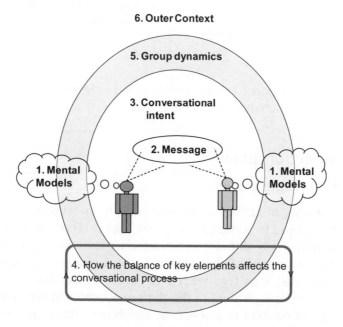

Figure 17.1: Managing knowledge-intensive conversations[1]

Table 17.1: Features of good and bad conversations

Features of bad conversations	Features of good conversations
1. There are status issues, such as one dominant source of power, or power struggles.	1. These conversations are between peers who trust or respect one another.
2. The personal risk participants are willing to take is low.	2. The personal risk participants are willing to take is high.
3. There is an uncertain ambience from the start.	3. The ambience at the start is either welcoming with reservations, or open and accepting.
4. The impact of the other's attitude on the level of anxiety is high.	4. The perception of the outcome is close to (or exceeds) the intent.
5. The level of intended reflection is low from the outset.	5. Those involved tend to reflect during the conversation.
6. There is much less listening than originally intended.	6. There tends to be more reflection than action-oriented judgement.
7. Across all four phases of conversation the level of playful discovery tends to be lower than intended and the focus on analysis tends to be higher.	7. The level of action orientation is higher than intended in both initiating and understanding conversations.
8. Bad conversations tend to involve more telling than listening/inquiry, particularly during the initiating and understanding phases.	8. Generally the level of playful discovery is higher in good conversations than in bad ones.
	9. Good closing conversations often show a higher level of advocacy than intended

These aspects are evident in what we identified as regular features of good and bad conversations, as summarized in Table 17.1.

Creating an action plan

Conversation planning framework

Improving the quality of conversations requires two investments in time. Firstly, take time to plan ahead for important or significant conversations (because of their impact) or for potentially difficult conversations. How can you most effectively manage the key dimensions of the process? Secondly, reflecting on conversations (particularly ones that didn't go well) after the event to learn for the future. Organizationally, this is equivalent to the "before action" and "after action" learning reviews used in relation to projects or significant initiatives. The framework that can be used to structure this planning for or reflection on conversations has four parts.

1. The *context and intent* of the conversation. This provides an important foundation to ensure that influential background and basic information is kept to the forefront of one's mind.
2. The *conditions* for the conversation. This is primarily around the emotional ambience and perceived degree of personal and business risk during the conversation. This will change during the different phases of a conversation.
3. The *status, dynamics, and actions* of those involved. This focuses attention on the balance of key variables that affect how well the parties relate. Thinking about how they are managed during the conversation can reduce misunderstandings and damaging interactions. Also included are the level of satisfaction with the process, outcome, and commitment to move forward. As well as the group dynamics and how individual contributions will be treated, the balance of different aspects of effective conversation needs to be considered.
   a. The ratio of listening to telling.
   b. The weighting given to playful discovery as opposed to analytic focusing.
   c. The balance of reflection to action-oriented judgement.
4. The *mindsets* of those involved. This is perhaps the most challenging part of the process but if addressed honestly will go a considerable way to determining how best to approach and manage difficult conversations or to learn from them. For example, what are the competing commitments of everyone involved?

> "I have used the framework for planning conversations. You can't be too prescriptive, but it is a good planning tool, and the more you use it, the more the process becomes natural. We are conducting expert interviews to capture knowledge and the framework has been useful in planning those interviews."
>
> *Alma Kucera, ex-HP Services*

> "The framework is designed to get more out of every conversation: not just formal meetings but chance meetings when you pass each other in the corridor. It helps open up the inner dialogue, so you ask yourself 'why am I entering into this conversation?' and 'what do I want to get out of it?'"
>
> *Juliet Brookes, Senior Information and Knowledge Manager, the National College for School Leadership*

The dynamics of bad conversations discourage open-mindedness, which clearly obstructs knowledge sharing. The emotional ambience and power structure between the participants seem to have the most influence on the ability of conversers to include a healthy balance of the aspects of good conversations.

A structured process has been created to help managers think through these issues in a systematic way. This involves working through each of the four stages of the framework in turn to help to understand the dynamics of a conversation. In Tables 17.2-17.5, key questions relating to each part of the framework are provided. These relate to planning ahead for a

Table 17.2: Understanding the context and intent of the conversation

The context and intent of the conversation creates conditions which influence what happens. Think through what you anticipate are key contextual issues that will more positively affect the outcome:

Organization/s within which or with whom the conversation/s will take
  place
Department/Division/s
What is the purpose of the conversation/s?
Who will be involved? (People/roles)
Who initiated it/them?
What is their authority/interest in doing so?
When, where, and how will it/they occur?
Is it intended to be a "one-off" or part of a series?
Formal or informal?
Any other pertinent information . . .

conversation. The same material can be readily adjusted for reflections on conversations that have already happened by slight adjustments to wording (in particular the tense of verbs).

The framework can be used by individual managers in developing their own practice of communication with others. For challenging conversations, it may take some time and effort to complete. However, the potential benefits are believed to be considerable in terms of learning, growth, and change. It is worth identifying the situations where the conversation has significant consequences and prioritizing use of the framework for these.

Real life stories

Although the "forced" discipline of reflecting on conversational events was time consuming and demanding, people who have worked through the framework consistently report that it has generated helpful insights about how their personal assumptions may have limited outcomes, and why conversational strategies did not work. Frequently the heightened awareness suggested alternative strategies which could be helpful in similar future encounters. Examples of the reflections of those working with the framework include the following:

> Analysing the conversation in a more compartmentalised way is helpful in making me think through what I'd be less inclined to do in future, and what I'd retain.

> Some elements of the reflection validated the approach I'd taken. Some elements I hadn't stopped to think about. Articulating them was useful to bring it to the forefront of my thinking.

Table 17.3: Identifying certain conditions

Certain conditions are known to shape the conversational process. Estimate the anticipated *emotional ambience* and *level of risk* of each condition against the scales defined:

The function of each phase of a conversation	Each function has a specific purpose or intent	Anticipated *emotional ambience* of the conversation 1. Defensive, divided, high resistance. 2. Uncertain and unconvinced. 3. Neutral. 4. Welcoming with reservations. 5. Open, accepting, with a willingness to continue.	Anticipated *level of risk* in what is being discussed Rate on a scale of 1-10 1 10 V. Low ⟷ V. High	
			Personal risk	Business risk
INITIATE *"I propose/ We need to start . . ."*	Explore possibilities			
UNDERSTANDING *"I believe this warrants attention/ We need to explore this further . . ."*	Create meaning/get buy-in			
PERFORMANCE *"I promise to/will act on . . ."*	Initiate action			
CLOSURE *"I accept/We can conclude/What has been learnt?"*	Embed learning			

Table 17.4: Anticipating the status, dynamics, and actions of those involved

The status, dynamics, and actions of those involved affect how a conversation progresses. Rate the anticipated Power Structure; balance of Listening/Inquiry to Telling; balance of Reflection to Action; and balance of Play to Analysis. Assess each of these for each of the conversation phases against the scales defined:

| The function of each phase of a conversation | *Power Structure* Assess each phase in terms of these 5 descriptions

1. Trust and respect among equals.
2. Affirming peers with loose ties.
3. A mix of individuals with no apparent structure/hierarchy.
4. Conflicting power struggles prevail.
5. Dominant source of power drives direction. | What is your anticipated/preferred balance of *Listening/ Inquiry* to *Telling*? (Rate EACH out of 10) | | What is your anticipated/ preferred balance of *Reflection* to *Action*? (Rate EACH out of 10) | | What is your anticipated/ preferred balance of *Play* to *Analysis*? (Rate EACH out of 10) | |

		Listening/ Inquiry	Telling	Reflection	Action	Play	Analysis
INITIATE							
UNDERSTANDING							
PERFORMANCE							
CLOSURE							

What is your anticipated level of satisfaction ...?

a) With the Process
1 (Very Low) - 10 (Very High)

b) With the Outcome
1 (Very Low) - 10 (Very High)

c) With the Commitment to move forward
1 (Very Low) - 10 (Very High)

Table 17.5: Considering your own and others' mindsets

Your own and others' mindsets will influence the outcome of the conversation/s. Think through the following dimensions and attempt to identify your own and the other/s' current mindsets:

The function of each phase of a conversation/s	What do I want to stand for in the conversation/s?	What do I want to avoid to prevent me fulfilling my commitment?	Are there any other competing commitments getting in the way?	Are there any big assumptions reinforcing my competing commitments?	What is your anticipated level of comfort/anxiety going into the conversation? 1. Very relaxed 2. Relaxed 3. Moderate level of comfort 4. Moderate level of discomfort 5. Very nervous/anxious
INITIATE					1 2 3 4 5
UNDERSTANDING					1 2 3 4 5
PERFORMANCE					1 2 3 4 5
CLOSURE					1 2 3 4 5

> I went in thinking I had to convince the other party, so spent too much time on telling and advocacy, if I had listened and inquired more I would have done better. This has helped me think about tactics for my next encounter.

> I find it difficult to temper what I am thinking and I don't allow enough time for playing with ideas. I focus far more on the analysis. My problem is that I have a strong tendency towards telling and advocacy all the time. (This was someone who admitted having problems convincing others and working in an adversarial environment)

> I don't allow much time for reflection in the conversations. I should also think more about difficult conversations in advance.

Two more substantial examples are summarized below. These were created through reflection on previous conversations using the framework. The examples represent large and small group conversations. One was considered to have gone well, and one was considered to have room for improvement.

A "good conversation" led by a project manager

Context: A planned three-hour conversation in October 2008 between eight project team members including the senior manager of the department and the project sponsor. This is a private sector organization.

Purpose: Initiated by the project manager to share and improve the project team's understanding of a specific part of the project, as well as improving the cohesion within the team. This was meeting three out of a series of four held in the company's headquarters in the USA.

Conditions: The level of personal risk to the project manager was judged to be quite high throughout, although the business risk was thought to be moderate. The emotional ambience was perceived as being "open and accepting" throughout.

Status, Dynamics, and Actions: The power structure started as "affirming peers with loose ties", but by the end strengthened to "trust and respect among equals". There was a high degree of listening and moderate level of telling throughout. At the outset there was a moderate level of reflection and higher level of action which increased significantly by the end of the conversation. There was a balance of moderate level of both play/creativity and analysis throughout, except during the performance phase when neither was high. There was a high degree of satisfaction with the process and commitment, but a lower level of satisfaction with the outcome as it was felt there was still more to do to reach the overall objectives.

Mindsets: The interviewee sought to create a focus for the topic, making sure that all ideas were properly captured during the performance phase, ensuring responsibilities were taken by the appropriate people, and subsequently ensuring that appropriate follow-up actions taken. The project manager felt positive about the clear definition of the objectives and required pre-work for the session.

Outcome: As this was the third session of four arranged as a series of related conversations, it was felt that the preparation involved had paid off and not just that the outcome for the project had been met, but that the project team had a greater understanding of their roles and how they could work more effectively together.

Key Learnings: Sound planning beforehand ensured that the outcomes were as positive as possible. Even though senior managers were present, a positive ambience was created where everyone was able to be open and honest about key issues. Participants' mindsets were more positive than expected at the outset, which enabled quicker and more direct resolution of key issues.

A "bad conversation" led by a knowledge manager

Context: A planned 45-minute conversation in June 2008 between two Associate Directors and the knowledge manager in the London headquarters. The knowledge manager was new to his role and the organization, which was in the private sector.

Purpose: To initiate a pilot Knowledge Management project (within the wider context of understanding the business in its environment). This was the declared top priority for the business. It was organized as a one-off session, but with the expectation that there would be follow-on sessions.

Conditions: The level of personal risk to the knowledge manager was judged to be quite high throughout, although the business risk was thought to be relatively low. The emotional ambience was perceived as being "welcoming with reservations" throughout.

Status, Dynamics, and Actions: The power structure was "affirming peers with loose ties" throughout. There was a high degree of listening and moderate level of telling during the first two phases of the conversation, but this reversed during the performance phase, as actions were being agreed. At the outset there was a low level of reflection and higher level of action and this continued until the end of the conversation. There was a high level of both play/creativity and analysis throughout, except during the performance phase when neither were high. There was a low degree of satisfaction with the process and outcome, although commitment of the knowledge manager remained high as it was still a company priority that matched his role.

Mindsets: The knowledge manager sought to create an appreciation of starting a journey for KM within the company. He also felt the need to demonstrate delivery of something tangible. The main thing he felt he did not do was get to know the individuals well enough as a first step (even though intuitively he knew this was an important step). What reinforced this perceived error was the project management culture which tended to put an emphasis on actions rather than process. Also, the Associate Directors were not KM experts and therefore doubted they could deliver what was required. As the knowledge manager was new to the company he could not judge whether they were correct in this assumption.

Outcome: This session was felt to not achieve its outcomes, although it was judged to be more successful in building relationships for the future.

Key Learnings: It was judged to be a "bad conversation" as it did not achieve its desired outcome. However, there were other positive outcomes achieved. On reflection, the knowledge manager felt he should have trusted his intuition more in not putting so much emphasis on actionable outcomes for this first conversation.

Top tips

✓ There are a number of ways in which the two frameworks (the planning and reflection versions) can be used:
  - To plan and/or reflect on a forthcoming one-to-one or group conversation.
  - To plan and/or reflect on a single conversation or series of conversations.
  - To reflect on a spontaneous conversation.
  - To improve group understanding/buy-in by suggesting individual members reflect on a group conversation, using their feedback to inform the planning of future group conversations.
✓ Using the frameworks does require a commitment of effort and time. Use them for conversations that have significant consequences in the first instance.
✓ Organizationally, using the frameworks can be considered as equivalent to the "before action" and "after action" learning processes used with projects. This embeds the view that learning from conversations is a legitimate business activity.
✓ The process becomes easier with use and therefore investing the time in practising is required in order to see the return of better knowledge sharing and knowledge-based decision-making.

The research and the team involved

This research was carried out during 2008 by a working group of members of the Henley KM Forum. Following a review of the literature, a survey was undertaken to explore the key variables associated with conversations and their inter-relationships. Forty responses were received. The results were used to support the design of interview questions. Nine interviews were undertaken, with each interviewee describing aspects of what they considered to be a bad conversation and a good one, creating 18 scenarios for further analysis. The research activities were intended to help managers understand the process and dynamics of effective conversations in the organizational context. They were not intended to provide prescriptive advice for a particular business.

Professor Jane McKenzie was the academic co-champion for this research. The member co-champion was Lucy Miller of the Ministry of Defence. The researcher was Mike Palmer from Henley Business School. Working group members included representatives from the following organizations:

AWE plc	*The British Council*
The Carbon Trust	*CSIP*
Department of Health	*HM Revenue and Customs*
HP Services	*Ministry of Defence*
Nationwide	*NCSL*
Oracle	*Unisys*

together with invited associates: Patricia Lustig (Visiting Executive Fellow, Henley Business School) and Richard Potter (Visiting Academic Fellow, Henley Business School).

Final reflections from the research

There was some evidence in the research that trust and mutual respect between the parties entering the conversation really does have a powerful effect on many elements of the process.[2] Firstly, it appears to make it easier to maintain a positive emotional ambience for knowledge sharing. Secondly, the conversers seem to be more prepared to use less direct routes to an outcome, pacing the conversation to engage in playful discovery and allow for plenty of reflection. The playful discovery in itself creates a positive emotional ambience which allows for more difficult aspects of the conversation later. Higher levels of advocacy and action orientation seem to be positively received without any damage to the interaction. Indeed conversers seem to gain sufficient confidence to increase the amount of telling above that which they originally intended. Others have argued for the power of mutual trust and respect as key elements in the process of tacit knowledge transfer[3] and critical to the initial phases of new knowledge creation. Often tacit knowledge sharing involves exploring ideas which may have business or personal risk, yet the evidence of good conversations suggests that even when the risk is high, conversers still have sufficient confidence to proceed with all the necessary aspects of a balanced conversation. Despite the fact that one might have expected that the level of stress associated with a high risk to have reduced the individual's mental availability, this does not seem to be the case. We saw that bad conversations often involved less personal or business risk. It is possible that concern over the risk may have encouraged people to prepare more thoroughly.

Notes

1. Based on Mengis, J. and Epler, M.J. (2005) "Understanding and managing knowledge-intensive conversations. A literature review and management framework", Universita

de la Svizzera Italiana, Faculty of Communication Services, Institute for Corporate Communications.

2. Read more about this in Isaacs, W. (1999) *Dialogue and the Art of Thinking Together*, New York: Currency Doubleday.

3. See for example: Szulanski, G. (1996) Exploring internal stickiness: impediments to the transfer of best practice within the firm, *Strategic Management Journal*, 17, Winter special issue, 27–43; Baumard, P. (1999) *Tacit Knowledge in Organizations*, London: Sage; Nonaka, I. and Konno, N. (1998) The concept of "ba" building a foundation for knowledge creation, *California Management Review*, 40(3), 40–54.

Chapter 18

Snapshot

One of the benefits of global organizations is their ability to offer a seamless service to customers around the world. They can also benefit from the ideas and learning opportunities generated by a diverse workforce. Yet, knowledge-related initiatives designed to achieve these objectives by "joining up" knowledge flows across national boundaries can be difficult to implement successfully. Part of the reason is that deeply embedded cultural preferences condition assumptions about how to do things and affect people's responses to what they are being asked to do.

Here we identify six factors that need to be taken into account when rolling out knowledge-related initiatives around the world: KM triggers and blockages; building relationships and networks; introducing structures, systems, and technology; performance management; introducing change; and communication. A series of questions have been created to help you understand how to tailor an implementation plan for an international knowledge initiative so that it is as effective as possible.

The research looked in detail at what these factors mean in Brazil, China, France, the United Kingdom, and the United States.

The implications of national cultural characteristics for key aspects of knowledge-related activities (such as the type of knowledge that is most easily shared, engagement with communities of practice, and how best to encourage knowledge sharing) are also considered.

Why this matters

Businesses are becoming increasingly global. They potentially gain from the opportunity this offers to access a larger pool of knowledge that everyone can benefit from. They can also serve global customers seamlessly – providing consistent quality and responsiveness wherever the customer is in the world. Yet, customers increasingly expect everyone in the organization to have the same information at their fingertips and the same knowledge about how to shape solutions to their problems.

"It's vitally important to take culture into account; you simply can't treat the whole world as if it were Britain or America."

Carolyn Lees, IT Director, Permira Advisers LLP

Frequently, organizations find it a struggle to share knowledge within a single country and culture. The difficulties are magnified significantly when attempting it across widely different cultures and distant geographies.

Physical separation, language, and time zone all affect how well people connect with each other for business purposes. The tacit element of knowledge, which is hard enough to share in a face-to-face situation, can be even more difficult when using email, phone, video, and other message forms. National culture adds another dimension to the problem because it introduces different personal preferences about aspects of knowledge practices, such as making use of knowledge that is already available, creating new knowledge, or sharing what we know with relative strangers.

Understanding the different dynamics and orientations that are part of each country's deep seated preferences means that we need to pay attention to different aspects of implementation, rather than assuming that a "one size fits all" approach is likely to be sufficient. Research recognizes some predictable patterns related to cultural preferences, but caution is required in using them. Understanding should not be allowed to degenerate into stereotyping; stereotypes are neither helpful nor accurate. Rather, the aim should be to improve understanding of the biases that could be encountered by managers seeking to extend knowledge-related initiatives across multi-national organizations.

What this means for your organization

The business advantage of a diverse global workforce is significant. It increases opportunity to distinguish the organization. Creative new solutions to existing problems, as well as more radical innovation, are all helped by bringing together knowledgeable people from around the world. Knowledge initiatives underpin the delivery of these opportunities, so it is worth spending time thinking about how to implement them as effectively as possible.

If knowledge-related initiatives are created in one part of the organization, how do you roll them out to other country operations? Organizations headquartered in one part of the world may feel they have taken a global overview in designing initiatives and programmes and therefore hope that country operations will be happy to receive them. However, the ease with which they will be accepted, adopted, and embedded into everyday practice could vary significantly. One of the main intentions of knowledge-related initiatives is to "join up" siloed knowledge bases and stimulate new thinking – yet if the implementation approach doesn't reflect the characteristics of the culture, this intention may never be achieved.

National culture has various general implications for knowledge-related initiatives. Being aware of them helps prepare better. Some of these are outlined below.

> "Different cultures often approach problems from different angles. Being able to effectively tap into that difference can make a huge impact on the value delivered by knowledge management initiatives."
>
> Marc Aafjes, whilst Global Head of Knowledge Management, Vodafone Group

- The starting point for knowledge initiatives is likely to be different in each country. It may be a matter of engaging individuals or groups depending on cultural authority preferences, it may be a question of adopting a structured approach or a flexible one, emphasizing innovation or efficiency, it depends on what is valued most in the culture. Tapping into the local cultural dynamics may result in greater success in the long run.
- The way knowledge initiatives are positioned and communicated also needs to vary. Senior management commitment and endorsement is always likely to be relevant, but in some countries it is essential. Different communication methods will also be more or less likely to be effective. Formal and informal approaches are received differently according to culture.
- Communities of practice must be approached differently in each cultural setting (see Chapter 10 to find out more about communities of practice initiatives). It may not be reasonable to expect close relationships between people to form in the workplace in all countries. In countries where this is the case, communities of practices may only ever be vehicles for information and explicit knowledge exchange, rather than more meaningful tacit knowledge exchange, which requires deeper trust.
- People need to be motivated differently to engage in knowledge-related activities. The whole range of explicit and intrinsic motivation tools should be considered. Simply including knowledge sharing in a management by objectives system may be fine for one country, yet in another it may not be particularly helpful.

National culture can also affect the organizational processes of knowledge creation, transfer, and utilization. Table 18.1 below summarizes some broad principles:

Table 18.1: Relating national characteristics to knowledge objectives

Knowledge creation	Knowledge transfer	Knowledge utilization
Supported by national characteristic to:	Supported by national characteristic to:	Supported by national characteristic to:
Be individually creative	Design and adopt structures and processes	Emphasize value delivered, in particular from existing knowledge
Entrepreneurial behaviours		
Risk taking		

those cultures with the identified tendencies are more likely to be successful in implementing the associated knowledge-related initiatives. Conversely if those tendencies are not inherent in a local culture, it suggests that managers need to pay more attention to encouraging and developing those behaviours when implementing locally.

Similarly, it may also be possible to map the type of knowledge being transferred against certain national characteristics. Tacit knowledge exchange is more likely in cultures that emphasize the importance of trusting relationships and the contextualization of knowledge. People are willing to spend time building sufficient common understanding that complex ideas can be shared. In contrast, more individualistic cultures in which close personal relationships are less prevalent in the workplace will probably be better at transferring explicit knowledge rather than tacit knowledge, probably adopting relatively depersonalized technology solutions more readily.

Creating an action plan

There are six factors that need particular attention when rolling out knowledge-related initiatives across national cultural boundaries. The managers responsible for the initiatives need to find out what these involve in each national culture by interviewing local managers and employees. Use the following as interview topics to help with this.

KM triggers and blockages

"Even within Europe, we find that national cultures have an influence on the extent to which people will re-use and contribute knowledge – further afield, it's even more noticeable."

Birgit Gotthart, European Portfolio and Knowledge Manager, HP Consulting & Integration

This relates to attitudes to important aspects of Knowledge Management, including individual and collective approaches to work, willingness to find new ways of doing things and the extent to which thinking and reflection are valued. Find out whether people:

- are expected to be independent thinkers and problem solvers;
- are receptive to change and willing to experiment and whether they are encouraged to take risks and experiment;
- are exposed to a lot of different ideas as a matter of course;
- are happy to adopt good practices from elsewhere;
- are allowed to make mistakes and learn from them.

Building relationships and networks

Deeper and more meaningful knowledge can be shared in closer relationships. It is therefore helpful to understand the extent to which trust and personal relationships underpin workplace activity. Find out whether there are:

- processes for reflecting on experience together;
- different ways for people to connect with colleagues around the organizations;
- spaces for social interaction and time allowed for it;
- activities that encourage networking and relationship building.

Introducing structures, systems, and technology

In a global organization, structures, systems and technology are necessary to join up operations around the world – creating the infrastructure that supports knowledge sharing. Yet, national cultures have different responses to standards, controls and procedures as well as to the adoption of new technologies. Find out whether:

- common practices are standardized to ease collaboration between different groups;
- people are trained in good practices and therefore have the skills needed to follow them;
- people participate in initiatives to continuously improve how things are done;
- people tend to use all the functionality of available technology;
- there is support for re-using solutions that have already been created, or a desire to produce something new.

Performance management

Finding the best way to encourage people to participate in the knowledge-related initiatives means understanding the cultural response to performance management options. Find out:

- the kinds of achievements that are recognized and rewarded;
- whether people and their achievements are publicly or privately recognized;
- the role that incentives play – financial incentives and incentive scheme gifts beyond usual salary payments;
- the extent to which objective setting is valued and used to manage performance;
- whether exposure to training opportunities is viewed as a reward.

Introducing change

First impressions count, so it is necessary to identify the most effective ways that knowledge-related initiatives should be introduced to a culture. What is the climate for change? It is important to know the level of awareness of external drivers for change, whether change tends to be driven from the top, and whether there is receptivity to new ways of working. Find out:

- whether there is a sense of urgency and challenge to do things differently;
- the extent to which there is a general understanding of the vision and objectives of the business;
- whether there is evidence of receptiveness to change and willingness to experiment;
- whether employees are expected to contribute to finding new approaches;
- whether new thinking from people outside the organization with different backgrounds is actively sought.

Communication

An important aspect of any change programme is communication. Hence, thinking about the cultural influences on effective communication is needed before moving forward with knowledge-related initiatives. Issues to think about include the channels for communication that tend to be preferred and the extent to which there is transparency about what is happening and why across all levels of the organization. Find out whether:

- there is widespread consistent understanding of the purpose, vision, and objectives of the organization;
- structured or unstructured communications are preferred. This includes whether certain technologies (such as email or the intranet) are used, and whether written or verbal communication is most effective;
- managers tend to communicate success stories and processes are in place to communicate lessons learnt to those who may need them in the future;
- there are preferences for hearing news from particular sources, for example, senior managers, local managers, trusted experts, or colleagues;
- whether translation into local languages is valued, or whether the corporate language is acceptable.

Real life stories

What the six factors mean in Brazil, China, France, the UK, and the USA is summarized in Table 18.2. These five countries were chosen because they were expected to exhibit considerable differences in bias towards knowledge initiatives as a result of distinct national cultural characteristics.

Table 18.2: What to consider in implementing knowledge initiatives in five countries (note "KM" stands for all knowledge-related initiatives and activities)

	KM triggers (and blockages)	Building networks	Introducing structure, systems, and technology	Incorporating KM into performance management	Introducing KM to the business	Communicating about KM
Brazil	Respect desire for creativity and independence by allowing local implementation of initiatives against broad principles. (Initiatives to improve knowledge re-use may need particular attention.)	Incorporate a high level of personal interaction into community design. Allow time for socializing. Virtual communities are less likely to be very successful.	Avoid highly structured and standardized initiatives.	Recognize creativity. May be less likely that recognition for efficiency improvements will be valued.	Build from existing teams and networks and engage local interest and involvement from the earliest stages.	Informal communication is most effective. Formal communication about KM initiatives could be less effective.
China	Work with groups to try new approaches, rather than with individuals. Build from the strong willingness to learn and improve business efficiency. (Team working initiatives may need particular attention.)	Ensure that sufficient time is allowed for relationship building. Communities likely to be most successful within a hierarchical level, rather than across levels.	Provide clear implementation guidelines. Avoid ambiguity and test understanding. Translate to local language when common understanding is essential.	Recognize the contributions of individuals and groups through visible awards, as recognition systems are very effective. Incorporate KM into the appraisal system.	Ensure senior management are visibly committed to KM initiatives.	Use respected senior people in country to communicate. Avoid forceful language in communication materials and link key messages to the business vision and values.

continued on next page…

Table 18.2 - *Continued*

	KM triggers (and blockages)	Building networks	Introducing structure, systems, and technology	Incorporating KM into performance management	Introducing KM to the business	Communicating about KM
France	Adopt structured approaches to KM as these will be more effective. (Open-ended (creativity-oriented) initiatives may need particular attention.)	Appoint a credible business champion to lead community initiatives. Design communities to have structured processes and boundaries.	Ensure there is senior management endorsement to make systems and tools more credible. Allow implications as well as factual data to be captured in databases.	Incorporate KM into company competency framework and include in performance management system.	Emphasize the role KM can play in supporting and dealing with change.	Place KM within a conceptual framework then translate to detailed implementation implications. Use formal communication methods.

	KM triggers (and blockages)	Building networks	Introducing structure, systems, and technology	Incorporating KM into performance management	Introducing KM to the business	Communicating about KM
United Kingdom	Motivate and gain commitment of individuals. (Knowledge sharing beyond known work groups may need particular attention.)	Start community of practice initiatives from existing informal networks.	To ensure adoption, think about how to follow through on implementation of systems and processes that need to be standardized.	Emphasize intrinsic rewards from KM by "selling" the learning opportunities and emphasizing career development potential.	Emphasize the role KM can play in delivering increased business performance.	Translate KM strategy into everyday implications. Use a range of communication methods to get messages across.
USA	Emphasize value proposition for individuals today. (Learning for possible future use may need particular attention, as might overcoming "not invented here".)	Virtual communities likely to work well. Explicit knowledge sharing most prevalent.	Sustain credibility by good content management. Database and online solutions likely to be adopted, as long they are clearly relevant to task delivery.	Emphasize extrinsic rewards from KM by making KM explicit in personal pay-related performance objectives.	Set targets that show how KM will contribute to delivering business objectives.	Communicate in written form mainly. Online and relatively formal communication commonplace. Communicate to employees via local managers.

Top tips

✓ Ensure that sufficient time is built into the implementation project plan to investigate the local cultural characteristics.

✓ Present the findings in a structured way around the six critical success factors for knowledge initiative implementation, assessing each country against these. This will help central teams see what the issues are likely to be in a global implementation programme.

✓ Decide what has to be the same everywhere and what can be tailored to local circumstances. For some initiatives, it may be most important that the principles are adopted and the details of the implementation can be varied.

✓ Ensure that there is follow through on the implementation. Some cultures may appear receptive and then quietly ignore the initiative!

The research and the team involved

This research was carried out during 2003 and 2004 by a working group of members of the Henley KM Forum. Following a review of the literature, 20 interviews were carried out with line managers in five countries to find out their perceptions of various factors and issues relating to Knowledge Management. The managers were drawn from six multi-national companies. As a result of detailed content analysis of the interviews, patterns were identified that were derived from national cultural traits that managers need to take into account in implementing knowledge strategies in the countries concerned. These practitioner guidance recommendations were reviewed and endorsed by KM practitioners and CKOs with global responsibilities. It was suggested that this research should be used as a template for future studies of other countries. However, it should be emphasized that there was no opportunity to test these recommendations directly in any organizations. They should therefore not be seen as prescriptive and should only be used as the basis for challenging thinking and preconceptions.

The Project was co-championed by Professor Emilio Herbolzheimer of Henley Business School and David Tullett of CGE&Y then Kevin Lehane of Orange. Working group members included representatives from:

Barclays	*CGE&Y*
Ericsson	*EZI*
Getronics	*GSK*
Hyder Consulting	*Nissan*
Orange	*RWE Innogy*
RWE Thames Water	*Unisys*
VT Group	

Research support was provided by Dr Roger Darby of Cranfield University and Dr Christine van Winkelen of Henley Business School.

Additional invited associates were: Andy Millward of Chestnut Consultants and John Burrows (formerly Buckman Laboratories).

Final reflections from the research

It is helpful to separate business culture from national cultural influences. Many large organizations have worked hard to develop a global business culture that reaches across operations located around the world. Putting effort into communicating corporate values and vision across the world creates a common language and focus that can help overcome other barriers. Adopting common systems, standards, and procedures to help manage the business has a direct impact on the deployment of knowledge-related initiatives. Corporate-wide information systems and a coordinated approach to training can be particularly helpful. Recruitment policy can also make a difference: multi-nationals seem to attract people with previous international experience. These employees are more willing to learn and adapt to the multi-national way of working. Overall, strong identification with the business culture can reduce the difficulties that could arise from national culture differences.

INDEX

Compiled by Indexing Specialists (UK) Ltd